To Jonathan,
from your
friend John Nichols!!

Always Remember Me

The Story of Jedidiah Lusk

CYNTHIA LUSK

Cyt Lusk

Copyright © 2014 Cynthia Lusk.

All rights reserved. No part of this book may be used or reproduced by any means, graphic, electronic, or mechanical, including photocopying, recording, taping or by any information storage retrieval system without the written permission of the publisher except in the case of brief quotations embodied in critical articles and reviews.

Credit for the cover image by Jedidiah Lusk.

WestBow Press books may be ordered through booksellers or by contacting:

WestBow Press
A Division of Thomas Nelson & Zondervan
1663 Liberty Drive
Bloomington, IN 47403
www.westbowpress.com
1 (866) 928-1240

Because of the dynamic nature of the Internet, any web addresses or links contained in this book may have changed since publication and may no longer be valid. The views expressed in this work are solely those of the author and do not necessarily reflect the views of the publisher, and the publisher hereby disclaims any responsibility for them.

Any people depicted in stock imagery provided by Thinkstock are models, and such images are being used for illustrative purposes only. Certain stock imagery © Thinkstock.

ISBN: 978-1-4908-3717-8 (sc)
ISBN: 978-1-4908-3716-1 (hc)
ISBN: 978-1-4908-3718-5 (e)

Library of Congress Control Number: 2014908713

Printed in the United States of America.

WestBow Press rev. date: 8/5/2014

DEDICATION

This book is dedicated to the family who was dedicated to Jedidiah- from birth, throughout his life, and until his death: my loving husband of over 28 years; Scott, my beautiful daughter; Jessica, my son; Justin, AKA "Mr. Perfect", and my mother; the incredible "Blue Nanny". Thank you all so very much for sharing Jedidiah!

CHAPTER 1

Sunday, February 14, 2010

"EEeugh! Don't you think that looks like chicken poop?" asked eight year old Jedidiah, as he kneeled on the frozen February ground. His voice, though weary, was tinged with curiosity.

"Justin's roosters have been out running around the yard, but THAT is my own vomit."

"Okay!" I said, as I scooped up my 68 pound son into my arms. "Now, let's get you to the hospital."

I had been carrying Jedidiah from our house just moments earlier when he warned, "Two, four, six, eight, I think I've got to regurgitate… PUT ME DOWN NOW!!" as I quickly lowered him to the ground.

"Blaugh!" went Jedidiah as he threw up for the fifth time that morning.

"Come on!" I stressed, "We've got to get you to the doctor!" as I heaved myself to my feet and carried Jedidiah to my waiting car.

"Are you coming Scott?" I yelled back to my husband who was just emerging from our house. "I am ready to go NOW!"

"But…," said Scott with a concerned look on his face, "We did not even get to open our Valentine's Day presents yet…" his voice trailed off as he opened the car door for me to put Jedidiah into the back seat of the running Subaru.

Jedidiah leaned weakly to the side while I connected his seat belt. Just that morning I noticed how pale his skin looked, and it frightened me. But even scarier than his skin color, was the size of his pupils in the middle of his deep brown eyes. They were abnormally large in the winter morning light.

Scott got into the front right bucket seat while I slid into the driver's seat. I turned on the CD player and pushed Jedidiah's favorite CD in while

1

accelerating down the quarter mile dirt driveway. We bounced over the rocks, splashed through a couple mud puddles, and came to a paved road. I turned the car left on to the county road while tossing a round plastic container to the back seat.

"Here, Jedidiah, take this in case you have to throw up again."

He looked up at me in the rear-view mirror with questioning eyes. "But don't you think my vomit REALLY DID look like chicken poop?" he persisted.

I slowed for the stop sign at state route Highway 70, looked both ways and made a right turn. "Okay, yeah," I breathed out. "So it was kind of like chicken poop."

"Well, didn't you see how it was a little yellow and some brown, but had that watery clear stuff all around it?" Jedidiah asked innocently.

Not in the mood to discuss the merits of chicken poop OR my son's vomit, I turned up the volume on the music CD. "Here, listen to the Kepple's. Your favorite song, 'Katie' is on next."

My mind was racing a mile a minute as I drove the 18 miles to the hospital in the nearest town of Quincy. "What could be wrong?" I silently screamed to myself, but wanting to yell out loud at the top of my lungs, WHAT'S WRONG WITH MY BABY???"

Just two days earlier, Jedidiah was acting like a normal little boy. He spent most of the day on Friday playing in the stream near our home in Cromberg, California. He splashed in the water, making dams and racing bark boats with his 15 year old brother, Justin. There was no school that day, due to a teacher work day. I left home and went to work, to ride snowmobile patrol with the US Forest Service on the Mt. Hough Ranger District of the Plumas National Forest.

I was to meet back up with the whole family in town that afternoon, at a Spaghetti Feed at the local high school. It was a fund raiser for the Quincy High School Wrestling Team.

When I saw Jedidiah again, he was skipping across the high school parking lot, the bottom of his pants soaked up to his knees. He saw me and ran over to grab my hand, and started swinging my arm.

"Jedidiah, your hand is FREEZING!" I gasped. "What have you been doing?"

He flashed a smile, "Oh just playing with Justin. We had a good day. But I kind of have a headache now."

I turned to his Dad, "Scott!" I scolded. "Why isn't Jedidiah wearing a coat?"

Scott shrugged, "He said he wasn't cold."

"But he is soaking wet and his hands are freezing!" I protested. We turned and went to the school cafeteria for the Wrestling Team Fund Raiser. We each consumed a large plate of spaghetti, some garlic bread, and a can of soda pop. We spent time visiting with friends, other parents, and students on the Wrestling Team. We all returned to our warm, cozy home that night with full stomachs, and happy memories.

Later that evening, Jedidiah insisted that he was seeing double. He told his Dad and me, "You guys both have two mouths, two noses, four eyes, four ears…"

"Really?" I asked, only partially believing him, as we were getting ready for bed. "Now you hop into the covers and say your prayers."

"Yeah, said Jedidiah, as his wavering finger pointed out the various locations of my multiple eyes, ears, noses and mouths.

I chalked it up to him being tired. What else could it possibly be? You know kids, I told myself, they have such vivid imaginations!

CHAPTER 2

"Slow down and pull up right next to the Emergency Room door," my husband insisted. "That way we don't have to carry him too far."

"Yep," I agreed as I swung the car around into the vacant parking lot, and slowed near the emergency entrance.

I put the car in park, jumped out and gently picked up Jedidiah as Scott held open the car door.

I carried him through the Emergency Room door, as a lady in official uniform was walking out. She frowned at my car's location and barked, "You can't park there!"

"I know!" I retorted. "I'll be RIGHT back to park it." Couldn't she see that I had a sick child in my arms? Like there was going to be a rush of vehicles right behind me, on that Sunday morning, in that small town, population of a whopping 5,000 people?!

I carried Jedidiah to one of two exam tables in the small ER, and went back to properly park the car while Scott answered questions to fill out the required paperwork. When I returned I was happy to see my RN friend, Debbie DeSelle, at Jedidiah's side, asking him questions on how he felt.

"And I keep throwing up and throwing up..." Jedidiah said, "And then everybody has four eyes and two mouths, and even two noses!"

"Does your head hurt?" asked Debbie.

"Yeah, kind of, but mostly I don't like throwing up."

Debbie continued her exam, shining a penlight in his eyes, then grabbed a small blood pressure cuff off the wall, wrapping it around his arm.

The ER Doctor came walking in, clipboard in hand. "Oh, it's probably just the flu. It's going around, you know." She turned around to eye me. "Are you his mother?"

"Yes, I am. But I don't think it's JUST the flu…"

She cut me off, "We have already had four or five kids in here this morning, all throwing up, with headaches, and all achy… With their parents all concerned. What makes you think he is any different?"

"Well…," I answered slowly, "If you'd take a closer look, you will see that his pupils are dilated."

Debbie stood next to Jedidiah, nodding her head up and down in agreement. "I think we should get him a CAT scan."

"Thank you Debbie!" I said, while eyeing the doctor back.

"Sounds good!" The doctor made a note on her clipboard, then briskly walked out, just as Scott came walking in.

"Front desk lady said there have been a bunch of kids coming in with the flu today. That's probably what it is," Scott said reassuringly.

"And he is very dehydrated, he needs an IV to get fluids in him" Debbie stated, "After he gets that CT scan."

"Huh?" Scott, taken aback, glanced from Debbie to me, and then over to Jedidiah.

"Uh, well yeah, I agree. I think we should get a look inside his head…. Just in case…" My voice trailed off.

My mother, a Registered Nurse who lives with us, had pulled me aside the night before to talk about Jedidiah. "You know, these three symptoms together; vomiting, headaches, and double vision, indicate increasing intracranial pressure. Since he hasn't had any trauma that we know of, falling or hitting his head, it could be something else…."

"But, I don't think he is having double vision now." Interrupting her, I went on, "Besides, that was on Friday night. I think he got over that." I remarked reassuringly.

"Are you sure? She looked at me, doubtful.

"I think so…." I said weakly. I didn't really know for sure, I just hoped he had. "Why, what else could it be?" Knowing I really did NOT want to hear the answer.

"Well, there are lots of different kinds of tumors and things that grow, putting pressure on the brain…" she began.

"Yeah" I nodded, walking away. I was right, that's was NOT what I wanted to hear.

5

Debbie and Scott were sliding Jedidiah on to a bed sheet, in preparation to move him over to a wheeled gurney. I stood staring, lost in thought. Jedidiah had a real bad headache about ten days previously. I realized, just then, what "sudden onset" really meant. He and I were sitting in the car at the local shopping center, waiting for Justin's basketball practice to get over, and then it would be time for Jedidiah's basketball practice. We just had returned from a visit to the Dollar Tree- one of Jedidiah's favorite pastimes while we were in town. He was taking his newly purchased toy out of the bag to play with it, when Jedidiah quickly clamped his hands to his head, "Owey, owey, OUCH!" He said. Then he rolled over on his side and yelled, "I am NOT kidding Mom, my head hurts!!"

Puzzled by his behavior, I calmly asked, "Like, just now? It hurts really badly, all of a sudden?"

"YES!" Jedidiah wailed. "Make it stop! Do something…now…please!"

Increasingly alarmed, I wondered just what to do. "Do you want some aspirin or something?" I asked.

Jedidiah flopped around in the back seat of the car, crying in earnest now.

A small wave of panic began to roll over me as I heard my son calling out in distress and I watched him writhe in pain.

"Wait a second," I told myself. "I am the grown up here, I can see he is in obvious pain. I can make a decision. I don't want my little boy hurting!"

"Jedidiah- you wait here, I told him. I will run inside Rite Aid really fast and get you some medicine to make it stop!"

"K….Hurry!" He squealed in high pitched voice.

I dashed in and grabbed some children's chewable painkillers, quickly paid at the counter, and ran back to the car. Shaking out three purple tablets, I climbed in the back seat. "Here Jedidiah, these are grape flavored. Eat them."

He could barely focus long enough to crush the tablets between his teeth, as I slid them in his mouth one at a time. I gathered Jedidiah up into my arms and rocked him until the pain lessened. Then we drove across the street to pick up Justin. Jedidiah did not feel like playing basketball that night. His headache did gradually go away, and did not return until Friday night.

CHAPTER 3

Scott was talking to Debbie as she prepared to hang the bag of fluid on the IV pole. "Okay, so we give him some IV fluids, make sure he is not dehydrated, then we can take him home?" he asked hopefully.

"Well," Debbie hesitated. "Let's just wait a bit and see what we can find out from the CAT scan results. Here, Mom, come hold his arm…"

"NO!" was all Jedidiah could say when he saw the needle and knew it was going to poke in his arm.

"It's ok," I tried to reassure him. "Just a little sting."

Jedidiah gritted his teeth. "Easy for you to say, Mom, when it's NOT your arm."

The ER Doctor appeared. "You might as well relax. We need to get the fluids in him and that will take a while. And I just sent off the CAT scan films to Reno for a Radiologist to read there. It will take some time from them to get back to us."

Scott looked at me, definite worry in his eyes, but he spoke encouragingly to Jedidiah. "It's going to be okay Jedidiah. You will be feeling great again in no time!"

The curtain moved aside and a young, tall, pretty girl walked in. Immediately, Jedidiah called out to her for help.

"Jessica! Sissy, come save me…They are trying to kill me with this huge needle!"

"Naw," said Debbie. "Nothing to it!" as she deftly slipped the needle into Jedidiah's forearm and adjusted the flow through the tube.

He didn't seem to react too much, so I loosened my grip on his arm.

"So, what's up?" The pretty girl asked.

Jessica was Jedidiah's big sister, and he definitely looked up to her. She'd turned 18 several months ago, and had moved out of our house and in with her boyfriend. Jedidiah really missed her recently.

"Well, Jedidiah had a CAT scan, and now he's getting all hydrated again. That's all I know," I replied. "We are waiting to hear..." I trailed off.

Scott chimed in, "He's just got the flu. Been throwing up so much he's dehydrated."

Puzzled, Jessica turned to me. "Then what is the CAT scan about?" Jessica and I had taken the Emergency Medical Technician class at the local college last year, so she knew that procedure was not part of the usual treatment for your average case of the flu.

"Can I see you a moment?" The doctor pushed the curtain aside and motioned for me to come out of the room.

"Be right back!' I told Jessica. Hoping for some reassurance that my son would be just fine, I followed her to the next room. The doctor turned to face me. "We got a call from the Radiologist in Reno."

"What? All ready?"

"Your son," the doctor went on, "appears to have something on his brain."

"What's that mean? A 'something'?"

"It means a lesion of some sort," she continued on. "And the radiologist in Reno recommends that we life flight your son to UC Davis to get it checked out."

"Whoa, wait a sec. You're going too fast for me. Life Flight? Isn't that for serious stuff? Wait...let me talk to my husband." I groped my way blindly back to Jedidiah's bedside.

"Scotty, c 'mere." I motioned Scott closer. I wanted to tell him away from our son so not to frighten him. "Doc says serious stuff. They want to Life Flight Jedidiah to UC Davis!"

"Huh?" Scott looked at me as blankly as I felt.

"Come here," I repeated. "Let's go talk to the doctor. Jessica can stay with Jedidiah."

Debbie was walking in as we were walking out. "Helicopter ETA is one hour. Let's get Jedidiah ready. And how much do you weigh, Cynthia? I assume you will be the one to fly with him?"

Scott and I stared at each other, dumbfounded. It went from the flu, to 'something' on his brain, to a life flight to UC Davis, that quickly? Just what was going on? How could we possibly comprehend what was going on?? WAIT ONE! I wanted to scream, this was all moving way too fast for me!

"uh,... uh ..." I stammered. I had never flown on a helicopter without my fire gear or tools. And I did not even have a travel bag packed and ready to go...

"Oh, I guess just me, myself, weighs about one hundred and forty five pounds." I mumbled to no one in particular. I was still trying to get a grasp on what this all meant. "And Jedidiah weighs sixty seven pounds."

I went back to Jedidiah's bedside and gazed down at him. He was so little, so cute, so young and he had always been very healthy. If fact he had been born right here in this very hospital, almost nine years ago. He had only been back for routine check-ups, vaccinations, and one round of stitches. Jedidiah was my baby! He was only eight years old. He was a happy, healthy, and robust, a normal, active boy. Kids like him aren't supposed to a have a "something" on their brain!

"So, what's happening, Mom?" Jessica broke into my thoughts.

"Debbie said they are going to Life Flight him to U.C. Davis." Still in shock, my words sounded hollow. "And I guess I'm supposed to go with him.

"What?" Jessica's eyes widened with surprise. "What's wrong with him? She looked down at her little brother with concern.

Jedidiah perked up. "Huh? I get to fly in a helicopter?" He seemed to be feeling a little better, and some of the color had come back into his face. "Wow, has anyone told Justin yet?"

"Why U.C. Davis Hospital?" I heard Scott question the doctor.

"Because they specialize in the treatment of children's medical emergencies," she answered flatly.

That did not sound good to me. Not good at all....

"Wop, wop, wop," I heard the helicopter approaching the hospital. Jedidiah was strapped on a gurney and was being wheeled down the hall, outside the door, and to the helipad. Scott, Jessica and I were all trailing behind. It was a bright winter day outside. I was glad it was not snowing, and thankful it was not foggy- either one would have made a helicopter approach and landing more difficult.

Debbie gave Jedidiah a special soft teddy bear for the trip, and it was tucked under his arm. She gave all of us special, warm, bear hugs. I got handed some earplugs, and Jedidiah got dark glasses to wear. Next thing I know, I was getting seat belted inside the back seat of the helicopter, and

Jedidiah was lying in the gurney in the left front. He just fit nicely into that spot. The Flight Nurse was next to me. The pilot was in the right front seat.

Soon we were lifting off and I was waving goodbye to the rest of my family as they got smaller and smaller on the ground at Plumas District Hospital. We flew over the Quincy High School and were gaining elevation to rise above the mountains surrounding town. I saw the white of the Quincy "Q" flash by, and saw the snow covered Claremont Peak approaching through the glass bubble at the front of the helicopter. I was holding Jedidiah's hand and I squeezed it tightly, hoping it was a reassuring gesture. I know the flight was exciting to him, but I sure wished it was under different circumstances for the both of us.

I wanted to talk to Jedidiah and point out some of my favorite landmarks down there on the forest we were flying over, but the loudness of the turning rotors prevented that. I saw the rocky bump of Little Volcano and the deep, dark chasm of the Middle Fork of the Feather River as we crossed over. I even caught a glimpse of the Pacific Crest Trail footbridge, where it spanned the Middle Fork near Deadman Springs.

A few minutes later a large body of water appeared below. The Flight Nurse pulled her headphones away from her ear, "That's Little Grass Valley Reservoir" she yelled, pointing out the window. I nodded in agreement. Yep, I had seen that from the air before.

Jedidiah's hand went slack in mine as he fell asleep. Apparently the medications given to him had taken affect. "Rest well, my little guy. I love you Jedidiah." I silently told him as I tucked his hand back under his seatbelt. "Who knows what the rest of this day will hold."

CHAPTER 4

We landed on the roof of the U.C. Davis Medical Center in Sacramento, California. Jedidiah was taken out of the helicopter, wheeled into the elevator and quickly shuttled down to the Pediatric Intensive Care Unit or "PICU" as it was called. I blindly followed along behind, my legs feeling as numb as my mind after 45 minutes of sitting stationary during the helicopter flight.

Jedidiah was efficiently transferred into a clean, waiting bed in the PICU. He was hooked up to all kinds of monitors, as nurses bustled about, tending to their business. I parked myself right next to Jedidiah, held his hand and watched the motion all around us, hardly able to comprehend what was happening. The Helicopter Fight Nurse turned over her notes and records to the PICU nurse, and with a quick wave towards me, said they were heading out. "Thank you," I was able to call out before the Life Flight crew disappeared out into the hall.

I felt completely abandoned, all alone, and scared in this strange place. I knew my son was in trouble, and I was frightened for him. I was at a loss as to what I could to do to help him. All I knew to do was to stay close, and keep tabs on what was happening. I had my cell phone, my charger, a notebook and a pen with me and the clothes on my back. That would have to do me for now. I would focus on Jedidiah, not my own plight of fright. I realized I needed to be strong for Jedidiah's sake.

I made a quick phone call to my brother, John Nichols. He lived very close by, in West Sacramento. It was good to speak with him! It sure made me feel a whole lot better. I knew he would do everything he could to help us out. John said he would come by the hospital tomorrow.

The whole night was a busy blur of nurses hooking up monitors to Jedidiah, wires and tubes going everywhere. Lots of sounds of machines beeping, kids crying, nurse's hushed voices, footsteps everywhere, and never a moment of still quietness. I must have dozed off a couple of times, but I knew I never fell into a deep sleep. Despite the exhausting day, I just could not get any rest. Who could possibly sleep in a time of mental and physical chaos, such as this?

CaringBridge Journal

Jedidiah's big sister, Jessica, began writing this for us, and we are extremely grateful!

Sunday, February 14, 2010

Mom took Jedidiah into the ER in Quincy. She and her mom, "Blue Nanny" were concerned that Jedidiah had been puking for two days and had a headache- they both knew those could be symptoms of head trauma. Plumas District Hospital took a CAT scan of Jedidiah's head and sent the results to a specialist in Reno who said, "Send Jedidiah to Davis immediately, 'something' had shown up on his CAT scan." Two hours later, Jedidiah accompanied by his mommy, was Life Flighted out of Quincy. Debbie DeSelle, the ER Nurse and family friend was very helpful and supportive the whole day. Thank you, Debbie! By the time I saw him, the IV was already in and he was excited about his first helicopter ride. Here's a picture of him in the COOL glasses he wore in the helicopter...;)

Monday, February 15, 2010

We learned that nothing in a busy hospital happens as soon as we want it to. An MRI had been ordered "STAT" that night, but didn't come until the next day. Jedidiah did a very good job holding still for the 45 minutes it took for the MRI. Mom stayed in the room with him and said it was a LOUD machine, sounded like a freight train. Jedidiah's headaches went from a 4 to an 8 (on a pain scale for 1 to 10) and he was given morphine. His level of consciousness went down and he slept most of the day.

Mom called while Justin was at basketball practice to update us. The MRI showed the tumor was deep inside the right side of his brain and was putting pressure on little pouches of cerebral spinal fluid, causing Jedidiah's headaches, double vision and vomiting. Dad and I sat in the car in front of Taco Bell, crying.

Mom's brother, John and his wife Stevie, live in Sacramento. They visited and made sure Mom has food and clean clothes. They continue to provide my parents with a home away from home. Thank you SO much for your help!

Tuesday, February 16, 2010

Dad drove down to Davis to be with Mom during Jedidiah's biopsy. Because Jedidiah was squeezed into the day's already scheduled surgeries, his surgery wasn't started until three. The biopsy, a high risk procedure in itself, had two purposes: 1. To take out a piece of the tumor in order to study it and find out exactly what it is, to know how to best treat it and, 2. To drill a hole into Jedidiah's skull that would be left open to relieve the intracranial pressure and allow the extra fluid to drain. The biopsy took over four hours and Jedidiah was moved into the pediatric ICU once it was over. The surgeon's primary assessment concluded that the tumor might be Glioblastoma multiformes or Astrocytoma. Tuesday ended with a lot of tears. Dad spent the night with Jedidiah so Mom could sleep at her brother's house and for the first time in two nights, she was able to get more than two hours of sleep.

Wednesday, February 17, 2010

Jedidiah woke up groggy and combative. Dad had several wrestling matches with him throughout the night. Jedidiah wanted to rip off the splint the nurses had on his right arm. After the pain medicine began wearing off the doctors discovered he could not move his left arm or leg. As the day progressed he regained control of his leg but still could not feel his arm. Physical therapy is not a priority until he is stable and out of the ICU. Mom took Dad's spot so he could drive home to watch Justin's last basketball game of the season.

Thursday, February 18, 2010

Dad drove Justin and me to UC Davis Thursday morning. This was the first time we'd seen our little brother since Sunday. We were lucky that he was coherent again and not on any pain medicine, but seeing him in that hospital bed was still pretty shocking. He was moved into his own private room in the ICU the night before. He's got tubes and wires going everywhere. On one side of the room are machines that monitor his vitals, on the other are three bags of fluids that are supplying him with hydration, dextrose and sodium, and underneath the TV that was playing cartoons was a table holding several teddy bears he's been given from well-wishers=)

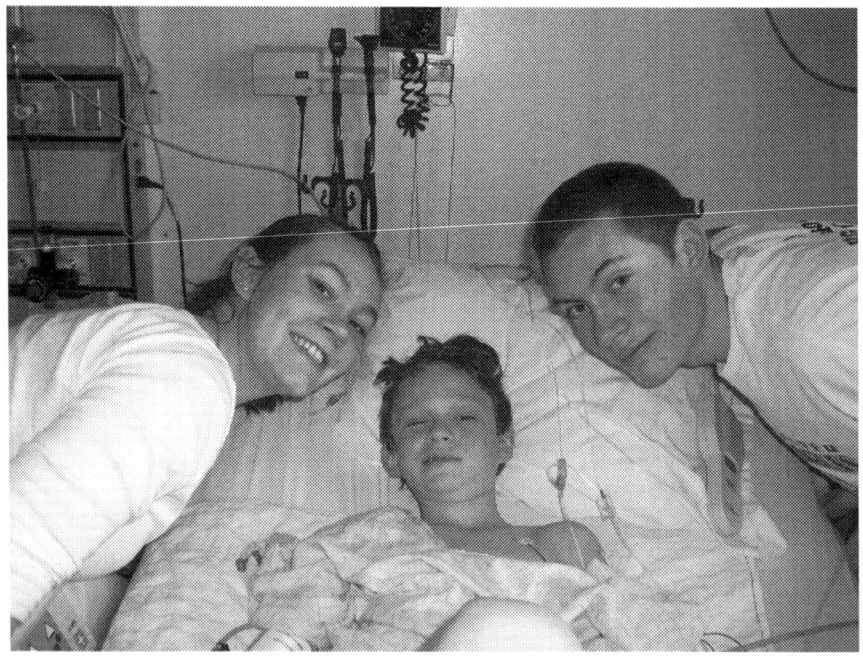

Jedidiah in UC Davis Hospital bed, with Jessica and Justin during their first visit.

Jedidiah still can't feel his left arm from the shoulder down or move his fingers when asked, but his hand twitches when he's unaware of it. So we know movement is possible although he doesn't think of that arm as part of his body anymore. One of his eyes is half-closed and the other is barely open and one side of his mouth droops.

If you ask how he's feeling his answer is, "I'm in the hospital, how do you think I'm feeling?" He is grumpy, and tired of the nurses poking, prodding and waking him up to shine a flashlight in his eyes every two hours. He REALLY wants to eat. He hasn't been able to for the past three days and he won't until the Speech Pathologist says his throat and esophagus work correctly. While I was there he demanded a Nerd Rope covered in chocolate, 28 Frosted Flakes and five jars of pickled okras!! Ha-ha, that's my little brother!...:) Despite his frustration and all the wires he's doing pretty good. I even got a kiss from him. =)

Dad and Justin went on a quest to get copies of Jedidiah's MRI to send to our Uncle Tim's friends- Neurosurgeons from Houston and San Francisco, leading brain tumor hospitals for a second opinion. Jedidiah was asleep by the time we left; he had been sedated to get a PIC. The PIC replaces the other three IV's he had in. The flexible noodle size silicone tube enters his vein in his right bicep and leads into his superior vena cava (in his heart). This is so he can receive higher concentrated levels on IV nutrition and medication.

Dad stayed with Jedidiah so Mom could take a break and visit her mom.

"Trust in the Lord with all thine heart, and lean not unto thine own understanding. In all thy ways acknowledge Him, and He shall direct thy patch." *Proverbs 3: 5-6*

Friday, February 19, 2010

Jedidiah is still in the PICU, which means he is not yet stable. Dad has been keeping an eye on all of his vitals as well as reading "Little House On The Prairie" out loud. Jedidiah will be in Davis until Monday at least. We are still waiting on the pathology labs to come back to know what kind of cancer it is, and how best to treat it. Good News of the day: the Speech Pathologist visited Jedidiah at 2:30 and cleared him to eat!!! After three days of not being allowed to eat (and two days of vomiting before that) Jedidiah can eat!!...J They gave him vanilla ice cream right away =). The special box of Frosted Flakes cereal he's been saving will have to wait a little while though. Right now he's limited to apple sauce, pears and ice cream, but he can eat =).

8:30 Update: Jedidiah got to eat his Frosted Flakes with Chocolate Milk =) and the Decadron he's getting is doing its job at reducing the swelling in his head, no more headaches or vomiting.

"Rejoice in the Lord always, and again I say rejoice."
Philippians 4:4

Saturday, February 20, 2010

More good news! Jedidiah's vitals were looking good enough last night that the nurses let him sleep the whole night through, no hourly flashlight checks…J He had a big breakfast of sausage, eggs, potatoes and cereal. At two thirty he was moved out of the ICU!!!! Mom and Nanny left Reno, (where they were at the American Endurance Ride Convention), to come visit Jedidiah and to celebrate being out of the ICU. Only one overnight guest was allowed in the ICU, and now both Mom and Dad can spend the night with the now stable Jedidiah. =))

Jedidiah is now in the Davis Tower, 7th Floor Pediatrics, Room 7789, Bed 1.

"And the peace of God which passeth all understanding shall keep your hearts and minds through Christ Jesus." Philippians 4:7

Sunday, February 21, 2010

Jedidiah moved his left arm!!! The surgeon came in and asked to shake Jedidiah's hand, and then asked Jedidiah to shake with his left hand. Jedidiah was able to do it!! He didn't even say it wasn't his. =) Blue Nanny (his grandma, Donnal, as the rest of the world knows her) has been helping Jedidiah move around more. Mom left for Cromberg tonight, has a long "To Do" list of stuff needing attention at home. Dad and Blue Nanny are staying with Jedidiah tonight. We're still waiting on the Pathology Lab to know what our next step will be. A meeting with Neurology and Oncology specialist is tentatively planned for Tuesday morning.

"I can do all things through Christ which strengthens me."
Philippians 4:13

Monday, February 22, 2010

9:30 AM- We should find out the results of the biopsy from the pathology lab today. Dad and Nanny are still with Jedidiah. We're all getting anxious waiting. Please pray for my Daddy, that he'll have the strength to carry on.

12:30 PM- Jedidiah has met with his Physical Therapist, Lisa, and Nutritionist, Terra. With Lisa's help, Jedidiah was able to stand today! Moved his left arm yesterday, stood today- we have progress. =) This is such a relief! When I saw him on Thursday, he couldn't roll over by himself and now he's getting back on his feet!...:) Dad has a whole list of exercises to help Jedidiah with later today to help build his strength and flexibility.

8:30 PM- Still no lab results!! Ugh...;/ Should get them tomorrow... please keep praying. In the meantime, Dad sent me tons of pictures to post today. Ha-ha, so there will be lots of new pictures up soon...;)

"I lift my eyes unto the hills; where does my help come from? My help comes from the Lord, the maker of heaven and earth."
Psalm 121: 1-2

Tuesday, February 23, 2010

3:00 PM- This morning, with the help of his Physical Therapist, Jedidiah got out of bed, WALKED to the chair, sat down while the nurse made his bed, and then walked back to his bed!! When I saw Jedidiah on Thursday, Mom had to roll him over and lift him up for the nurse to change the sheets. We're all so proud and happy for Jedidiah! =)

Mon left Cromberg at ten to drive back down to Sacramento. Her cell phone is breaking though, so I haven't heard from her yet.:/ And we are still waiting on the Pathology Lab- I'll update all of you just as soon as I find out.

5:00 PM- So, it's looking like there won't be any news. Again. :/ Doctors said Jedidiah is their first priority. We haven't gotten results yet because the doctors are still deliberating with each other to determine the best method of treatment. So, we should know tomorrow! In the meantime, Jedidiah keeps getting stronger. Mom is staying with Jedidiah tonight, so Dad and Blue Nanny can go back home.

9:30 PM- Jedidiah got his stitches out today. His scalp wounds are healing nicely.

"Cast your cares upon the Lord, for he cares about you."
1 Peter 5:7

Wednesday, February 24, 2010

Okay, so no results. But Mom said it's okay because the doctors are just being diligent and making sure they choose the best treatment for Jedidiah. And this has not been wasted time. Jedidiah continues to get stronger and healthier each day. Today he walked a couple more steps, assisted by Physical Therapist, to put a Scooby Doo sticker on a piece of paper on the wall!...;) The therapy has been wearing him out though. Jedidiah has been sleeping lots, and cuddling with his Mommy...J

The steroids they have him on to reduce the swelling in his brain, also do increase his appetite... A LOT! Ha-ha, he's been demanding corndogs in addition to each meal. Corndogs, and chocolate eggs...;) Jedidiah continues to get and feel better!

If you know my parents, you know that they were both smokejumpers (crazy people who jump out of perfectly good airplanes to fight forest fires). Some of their old jumping buddies heard about Jedidiah and the story spread. Now there are Smokejumpers throughout the west who will be "Jumping for Jedidiah" this summer.

Tonight Jedidiah was moved to his own private room. It's much quieter. Mom says she thinks they both will finally get some good sleep.

"Have I not commanded thee? Be strong and of good courage; be not afraid, neither be thou dismayed; for the Lord thy God is with thee withersoever thou goest." *Joshua 1: 9*

Thursday, February 25, 2010

The doctor said not to expect any results until next week. The biopsy sample was sent to an outside lab for another opinion. The doctors at UC Davis are doing lots of research and making lots of calls to figure this thing out! In the meantime they have also reduced the steroid, Decadron, (Jedidiah is on this to reduce the swelling in his brain). Because of that medicine, he is super hungry ALL the time. So, they are trying to find the right balance. Right now he is on 2 mg. every six hours. Jedidiah continues to work with his Physical Therapist- walking assisted across the room.

Here is a silly anecdote from this morning:

Setting: Mom and Jedidiah watching the morning news.

Newscaster: "A Killer Whale in Florida killed its trainer yesterday. This is the third person who has succumbed to such an accident…"

Jedidiah: Well, DUH! Isn't it obvious? They are NOT called KILLER whales for nothing!!"

Ha-ha, that my little brother for ya!!...;)

Jedidiah was also visited by the Therapy Dog, Rosy, who cuddled up in bed with him =). Rosy is a four year old Golden Retriever who is one month pregnant!

"Fear thou not…I will strengthen thee…I will help thee."
Isaiah 41:10

Friday, February 26, 2010

Mom and Jedidiah had a very busy day today, wheeling Jedidiah all around the hospital to get Jedidiah a "dilated eye exam". (Picture of him wearing the protective sun glasses after getting his eyes dilated.) Mom lifted him in and out of the wheelchair most of the morning. The Ophthalmologist told Jedidiah he had a very strong mom. Nothing could be truer =).

Dad, Blue Nanny and I are all driving down to Sacramento tomorrow to visit Jedidiah. Justin will join us on Sunday. He is riding down with his Track Coach and family friend, Coach Hannah.

"The name of the Lord is a strong fortress; the godly run to him and are safe." Proverbs 18:10

<u>Saturday, February 27, 2010</u>

Dad, Blue Nanny and I made it down to Davis today. Sure was good to see Mom and Jedidiah! His room is filled with presents and pictures of family. A HUGE "Get Well" card is hung with medical tape on the bathroom door. Dad brought more pictures to hang, lots of cards and presents from friends and family and the eighty seven pounds of food Jedidiah requested!!...:)

I even got to feed Jedidiah a lunch of ravioli, soup, roll, fruit cocktail, pureed prunes, apple juice and chocolate milk! Jedidiah would stick out his tongue to let me know he was ready for another bite, ha-ha, he was like a little, baby birdy. Lunch wore him out though, he's so uncomfortable from lying in bed for two weeks. His new quote is, "there is no such thing as too many pillows!" We stuffed at least seven pillows all around under him, but that kept making him slide down the bed. So it was a constant battle trying to keep him from sliding down, but also keep him comfortable.

Right after lunch the nurse took Jedidiah off of IV fluids. He's now able to drink enough to stay hydrated, take oral salt tablets to stay balanced and is also on oral Decadron. Serious talk about releasing Jedidiah from the hospital has begun. We're hoping for Monday or Tuesday. Then Jedidiah would have a week or so at home before starting his treatments.

Nanny and I are spending the night at the Best Western directly across the street from the hospital. We're planning on having a Family Meeting tomorrow with the doctor.

<u>Sunday, February 28</u>

The Hannah Family came by today, bringing Justin and lots of goodies for Jedidiah. It was great to have them visit. After they left, the Physical

Therapist, Lisa, came in to show the whole family how to help transfer Jedidiah from the bed to the wheelchair. The biggest news; however, was that the pathology lab report came back.

Dr. Z explained to us that Jedidiah has Glioblastoma multiformes, a high grade tumor. This tumor does not respond well to the known treatments, but luckily it does not spread to other parts of the body. I found two websites that have been helpful to better understand his diagnosis: http://emedicine.medscape.com/article/1156220 -overview is more of a brief summary while http://brain.mgh.harvard.edu/patientguide.htm is lengthier.

We should find out Monday when Jedidiah will be able to come home.

Monday, March 1

Oh my goodness, reading all the positive messages in the guestbook was the highlight of my day! I know they mean so much to my parents and Jedidiah when they read them from the hospital. Thank you all SO much.

But about Jedidiah, he should be getting out tomorrow. The nurses helped Dad book a room at Kiwanis for Mom, Dad and Jedidiah for Tuesday and Wednesday night. Kiwanis is similar to the Ronald McDonald house and is only three blocks from the hospital. Thursday morning Jedidiah has a radiation consultation, where they will make a mask of his face to help with the planning of his radiation treatment.

Hopefully then Jedidiah will be coming home for a week or two, during which he will still need 24/7 care. During this time, the radiologists will be planning his treatments and Jedidiah's brain will continue to heal from the biopsy.

Once they are ready for him, Jedidiah will go back to Davis to begin his treatments. In addition to the hour long radiation sessions Monday through Friday, Jedidiah will also be on an oral chemo medication, Temodar. This drug is supposed to increase the tumor's susceptibility to the radiation and is supposed to be an improved version of chemo, as to not cause as too much negative side effects.

After six to eight weeks of this, Jedidiah will get an MRI to see how the tumor is reacting. If all works out, he will start physical rehab to start practice walking again.

So… that's the plan. You now know as much as the family does. I'll keep ya posted.

Tuesday, March 2nd

The hospital celebrated Dr. Seuss' birthday today in a very big way! Jedidiah had green eggs and ham for breakfast and was then visited by a life-sized Cat In The Hat, who performed a song and dance!! Jedidiah got a stuffed Cat In The Hat to keep.

But there has been a change of plans…

Jedidiah woke up our parents last night with incoherent babbling and lots of wriggling. The nurses thought it could be a symptom of withdrawal from the Decadron. But because of this and the fact that he hasn't had as much control over his left arm the past couple of days as he did just a few days before, they scheduled a CAT scan for him.

So this afternoon, after physical therapy Jedidiah had a CAT scan to check on the swelling in his brain since they reduced the amount of anti-inflammatory steroid, Decadron, he was getting. The CAT scan revealed increased pressure in his brain. He then went in for an MRI. The good news is the pressure was not caused by bleeding, but the bad news is the tumor has grown. This is what is causing the increased pressure. The tumor has grown from 4.5 cm by 5.5 cm to almost 6 X6 cm now.

The doctors have increased the Decadron again. Jedidiah has not been discharged today. The doctors are trying to start the radiation and chemo treatments sooner than originally planned. Jedidiah probably won't be coming home soon. But Jedidiah has been alert and focused all day. Mom and Dad are both down there with Jedidiah. I even got to talk to him on the phone today. He tried saying he loves me more than I love him! But that's not even possible!! Thank you all for your continued love and support.

Thanks, Zach, for today's Bible verse:

"So do not fear, for I am with you; do not be dismayed, for I am your God. I will strengthen you and help you; I will uphold you with my righteous right hand." Isaiah 41:10

Underline: Wednesday March 3rd

2:30- The MRI last night showed Jedidiah's tumor has nearly doubled in size since he was admitted at U.C. Davis. The doctors met this morning to re-plan his treatment. Jedidiah is going into emergency radiation this afternoon, after which he will be re-admitted to the PICU and be closely monitored.

5:30- Paula Buus (who babysat all three of us Lusk kids) celebrated Dr. Seuss' birthday yesterday here at the dentist's in Quincy as well. Pictured is her, dressed as 'Sam I Am', with her grandson who thought she looked like a "dork". I had to post this picture so Jedidiah could see her too.

Oh, and Angie, in regards to your question on where to mail cards: I would say send them to our Cromberg home address still. One of my parents is always going back and forth. I think the cards will make it to Jedidiah safer and faster that way.

"My little children, let us not love in word, neither in tongue; but indeed and in truth." 1 John 3:18

Thursday, March 4th

Here is the latest as I understand it:

Yesterday's radiation appointment took over five hours, including the ambulance ride to and from the hospital to the radiology department. First they made a plastic mask of Jedidiah's face and head. Then he had a CAT scan that's connected to the radiology computer. The radiation was performed in a room with six-inch lead walls. Jedidiah had two minutes of broad scale radiation to each side of his head. Due to time sensitivity yesterday, the radiologists did not have the time to pinpoint just the tumor with the radiation. The broad scale radiation also hit the optic nerve and motor function part of his brain. But stopping the tumor's growth as soon as possible is the Main Priority!

Jedidiah has been babbling incoherently during the night, but alert during the day. His Doctor's orders are for him to eat and sleep. Jedidiah's treatments are taxing on the little guy. He started taking Temodar, the chemo medicine last night and wasn't able to hold down his breakfast this morning. He had another radiation appointment this morning at 0700. He will go again tomorrow and spend the weekend recovering.

Now he is eating pizza and strawberry ice cream! The doctor said he will be able to move out of the PICU and back into his own room soon. Phew!!

I am sorry I haven't been able to read through all of the On-line Guestbook and reply. But we appreciate everyone's encouraging messages. Thank you.

"God is our refuge and strength, an ever-present help in trouble. Therefore we will not fear; though the earth give way and the mountains fall into the heart of the sea, though its waters roar and the mountains quake with their surging." Psalms 46: 1-3.

<u>Friday, March 5th</u>

Jedidiah had his third radiation treatment this morning. The radiologist finished the complex 3-D map of his brain in time for this morning's treatment. With this map, they are able to pinpoint the tumor's location and just radiate that specific area. The radiation treatment takes just a few minutes and is painless- just like an X-ray. The experts program the waves to be high enough to kill the tumor, but just low enough to spare the healthy brain tissue. Dad explained to me that radiation is an electronic impulse between negative and positive poles. Jedidiah continues to take the chemo medicine Temodar to weaken the tumor's defenses against the radiation. Jedidiah will continue treatments as an inpatient in the hospital (instead of being able to come home during the weekends or staying at Ronald McDonald's) for a while so the doctors can still monitor him closely. But he is out of the PICU now and back into a private room of his own!

Mom is coming home tonight to sign Justin's Driver's Permit stuff and is staying until Sunday. It's so great of Dad to make sure she gets a break. Dad's staying with Jedidiah this weekend to keep him company. Jedidiah's getting a break from the radiation during the weekend.

Picture of Jedidiah and his radiation mask. This mask helps him hold still during his treatments so the radiation can be pinpointed to hit just the tumor.

"We are afflicted in every way, but not crushed. Perplexed, but not driven to despair. Persecuted, but not forsaken. Struck down, but not destroyed." 2 Corinthians 4:8-9

Saturday March 6th

No radiation today. Jedidiah has been busy eating and sleeping. He holds coherent conversations with Dad. Jedidiah tells stories of all his best memories. Aunt Linda had the final answer when Dad and Jedidiah couldn't remember if we had fondue at Camp Grandma in Idaho or during a camping trip to Moab. It turns out they were both right!

Our cousin, Christy, came up from Santa Barbara to visit Jedidiah today.

Mom, Nanny, Justin and I all met for breakfast at the all you can eat biscuits and gravy hosted by Bikers of Northern California. Half of the proceeds are being donated to benefit Jedidiah! Thank you for all of your generous contributions.

"So we do not lose heart, though our outer nature is wasting away, our inner nature is being renewed every day." 2 Corinthians 4:16

Sunday March 7th

Jedidiah had a pizza party with his Uncle John, Aunt Stevie and Cousin Christy last night! He still woke up three times during the night for "midnight snacks". Today was a restful day for Jedidiah. He hung out with Uncle John during the morning while Dad took Christy out for Breakfast. Mom is now back in Sacramento, hugging Jedidiah.

"For I am sure that neither death nor life, nor angels, nor principalities, nor things present, nor things to come, nor powers, nor height, nor depth, nor anything else in all creation will be able to separate us from the love of God in Christ Jesus, our Lord." Romans 8:38-39

Monday March 8th

Jedidiah had his fourth radiation treatment this morning. The doctor warned he'd get worse before he can get better. The radiation made his right hand uncoordinated, and he is unable to speak. We are looking forward to the getting better part. Jedidiah is slowing talking again though.

Both Mom and Dad were there when the Plumas County SWAT Team stopped by to visit Jedidiah!! Deputy Shawn Webb had a GBM tumor (the same kind Jedidiah has) nine months ago and is back to work now, after undergoing similar treatment. Jedidiah got a SWAT t-shirt of his own.

"Praise be to the God and Father of our Lord Jesus Christ, the Father of compassion and God of all comfort, who comforts us in all our troubles, so we can comfort those in any trouble with the comfort we ourselves have received from God." 2 Corinthians 1:3-4

Tuesday March 9th

When the doctors said the tumor had grown, they meant it has gone from the size of a cashew to the size of a walnut. As the tumor grows, it puts more pressure on his brain. The fact that the tumor is growing on a part of the brain that controls motor function, does not help Jedidiah. The pressure caused by the growing tumor is what's causing Jedidiah to lose motor skills and see double. The radiation treatments are supposed to kill tumor cells, but that also causes swelling. The steroid, Decadron, is supposed to help keep the brain swelling to a minimum. The doctors have started radiation treatments quickly, to try to kill the tumor as quickly as possible. The good news is all the bad side effects Jedidiah is experiencing now are reversible.

Jedidiah enjoyed visiting with Christy. Now she is going to go spy on his big brother Justin for a while, and will report her findings back to him. Jedidiah is more than happy to follow the doctor's orders to eat and sleep. He also continues to tell stories to Mom during the afternoon. He made up a new joke as well: Question: "What is the main ingredient for pancakes?" Answer: "The Pan, of course!" Ha ha ha…he has always been a silly guy!

Wednesday, March 10th

A correction I need to make: Jedidiah not only received a new t-shirt from the Plumas County SWAT Team, but he also received a REAL, Tactical SWAT Team Jacket! Here is a photo of Jedidiah in that jacket. Jedidiah was officially Deputized! He looks the part, because he IS now a part of the Plumas County SWAT Team. How cool is that?!

Physical therapy has been added back to Jedidiah's daily schedule. He met with Lisa today to stretch out his muscles and joints.

Jedidiah heard the Polka Dot is open now in Quincy! He is looking forward to coming home and ordering Blue Goo in a cone, dipped in chocolate!!

Jedidiah has his up days and his down days…today it seems to be a down. Please join our family in praying and sending positive thought to Jedidiah at seven tonight.

"Having no anxiety about anything, but in everything by prayer and supplication with thanksgiving let your requests be known to God. And the peace of God, which passes all understanding, will keep your hearts and minds in Christ Jesus." Philippians 4:6-7

Thursday, March 11

Yesterday Jedidiah worked on balancing while sitting up. Today he met with the Occupational Therapist, Kate, to practice standing. Mom said they both have been sleeping pretty well lately, from 10 PM to 5 AM. It sounds too early for me! The anti-nausea medicine has been working well; Jedidiah is able to hold down all of his food. He's just been very tired. He has an MRI scheduled Monday.

Cousin Anna found out there is a brand of snowboarding clothes named after Jedidiah!

"I can do all things in Him who strengthens me." Philippians 4:13

Friday, March 12th

Jedidiah finished his eighth chemo and radiation treatment today. He then had physical therapy. After lunch he's going to meet with his Occupational Therapist. He's been a busy boy and is glad to have the weekend off to recuperate. Dad is driving down there this afternoon bringing get-well cards and presents!

"The Lord is gracious and compassionate; slow to anger and rich in love. The Lord is good to all; he has compassion on all he has made." Psalm 145:8-9

Saturday, March 13th

Jedidiah's doctor wrote a prescription for sunshine!! Mom and Dad wheeled Jedidiah outdoors into the sun today! Jedidiah's spirit is still there, he's just tired from all the medication and the tumor's pressure on his brain. He still sees double, cannot speak, is uncoordinated and a little confused, but he has stabilized over the last three days. He'll rest and spend time with our parents this weekend. The MRI on Monday will determine his treatment for the next couple weeks.

"Let us not grow weary in well doing, for in due season we shall reap, if we do not lose heart." Galatians 6:9

Sunday, March 14th

Jedidiah enjoyed another leisure stroll around the outside of the hospital today, being pushed in his wheelchair by Mom and Dad, accompanied by Uncle John and Aunt Stevie. He wore his "No Fear" shirt that Nano sent. Mom went home last night and will return to Sacramento tomorrow morning in time for the MRI results. We are hoping for the best- that the radiation and chemo have stunted the tumor's growth. We are hoping Jedidiah will be able to continue his treatments as an out-patient. If so, he will be able to stay at the Ronald McDonald house during the week days and return home on the weekends. Please pray for this with us.

Jedidiah has enjoyed his visitors this week: Coach Elliot Smart, of the Johnsville Junior Ski Team (or JJST- for short) stopped by on Thursday to say hi. Yesterday Coach Richard brought his gang of former "Fire On Ice" JJST Racers. (Everybody who knows about JJST, knows that "Fire On Ice" is THE Fastest team! It MUST something to do with the coaching...) Natalie Kepple also stopped by to see Jedidiah. She sings Jedidiah's favorite song, "Beautiful Katy." Jedidiah would sing along to that song on the way to the bus stop almost every morning since getting that C.D. Thank you all! It means a lot not only to Jedidiah, but to our whole family.

"May your unfailing love rest upon us, O Lord, even as we put our hope in you." Psalm 32:22

Monday March 15th

Jedidiah's MRI was this morning. The preliminary results that were "expected soon" at eleven, actually came around one. Two doctors had two different opinions; one said the tumor has grown slightly, while the other said it does not appear that the tumor has grown at all. They both followed up their encouraging news with the statement, "This is the fastest growing GBM we've ever seen!" We have heard THAT before...Sheeze, those silly doctors. BUT, we are taking "slow to no growth" in one week, compared to the "doubling in size the first two weeks" as a HUGE improvement! No official word from the doctors yet, but to me, it means that the radiation and chemo treatment ARE working. They are not just torturing Jedidiah with these procedures, it's paying off. Now we need that tumor to start shrinking!!

The doctors were still deciphering the MRI during rounds at six o'clock. They will have all the results in the morning. They did suggest to Dad that he should start looking into any openings at the Ronald McDonald house. We are staying positive that Jedidiah will be able to come home this weekend in time for his brother's birthday party. Jedidiah is looking forward to playing board games with his family the week after his ninth birthday,

Mom drove back to Sacramento this afternoon to relieve Dad. She had quite the surprise today. After loading up the truck with bags of animal feed at Pet County Feed and Tack store in Quincy (with bags of food for ALL the different animals at our house) she was told the bill was already paid and taken care of!! Thank you to whoever is responsible! That was really nice.

Pictured is Jedidiah working hard with his Physical Therapist. He worked on bridging today; using his feet and legs to lift his torso off the bed. This maneuver strengthens his legs and core muscles as well as making it easier on Mom and Dad to move Jedidiah.

"Those who wait on the Lord shall renew their strength; they shall mount up with wings like eagles, they shall run and not be weary, they shall walk and not faint." Isaiah 40:31

Tara, thanks for sending this Bible verse. You have perfect timing.

Tuesday, March 16th

Jedidiah is getting a new radiation mask made tomorrow. His cheeks have gotten chubby and swollen from the Decadron and the mask he has now no longer fits comfortably. This evening one of the doctors brought in a portable machine to show Mom the latest MRI. He compared yesterday's MRI to the one taken a month ago when Jedidiah was first admitted. The tumor has grown from 3.1cm by 4.2cm, to 4.5cm by 5.6cm. Mom said the numbers meant little to her, compared to seeing the picture of how much room the tumor takes up inside Jedidiah's skull. The radiologists are again working on refining the targeted area and will use the data by Monday.

Talk about discharging Jedidiah began again! Of course the actual discharge process is complex and includes lots of paperwork from various departments and professionals throughout the hospital...But it is the beginning of getting Jedidiah home and my parents out of that hospital, and for that, I am Thankful!!!

Wednesday evening, Uncle John is staying with Jedidiah so Mom and Dad can go to watch Justin's first track meet of the season.

"This is my commandment, that you love one another as I have loved you." John 15:12.

Wednesday, March 17th

Happy Saint Patrick's Day! It seems to be a lucky day! We just got the news today that Jedidiah will be discharged from the hospital tomorrow!!! They'll spend Thursday night at Uncle John's and leave Sacramento after Jedidiah's radiation treatment Friday morning. Dad will drive and Mom will sit in back with Jedidiah to help hold him up during the three hour ride home. We're all so excited Jedidiah will be home for his big brother's birthday!

(I do have to temper this good news though, with a warning- Jedidiah is coming home in a wheelchair. He cannot sit up by himself, much less stand. He wears a diaper. His left arm is still immobile and he does not talk much. I don't say this to scare anybody, or to sound negative, but simply to remind everyone that Jedidiah will not be able to play yet. As Dad says, "It's just like when he came home from the hospital as a tiny baby. He is too delicate to play with yet.")

Jedidiah will return to Sacramento on Sunday evening to continue his chemo and radiation treatments during the week.

I want to thank Lisa Kelly for organizing the Johnsville Junior Ski Team Fundraisers for Jedidiah! I know there were countless others who donated items for the raffle, sold tickets and more…I am sorry I don't have all your names, but thank you!! Finally, thank you to all who bought tickets! The JJST made an outstanding amount of money!! The community's support is incredible!!!

Jedidiah had another pretty cool visitor today- Jon Brockman, #40 from the Sacramento Kings! (Basketball Team, I think?…) He even gave Jedidiah his autograph.

"For I know the thoughts I think toward you, says the Lord, thoughts of peace and not of evil, to give you a future and a hope." Jeremiah 29:11

Thursday, March 18th

Mom, Dad, Uncle John and Aunt Stevie had a long and stressful day today, but their hard work paid off. At five o'clock, Jedidiah was released from the hospital after almost five weeks!!! They are spending the night at Uncle John's, going to radiation in the morning and then driving home. Jedidiah gets to spend the weekend at home before returning to Sacramento to continue his chemo and radiation treatments.

Picture of Jedidiah yesterday with a smaller therapy dog.

"We are afflicted in every way, but not crushed; perplexed, but not driven to despair; persecuted, but not forsaken; struck down, but not destroyed.” 2 Corinthians 4:8-9

Friday, March 19th

Jedidiah is home, Hurray!! They left Sacramento around 11 AM and made it home with enough time to get Jedidiah situated and feed the horses before picking up Justin from town. Jedidiah is upstairs in Mom and Dad's bed for tonight. They're going to look into getting a small hospital bed from a Forest Service friend, to put downstairs to create a new "room" for Jedidiah in our living room. We are hoping the wheelchair will make it possible for him to sit at the dinner table to eat with our family.

"Likewise the Spirit helps us in our weakness, for we do not know how to pray as we ought, but the Spirit himself intercedes for us with sighs too deep for words.” Romans 8:26

Monday, March 22nd

Yikes, I've fallen behind with my updates this weekend. I was busy in Cromberg, visiting both brothers! So, I'll do Saturday and Sunday on one journal and do Monday's later this evening.

Saturday, March 20th was Jedidiah's second day home and Mom's "Work Party". She had some Forest Service people come help cut trees, rake pine needles and burn the debris around our house to make it fire safe. Thanks to those who came to help!! I had a good time showing up after all the work was done. Jedidiah's teacher visited and played the recorder. She teaches all her students to play. Jedidiah learned how to play several songs in her third grade class, including, "Jingle Bells." Last December he could play these by memory. We hope he is able to play them again soon!

Shawn Webb and his daughter also stopped by to visit. Thanks, Shawn! You and your family are a real inspiration to us!! We sure do appreciate you.

Meghan from Great Northern donated five bags of "Adult Sanitary Pants" or diapers. Granted, it's not a very glamorous gift to give, but a very useful one for us! Thank you.

Sunday, March 21st we celebrated Justin's Sixteenth Birthday!!! Jedidiah wore a birthday hat and celebrated with us while Justin opened presents. Mom brought the baby goat, "Bucky" out to say hi to Jedidiah. It was super cute! Justin received an awesome birthday present- several people volunteered to help fix up the old International Scout so he can drive it!! Thank you to Dan and Andrea Seiler, Susan Bergstrand and Ryan Nuepen. (Sorry about any possible misspellings.)

"We know that in everything God works for good with those who love him, who are called according to his purpose." Romans 8:28

Monday, March 22nd

Happy Anniversary Mom and Dad!!!

They left for Sacramento yesterday afternoon and checked into the Ronald McDonald house that evening. Mom and Dad were both there to wheel Jedidiah the eight blocks from the R.M. House to the Radiation Center for his treatment. The night before Jedidiah had not been talking and did not recognize Mom or Dad, but today was a better day! Dad told Jedidiah to roll all the way over instead of rolling only halfway over and getting stuck on his tummy. Jedidiah then rolled over three times! It may sound silly, but that is great mobility for him. Jedidiah also asked to have a picnic lunch outside! Jedidiah moving and talking more is always wonderful.

Picture of Mom and Jedidiah at the Ronald McDonald House.

Tuesday, March 23rd

Wow, I just can't say it enough: Thank you for all your continued support!! Quincy has the greatest amount of love and kindness per capita than anywhere else. Even with our insurance, the cost of Jedidiah's medicine and treatment is astounding. The community has also poured out its love as financial support. There are SO many people who have taken the initiative to help, without asking for any recognition. Thank you to whoever set out the Donation Cans in businesses around town. Thank you also to Pangaea's and everyone (I know there is a lot of you!) who are organizing the "Friends of Jedidiah" dinner on May 22nd, to the FRC Rodeo Team- who are planning to host a rodeo for Jedidiah's benefit on May 12th, and to the Plumas Christian School- who are planning a play to support Jedidiah. We appreciate ALL of this! Also, most importantly, thank you for all the prayers, love, hugs and emotional support! There is no way our family would be able to make it through this without all of your help, thank you!!

Speaking of support, Coach Kim from Johnsville Junior Ski Team visited Mom and Jedidiah this morning. She helped Mom cook breakfast after walking with them to Jedidiah's radiation treatment. Kim also brought Jedidiah two pet goldfish! Mom says she is adjusting to being at the Ronald McDonald House. It's NOT a fun place for her, but it does beat the hospital.

Picture of Jedidiah, Mom, Justin and Kyra (Justin's friend) at Justin's Sweet Sixteen Birthday Party.

"Blessed is the man who perseveres under trial, because when he has stood the test, he will receive the crown of life that God has promised to those who love them." James 1:12

Wednesday, March 24th

Oh my goodness, there are lots more people to thank!!!

Bill Hopman drove to Sacramento today to give Mom a Laptop computer to borrow. Now Mom will be able to keep up with and reply to the messages in the CaringBridge Guestbook. Bill even helped set up a personal email account for Mom (her first one ever, outside of work!). The laptop is for more that providing Mom a way to stay in touch, it will also help provide entertainment for Jedidiah.

Picture of Bill Hopman showing Mom how to use the new computer.

Brian Woods, owner of Quincy Tow and driver of 3A Stock Car, picked up the Scout yesterday to check out the transmission. He has also offered to drive Jedidiah in his stock car during the "Hot Laps" this summer.

Jedidiah is stoked!! Bill Coates, owner of Delleker Les Schwab, checked the Subaru's front and rear brakes- no charge, Mom and Dad have been taking that Subaru through the canyon to Sacramento, numerous times these past five weeks. You can imagine how important good brakes are for us! Mr. Transue donated his time and labor and his backhoe during the work party on Saturday. The Forest Service employees from Beckwourth Ranger District have taken turns providing hot dinners for Dad, Justin and Blue Nanny every Wednesday.

Thank You! Thank You! Thank You! Thank You!

Again I find myself thanking Coach Kim Wilbanks. She is a JJST Coach and even helped teach Jedidiah how to ski. I received an email from her today about the "Ski for Jed Day". She has planned an awesome fundraiser and wants to get the news out, so here is the inside scoop:

I don't know if you were aware of this but I have been working on a fundraiser for Jedidiah- "Ski for Jed Day". I am going to give beginner ski lessons at Soda Springs for $30. each on March 27th. I can do 30 people, which could raise $900.00 for Jedidiah IF I can find people wanting lessons. (Equipment rental is free- donated by shops in Truckee.) It's a good deal, as a comparable lesson at North Star is $90. (And I have more training and certification than most of their instructors!!)

Also, I asked Soda Springs if they would help out with the tickets, and they did me one better- they GAVE me 100 lift tickets, good for the rest of the ski season!!! I am selling these tickets for a discounted price- $20. Each, which could bring in an additional $2,000!!!. These tickets (and the lessons) are available at:

Quincy- Plumas Parks & Rec Office
Greenville- Evergreen Market
Portola- Valu-Wise
Loyalton- Dr. Walker's Office
Chester- Chester Progressive Office

It's completely incredible how everyone is using their unique talents and abilities to continue to help out our family. **Thank you all!**

Jedidiah continued his radiation and chemo treatments today and continue to follow the doctor's orders to eat and sleep. Mom laid a blanket on the ground today and they both practiced rolling around. He is getting stronger and wanting to move around more, which is a great sign! I know they had an appointment with Dr. Z this morning. I haven't heard how that went but I have learned that no news is good news!

"For God so loved the world that he gave his only begotten son, that whoever believeth in Him shall not perish, but have everlasting life." John 3:16

Thursday March 25th

Jedidiah completed his 16th radiation and chemo treatment today. Because Friday is "Cesar Chavez Day" for the State of California, the treatment center will be closed. Bad for killing the tumor, but good for Jedidiah's birthday weekend! Dad will drive to Sacramento to bring Mom and Jedidiah home Friday. All the cousins are convening in Cromberg on Sunday to celebrate Jedidiah's Birthday.

Picture of Nurse Terri with the family and the HUGE box of Lucky Charms cereal that she got for Jedidiah! Also, I added a couple new photos to the website- feel free to check 'em out.

"Jesus answered, 'I am the way and the truth and the life. No one comes to the Father except through me'." John 14:6

Friday, March 26

I went out to Cromberg for dinner with the WHOLE family tonight! We had meatloaf and mashed potatoes made by the Collins Family. Thank you guys, it was delicious!

Jedidiah's hair is falling out on the sides. It looks like he has half a Mohawk now...

This morning Mom said, "Jedidiah, hug me." Jedidiah rolled all the way over, put his arm and leg around his mommy and smiled!!! This evening Jedidiah hugged both me and Justin on the couch. Jedidiah was definitely responsive today. When I asked him if he wanted to stay on the pillow or lay flat, he answered, "I want to stay on the pillows." When I was adjusting him on the pillows, trying to keep him comfortable, he leaned forward and "bridged" when I asked him to. I was so impressed!

Justin was being sweet and kissing on his little brother. Jedidiah, acting just like his old self, mumbled, "Oh I hate it when my brother kisses me." Ha-ha!! I almost started crying. It was SO great to hear Jedidiah acting like himself! Jedidiah's been physically stable, which is enough to be thankful for. But to hear his voice and to enjoy interacting with him again, is nothing short of amazing!!! Jedidiah was worn out by the time I left to go home. I am sure he'll sleep good tonight.

"If you declare with your mouth, 'Jesus is Lord' and believe in your heart that god raised Him from the dead, you will be saved." Romans 10:9

Sunday March 28th

The WHOLE Lusk clan came to Cromberg to celebrate Jedidiah's ninth birthday party! We had people flying from Washington and Southern California, and driving from Northern Idaho and Oregon, but they ALL made it!

Aunt Linda brought a race car piñata and chocolate cake. Christy and Dad helped Jedidiah bust open the piñata! Wawee (the nickname for Dad's Mom) brought at least fifteen cans of Silly String and we had an epic battle. The chocolate fountain from April Keenan was a huge hit! Jedidiah's friends Nano and JD also stopped by. (Jedidiah waved goodbye to them when they left!!)

Dad and Linda are staying with Jedidiah this week. Before they left, mom gave Jedidiah, "Too Many Kisses" which made him giggle… It was the greatest sound!! Jedidiah waved AND giggled- it was an awesome day! Thank you all for making the effort to come to visit for Jedidiah's birthday party. It was SO much fun!!!

Pictured are all of us cousins surrounding Jedidiah. I have several other pictures from the party, but for some reason they are not uploading right. Hopefully they will be up tomorrow.

"Judge not, and you will not be judged. Condemn not, and you will not be condemned. Forgive, and you will be forgiven. Give and it will be given to you." Matthew 7:1-2

Monday, March 29th

Dad and Linda took Jedidiah to his radiation treatment in the morning and the cousins stopped by later. It snowed in Cromberg, but it was sunny in Sacramento. Jedidiah asked Dad to put him in his wheelchair to go outside. Jedidiah was aware of where he was, who he was, accepting of the fact he needs a wheelchair and he wanted to go outside to enjoy the sunshine! Before bed, Jedidiah and Uncle John practiced rolling around on a blanket on the ground.

The doctors said the brain is not designed to carry away dead cell material like the rest of the body, and shrinking a GBM tumor takes time- months, if not years. The short term goal is to stop the tumor's exponential growth. Jedidiah still has double vision and limited mobility but his level of consciousness has improved and he remains a fighter.

Picture of all us cousins having a Silly String fight during Jedidiah's birthday party.

"Heaviness in the heart of a man maketh it stoop; but a good word maketh it glad." Proverbs 12:25

Tuesday, March 30th

Happy Birthday Jedidiah!! He is officially nine years old today! It was cloudy this morning so Dad, Linda and Jedidiah took the shuttle to the radiology center. Dad thinks he should get a new truck-C4500 4x4 with sleeper, lift and snowplow- kind of like that shuttle bus, ha ha!

Mom took the baby goat, "Bucky" to Mrs. Lemnah's third grade class today. The students found him adorable! The entire class sang, "Happy Birthday" and played their recorders for Jedidiah over Mom's cell phone. Jedidiah asked them to play more!

Tuesday night was also the Johnsville Junior Ski Team Awards Night. Mom and Justin went on Dad's and Jedidiah's behalf. Jedidiah's ski racing team awarded him the "Coach's Award" and the entire JJST gave Jedidiah a new award, called the "JJST Hero Award Trophy," AND they gave him a Standing Ovation! The Ski Team has SO many wonderful people behind it, who have been so incredibly supportive. Thank you all!!!

Other highlights of the day include: Jedidiah using the big potty, and reaching out, grabbing a muffin and feeding himself. We're all so very proud of him!

Picture of Jedidiah and his Aunt Linda enjoying the sun.

"I will not leave you comfortless: I will come to you." John 14:18

Friday, April 2<u>nd</u>

Jedidiah finished his radiation treatment for the week. He gets two days just to relax now. He impressed his doctor on Wednesday with how much he's been talking this week! Jedidiah made Aunt Linda cry today when he told Dad he loves him. He has been laughing a lot too! Dad sent videos of Jedidiah laughing from "Too Many Kisses" from Dad, and of Linda reading the big joke book, "Jokelopedia" Jedidiah got for his birthday from Jesse, Bri, Gavin, Emma and Danny Whitley (Thank you So much, Jedidiah just LOVES that book!)

They made a new radiation mask for Jedidiah this morning, again, lol! This time they padded the cheeks so hopefully this mask can last a little longer with his continuously growing cheeks. At Jedidiah's appointment on Wednesday, his doctor said they are planning on stopping radiation in about two and a half weeks and then doubling the Temodar- the chemo medicine he is on now. Also, they want to add an adult kind of chemo medicine. As I understand it, both chemo treatments will be in pill form, so I think Jedidiah might be home more, which is very exciting.

Not only has Jedidiah been talking, laughing and rolling lots, he also stood for a second during a transfer to the potty yesterday. He also has been asking for the urinal. He is much more aware and much happier. Thank you for all your continued love and support.

Also, thank you very much to Aunt Linda for helping Dad and Jedidiah all this week. We Love you Linda!!!

"*Make a joyful noise unto the Lord, all ye lands.*" Psalm 100:1

<u>Saturday, April 3rd</u>

Linda told a funny story that Carli text her, and it made Jedidiah laugh and laugh! It seems that when the Williams Family returned home after Jedidiah's birthday, their dog, Max, was so happy to see them he "wee-weed" all over our cousin, Cole. Jedidiah thought that was just the funniest story he had heard in a long time!

Uncle John is watching Jedidiah tonight so Mom and Dad can ride together in the fifteen mile Nevada Derby tomorrow. It's a horse endurance ride near Reno. Thanks Uncle John!!! Jedidiah was asking for his mommy tonight (well, okay- he was really yelling and hollering for Mom). It must have been very hard on Uncle John, but Mom said it is something he has been doing lately, even when she IS there.

This is why it is SO great that Jedidiah's been saying stuff like, "Dad, I love you!"

This has been hard for all of us, but there still are small miracles in every day, you just have to look.

The picture is from Wednesday night, when Mom and Justin went to the Johnsville Junior Ski Team Awards Night- accepting Jedidiah's Hero Award Trophy.

Justin, I and my boyfriend, John, are leaving for Santa Barbara tomorrow to enjoy the sun at our Cousin Christy's house for Spring Break! Updates may not be as often this week, but hang tight; there'll be still coming...

"*Open the gates, that the righteous nation may enter; the one which keeps faith.*" Isaiah 26:2

<u>Sunday April 4th</u>

Happy Easter!! Dad and Mom had fun at the endurance ride yesterday. It was snowing outside of Tahoe and chains were required over I-80 on Donner Summit today. Mom made it through the snow and back to Sacramento tonight. Dad said that Jedidiah is mentally himself 25% of the time now. Well, that is a 25% increase over what he had when radiation began. When Mom showed up tonight, Jedidiah said he missed her, and then asked her to read a joke to him.

Picture of Mom and Jedidiah reuniting after Mom's week off. Thank you Aunt Linda and Uncle John for helping to make that possible!

"The angel said to the women, 'Do not be afraid, for I know that you are looking for Jesus, who was crucified. He is not here; He has risen, just as He said'." Matthew 28:5

Tuesday, April 6th

Jedidiah has nine more radiation treatments left!! Then he will change to chemo pills at home. Hopefully! ...Sounds like a good plan to me though!! He's still himself mentally around twenty five percent of the time. Mom is with him this week and they continue their routine of treatments, eating and sleeping.

Picture of Mom and Dad at the Endurance Ride Sunday. Thank you again, Uncle John, for staying with Jedidiah so they could spend the time together and do that.

"So I always take pains to have a clear conscience towards God and towards men." Acts 24:16

Saturday, April 10th

Wow, it's been a while since I've posted. Sorry about that. I've been on vacation and haven't had working internet. Justin, John and I stopped by to visit Jedidiah on our way home from Santa Barbara yesterday. It was my first time being at the Ronald McDonald House. Jedidiah, Mom and Blue Nanny are all spending the weekend there. Justin brought back souvenirs for Mom and Jedidiah, including a bunny lollipop. Jedidiah giggled and giggled about the fact that he was "eating a bunny's face". It was adorable! He kept asking me to read more jokes from his Jokelopedia book. He already knew most of the answers to the riddles too!! We stayed for dinner. Aunt Stevie made delicious homemade macaroni and cheese. Justin and I took turns feeding Jedidiah the pumpkin pie he was so excited for. Jedidiah has six more radiation treatments starting Monday.

Picture of us three siblings hugging!

"And these three remain: faith, hope and love, but the greatest of these is Love." 1 Corinthians 13:13

Sunday, April 11th

Jedidiah is given anesthesia before every radiation treatment so he'll stay completely still throughout the entire treatment. Those of you who have been under anesthesia know how waking up from it can be tiring and confusing. This feeling is only added to the effects Jedidiah already feels from the tumor. Since he doesn't have radiation, and therefore anesthesia, during the weekends, Sundays are usually his best days. Today he thoroughly enjoyed Blue Nanny reading him jokes. The two cuddled up and giggled up for hours. Jedidiah asked Nanny to call. So, I got to talk to Jedidiah today! He said he loved me, thanked us for visiting and asked us to visit him again! It was great to hear from him!! Another exciting part of yesterday's visit was seeing Jedidiah using his right arm and hand again. He picked up the sea shell Justin brought back from Santa Barbara. He smelled it and listened to it. He said it smelled funny, like sand, and he heard the sound of the ocean through the shell.

Picture of Blue Nanny and Jedidiah reading jokes. Just look at that smile!!!

"Whatever you have learned or received or heard from me, or seen in me- put it into practice. And the God of peace will be with you." Philippians 4:9

Wednesday April 14th

Dad made it to Sacramento last night. This morning, all three of them went to Jedidiah's treatment (only three left now). Afterwards they went to Jedidiah's weekly appointment at the Cancer Center. At the appointment, Mom learned how to change Jedidiah's PIC dressing. Now she will be able

Always Remember Me

to do that at home instead of having to go to Sacramento every week to have it changed. Jedidiah also went to the Dermatologist to get the rash on his chest checked out. They took a biopsy of it to see whether the rash is an infection, or just a reaction from the drugs Jedidiah is on, The doctor thinks it is most likely the latter, but it is better to be safer that sorry.

Dad ordered an "Extremely Comfy" lounge chair from Cabala's for Jedidiah. Now Jedidiah is finally able to lie comfortably! Thanks, Dad!! The three of them enjoyed the sunshine this afternoon after their busy morning of appointments. Jedidiah talked, sang, read jokes, and told his parents how much he loves them! Jedidiah said he was having fun and also asked to go to the zoo now.

Picture of Jedidiah relaxing comfortably for the first time in two months! In his new chair his Dad got for him.

"Being confident of this very thing, that He who has begun a good work in you will complete it until the day of Jesus Christ."
Philippians 1:6

Saturday, April 17th

Jedidiah has shown immense improvement the past couple days. He has been wiggling his left fingers and toes, singing, holding conversations, declaring he will walk again and even reciting the L O N G poem, "The Cremation of Sam McGee". We are all SO impressed with him!!

Jedidiah called me again last night from Uncle John's house. They were having a BBQ and Jedidiah was feeding himself corn on the cob and ribs! Jedidiah's portrait, "My Green Picture" debuted on the front page of the Feather River Bulletin (Quincy's weekly newspaper). When I told Jedidiah about it he said, "Now I'm famous!" He has always been a silly guy. He asked me to put Justin on the phone, but I had just dropped Justin off at home in Cromberg. Jedidiah is excited to see his big brother again!

Have you guys seen the new bracelets the High School students are sporting? They say, "Always Be Positive" on one side and "For Jedidiah" on the other! The Leadership Class of Quincy High is the force behind this. Our family is already clamoring for their own bracelets. Big thanks to Hannah, ASB President at Quincy High for this great idea!

Mom, Dad, and Jedidiah enjoyed pizza and ice cream this week, thanks to the Holten Family. That was awesome of you guys!

Mom drove to Yuba City today to watch Justin's track meet. Justin placed second in the mile with a time of 5:09! Mom is driving Justin and I back to Sacramento early tomorrow for a family trip to the Sacramento Zoo!! We will be all together Monday morning for Jedidiah's LAST radiation treatment. We are all SO excited!!

Picture of what Jedidiah's radiation treatment room looks like.

"There, in the presence of the Lord your God, you and your families shall eat and shall rejoice in everything you have put your hand to, because the Lord your God has blessed you."
Deuteronomy 12:7

Sunday, April 18th

The zoo was Awesome today!! We are all worn out from having so much fun! Jedidiah was most excited about seeing a zebra, a giraffe and a crocodile, and we saw all three...and more! Jedidiah even got to feed a giraffe today! He is doing SO much better now, compared to the last time I saw him. He showed Justin and I how much he can move his left leg and wiggle his left fingers! He has declared he will walk again, It is such an incredible feeling to be able to have conversations with him again!!!

Unfortunately my camera batteries died, so no picture of Jedidiah feeding the giraffes tonight. Be ready for one tomorrow. Good night and sleep good!

Monday, April 19th

We're home!! We celebrated Jedidiah's last radiation treatment this morning with lots of sweets! Two men who work at the radiation treatment center, Rick and John, brought donuts and apple pastries to share with us. After Mom changed Jedidiah's PIC dressing at his last appointment for three weeks, we all went home! Jedidiah has three chemo and radiation free weeks ahead of him!

Picture of family at the zoo yesterday

Wednesday, April 21st

I'm so excited! I get to spend all day tomorrow with Jedidiah. I'm filling in for Mom so she can take three of her horses to get gelded, while Dad is at work. Jedidiah is a fun guy to spend time with! Monday night we celebrated his homecoming with a meal of shrimp, and a family board game of "Life".

Tickets are now available for the Lasagna Dinner at Pangaea's for the "Friends of Jedidiah Celebration" May 22. Information is in this week's newspaper. I believe tickets are for sale at Pangaea's, Epilog and one other location...

Tickets are limited but the dinner will be followed by desserts, a music performance, slide show, silent and live auctions Extravaganza at the Vet's Hall in Quincy (No tickets are required!!) Music and silent auction begins at 5:30. Jedidiah's classmates from Mrs. Lemnah's third grade class will be giving a special performance as well as many other talented local musicians including the QHS Band and the Keppel Family (who sing Jedidiah's favorite song, "Katy"). It's going to be a fun-filled night!

Attention Lusk Family: (including Williams and Chavis) I mailed out your, "Always Be Positive For Jedidiah" bracelets today for everyone. Start checking your mailboxes soon...

Today's picture is of Jedidiah and Dad feeding the giraffes at Jedidiah's trip to the zoo. Sorry it's only the backs of their heads though, lol, that's all I could see. The boys got to go into the special fenced off feeding area.

"But when the Holy Spirit controls our lives, he will produce the kind of fruit in us: love, joy, peace, patience, goodness, faithfulness, gentleness and self-control." Galatians 5:22

Friday, April 23rd

Yesterday was a blast! I spent all day with Jedidiah. =) I cooked and cooked and fed and fed and fed that guy. Talking the whole time of course! It was so great having a conversation with him! I was nervous about being able to lift and move him, but I successfully transferred him from the chair to the bed, back to the chair, to the potty and then back to the bed! I was SO proud of not dropping him. Of course my transfers weren't as smooth and skillful as Mom and Dad's but Jedidiah was very patient with me. I was so worn out that once Justin showed up, I took a nap next to Jedidiah. It was a wonderful day!!

Today we had a Bonfire and S'More Party. Jedidiah split the wood for the bonfire all by himself! He used the wood splitter (He got to move the lever). Ha ha, it was great fun! Jedidiah then started a competition of who could make the best S'More. Of course, he was the judge! John, Justin and I all tied for first place, but I think Jedidiah was the real winner there. Ha ha. Jedidiah wanted to practice standing, so Dad helped. Jedidiah stood up twice while I was there and practiced moving his left leg forward and back. We were all SOO impressed! After I got home, I got a picture message from Dad, of Jedidiah in his go-kart. Jedidiah took it for a lap around the driveway! After that he sat on his snowmobile to make sure it still worked. It does. He is One Tough little guy- very determined and very spirited!!.

"The Lord is my strength and my song; he has become my salvation. He is my God, and I will praise him, my father's God, and I will exalt him." Exodus 15:1-3

Sunday, April 25th

Yesterday Jedidiah went to the first Stock Car Race of the season! It was his idea and he was so excited to be there. He sat in the front row and waved at all the drivers as they went by. They announced over the loudspeaker that all of the tips from the concession stand were going to Jedidiah. Thank you American Valley Speedway and supporters!

Tonight we all had a BBQ dinner and a bonfire again. It was Jedidiah's idea. Ha ha, he loves judging the s'mores Justin and I make for him.

Jedidiah is going to school tomorrow! He is excited to get to see his friends without having to do homework.

I have had several requests for a new "To Do List". The biggest thing our family needs help with now, is building a wheelchair ramp up the stairs to our front porch. That would be awesome!

Picture of Jedidiah and Dad bundled up at the races.

Monday, April 26

Jedidiah got to see all his friends at school this morning! He explained to them that the medicine he is taking, Decadron, is what makes his cheeks so puffy. Everyone was curious but polite and mostly just excited to see him again! He used his right hand to play, "Mary Had a little Lamb" and "Hot Cross Buns" on the recorder with his classmates. He practiced fractions and writing his name in cursive and left after lunch recess. A great day at school and NO Homework! He is going back to school Wednesday afternoon.

This afternoon, Mom and I rolled Jedidiah all around town running errands. Jedidiah's highlight was eating a Meatball Marinara sandwich with pepperoni from Subway! Ha ha, he was SO excited to eat it.

Has anyone seen a small black kitten up for adoption? Dad gave Jedidiah a coupon for one for Christmas, but we have not found one yet. PAWS in Quincy only has grown cats for adoption right now. So, we are looking for one! Jedidiah said, "A fat one or a super skinny one is ok, but medium is the best." Please send me an e-mail if you have seen a kitten matching this description!

Wednesday, April 28

Oh man, Jedidiah had an awesome, adventure packed day today!...;)

Mom took him to school for the afternoon. Instead of math like Monday, they had an art lesson!

After that, Jedidiah returned to "Wild Wednesdays", an afterschool group that meets once a week at the Library. Jedidiah's gone to Wild Wednesday all school year and several of the projects he's made there still decorate the house. Today there was a special musical performance. Dad and I had fun singing along with Jedidiah!!...:) Jed is looking forward to going next Wednesday!

As if that wasn't enough excitement for one day, Shawn Web's visit turned into a front seat ride in a Real Sheriff car!!! Ha ha, Jedidiah was SOO excited, it was adorable! =) I got locked in the back seat and we drove to Rite-Aid for ice cream, Jedidiah's all-time favorite!...;) Thank you Rite-Aid for the treat!

All in All, a Wonderful day for Jedidiah!! Thank you all for helping making it possible!...:-)

Picture of Shawn Web with the family, eating ice cream at Rite-Aid!

"Give thanks to the LORD, for he is good; his love endures forever." 1 Chronicles 16:34

Oh my goodness. I've fallen way behind on updates. Not because Jedidiah hasn't been up to much, but because they've been so busy. So, I'll try to catch up on these last four busy days.

Thursday, April 29th

Mom and Dad took Jedidiah to Sacramento for a short Doctor's appointment regarding supplies for the PIC and to ask if the amount of Decadron Jedidiah's on could be reduced. (Decadron is the steroid used to reduce the swelling in his brain, but is what has made Jedidiah's face swollen and what makes him feel so hungry all the time.) Upon arrival, the doctor looked at Jedidiah, ordered an emergency CAT-scan and mentioned a potential overnight hospital stay. Jedidiah burst into tears, he didn't want to be stuck back in the hospital again, especially when his kitten was coming tomorrow! Amazingly, Jedidiah quickly pulled himself together. Within thirty seconds he stopped crying, saying he was embarrassing himself in front of the nurses, and that since crying wouldn't fix anything, they could do whatever they needed to. Wow, he sure is tougher than me!! The CAT-Scan showed no blood clots and the PIC was still positioned correctly! Thankfully they were able to come home that night!! And the Doctor did reduce the amount of Decadron. Jedidiah now takes the same dose, but only twice a day compared to three. Most certainly a happy ending to a worrisome day, But most amazing is Jedidiah's mental toughness!!

Friday, April 30th

I spent the day with Jedidiah while Mom and Dad went for a horse ride. Jedidiah's Christmas wish for a kitten finally came true. At eleven, Linda and Mike Hoover brought over the little black kitten they had picked up in

Reno for Jedidiah. Jedidiah was SO excited and said the kitten was exactly what he expected it to look like. =) Because the kitten is such a fast little guy, Jedidiah decided on the name, "Black Lightning". While shy at first, Black Lightning soon came out and played with his favorite toy, right next to Jedidiah's chair. The two spent the afternoon meowing at each other. Mike and Linda, thank you SO much!

Saturday, May 1st

The family all finished the 2nd Quincy High School Annual Fun Run/walk to support the track team. They took off from the high school early Saturday morning and finished at the track at the College. With Dad's help, Jedidiah won first place in the wheel chair category and received a QHS track back-pack! Afterwards they took him to Polka Dot for that blue-goo ice cream he's been wanting for so long. =) And to top off that perfect day, Jedidiah went back into town that night to watch the races! Phew, what busy and exciting day…;)

Sunday, May 2nd

This Sunday was another work party at the Lusk Family Farm. Thank you to everyone who came and helped. This morning Jedidiah did a physical therapy stretch with his left arm by himself. And later, he sat up by himself! He is steadily gaining back his old strength!
Thank you all for your continued prayers and support!

Monday, May 3

Jedidiah went to school today, Then he went to the Boy Scout meeting where they got to see inside of an ambulance! I got to spend four hours with Mom and Jedidiah this afternoon, going to the Boy Scout meeting and getting Jedidiah's favorite Meatball Marinara sandwich from Subway again. Tomorrow Dad is going to skip work and take Jedidiah crawdadding in Taylorsville. Shhhh…. Don't tell his boss.
A week ago I said on this website that we needed a wheelchair ramp for our house. The ramp is already built!! Thank you to Dennis and Justin

Barker for building it! I have a picture of Justin Lusk pushing his little brother up the new ramp and straight to the front door. This will save Mom's back SO much! Now she won't have to carry Jedidiah up and down the front steps every day. THANK YOU!

Friday, May 7

The Barkers came back on Tuesday and added rails to the wheelchair ramp they built for our porch. Jedidiah was busy supervising Mom and Dad stacking the new shipment of hay.

Jedidiah spent Wednesday at school and had his favorite Subway Meatball Marinara sandwich for lunch. Then I met him at the Plumas County Library for Wild Wednesday where we made a Mother's Day card and played a tag game called, "Wolf, Wolf". Ha ha, you should have seen me pushing Jed in his wheelchair as fast as I could across that bumpy lawn! It was great fun. Jamie brought a special treat for us all, donuts from Papa's Donut House- another of Jedidiah's favorites!

Thursday Dad and Mom took Jedidiah crawdadding in Taylorsville. This afternoon is the Boy Scouts Blue and Gold event. Jedidiah has been looking forward to that for weeks now. I will put pictures up tomorrow evening.

We are celebrating Mother's Day tomorrow. Mom is leaving on Sunday for Oregon for two weeks. Thankfully, her boss is very understanding and that will be the biggest block of time she will have to work this summer. Meanwhile, Dad and his sister, Julie, are taking Jedidiah back to Sacramento Sunday evening for his MRI Monday morning. Jedidiah has several appointments throughout the week but IS returning Wednesday night for the FRC Rodeo!

Picture of Jedidiah sitting with the other Wild Wednesday kids who were tagged in the "Wolf, Wolf" game and had to sit inside the Wolf's Den.

Monday, May 10th

Ok, so I was wrong about the Boys Scout Blue and Gold thing, which is why there is no picture of it like I promised. But we all enjoyed a busy Mother's Day Weekend. Saturday Morning, Justin and Jedidiah made breakfast in bed for Mommy. Jedidiah scrambled the eggs all by himself! I spent Saturday night at the house and had a big family dinner with Bobby, Wawee and Aunt Julie (Dad's parents and big sister) who are staying the two weeks Mom's gone. On Sunday, Dad, Bobby, Wawee and Julie left for Sacramento in Bobby and Wawee's R.V. Dad did a Great job keeping track of time and they departed on schedule. A very rare event in our family and certainly not a trait that I inherited...;) Mom might not have left quite on time, but she and I did find the time to plant Mother's Day flowers together. =) Jedidiah had his MRI early this morning, we will find out the results on Wednesday. Everyone think Small!...:)

Here's a picture of Jedidiah and his new Kitten, "Black Lightning", who has become very playful and friendly. He even curls up and naps right next to Jedidiah. =)

"Don't panic, I am with you. There's no need to fear for I am your God. I will give you strength. I will help you. I will hold you steady; keep a firm grip on you." *Isaiah 4:10*

Tuesday, May 11th

Today Jedidiah showed Bobby, Wawee and Aunt Julie around the Zoo!...:) The Lioness who stared at Jedidiah and licked her lips during our last visit rushed the fence today- right at him!!

Tomorrow is a busy day for Jedidiah. He has several appointments including learning the results of the MRI. And then they're driving back here to make it to the Feather River College Rodeo in his honor at 5:30. It's at the college and admission is free, I hope to see you all there!!!...:-)

Picture of Jedidiah at the zoo with his grandparents, Bobby and Wawee, and Aunt Julie!!

"A Cheerful heart is good medicine." *Proverbs 17:22*

Wednesday, May 12

Oh my goodness, Jedidiah's Rodeo was a Blast!!! Jedidiah arrived in style; Grandpa Bobby drove the RV all the way up to the rodeo stands.

Everyone stood and clapped when Jedidiah got out. We then took him up to the Announcer's Stand, for the best seat in the house!

Not only did Jedidiah arrive in style, but he also arrived PIC free! That's right, his PIC, the tube that goes directly into his heart- the tube that has been in him for over two months, is OUT!! We have a swimming trip planned for Friday. The other great news came when Dr. Z analyzed Jedidiah's MRI from Monday. He said the tumor is visibly smaller! The radiation treatments worked! The tumor is now twenty percent smaller than it was when Jedidiah started his emergency radiation treatments almost two months ago. Thank you God!

Jedidiah had several appointments this morning in Sacramento but Dad, Bobby, Wawee and Aunt Julie rushed him home, and made it to Quincy just in time to watch the Bull Riding!! After the rodeo, during the cowboy meet and greet, all of the competitors lined up to shake Jedidiah's hand! Austin Carrasco gave Jedidiah the first belt buckle he ever won, saying it brought him good luck and hoped it would do the same for Jedidiah. Then Mert Bradshaw gave Jedidiah the All Around buckle he just won. Thank you guys, that was SO cool!! Jedidiah then posed for a photo with two of the pretty cowgirls.

We laughed and laughed when members of the Quincy High School Track Team, including my brother Justin, raced some of the cowboys in a foot race,,, and lost! Ha ha, of course the rodeo guys stole and hid their competitor's shoes, but it was all in good fun! Unfortunately, Mom had to be in Oregon this week, but we sent her so many pictures and updates, it was almost like she was here.

Thank you a TON to Jesse Segura, the Feather River College Rodeo Team Coach and the Rodeo Team members. Thanks also to the QHS Track Team and the FRC Softball Team for selling bracelets and raffle tickets. Last but certainly not least, Thank You to all the community members who came to attend. The support here is truly amazing! Words cannot even adequately express how much this means to our family.

Monday, May 17

WOW! This weekend was a whirlwind of fun!!!

Friday, John, Justin, Kyra and I left for Reno after school. Mom left Oregon early that morning and we all met up with Dad, Bobby, Wawee, Aunt Julie and Jedidiah at the Peppermill Island Buffet!! This has been Jedidiah's plan for three months now! He was so angry about not getting to eat for days before and after his biopsy. He asked Dad to take him to the all-you-can-eat buffet with the cousin once he gets out of the hospital. The cousins are coming down for the official "All You Can Eat, Sleep and Swim Weekend" Memorial weekend but Jedidiah wanted to do a trail run this weekend!! ha-ha, that boy knows exactly how to get what he Wants!…;)

You should have seen Jedidiah swim!!! I thought for sure that we'd all sink after eating that much at the buffet! But Jedidiah was off in bobbing around all by himself in a matter of minutes!! Mom and Dad just wheeled him to the edge of the pool and lowered him down the stairs. Their teamwork made it look easy, but trust me, it isn't. They both supported him in the water at first, but he was eager to be free, so they slowly loosened their grips. We were all astounded to see Jedidiah standing on both feet in the pool, all by himself!!! He could bob, he could hop, he could stand, he could walk, he could run, and he could swim!!! He enjoyed doggy paddling around and soon started a game of tag! My favorite part was getting a real hug from my baby brother for the first time in over three months!!…:) We all spent the night at the Peppermill, compliments of Aunt Julie. =)

Jedidiah swimming with his sister, Jessica, in the pool at Peppermill in Reno, Nevada

Saturday morning we ate breakfast at the buffet before swimming Again!! Jedidiah slept Good Friday night and was ready to go all over again!! It was incredible seeing him use his left leg and arm so much. And to see him standing, I'd almost forgotten how tall he is!...;) Before leaving Reno Jedidiah said, "This weekend has been EXTREMELY fun, and we still have the races!" ha-ha, he loves watching the stock car races at the fairgrounds!! The whole family attended, thanks to Curt Neiman and American Valley Speedway for the Family Season Pass!! Guess where we'll be most Saturday nights? At the races!...;) Every Saturday there's a race, Jedidiah is Sure to be there!! Jedidiah has been SO looking forward to riding with Joe Woods in the 3A car for hot laps and on Saturday Jedidiah got to meet the fifteen year-old driver. The two posed for a picture together before the main event. Thank you Joe, Jedidiah can Not wait!...:)

Sunday the family met at the Fairgrounds to watch Nanny and I ride our horses. Zenda was also there and her brother with his limo! Jedidiah saw the limo driving around a couple times before asking to go over and look at it. Zendra's brother gladly let us ride in his limo!! Dad, Mom, Jedidiah and I hopped inside, it was the first time being in a limo for all of us. Jedidiah sat upright by himself the entire drive. We were excited about the red leather seats, all the buttons, the window between the driver and us that rolled up, the stereo and especially the TV!!! Jedidiah had me take pictures of everything, saying, "Justin is going to be So jealous." Ha ha, it was a wonderful surprise to be able to do that. =) Mom left for Oregon, her last week this month. We were all sad to see her go, but are excited to see her in only four more days!

Monday Aunt Julie is taking Jedidiah to school today =) And following the regular Monday routine, after school they are going to a Boy's Scout meeting and then ordering Meatball Marina sandwiches from Subway!...:)

Picture of us at the races, Thank you Curt Neiman and American Valley Speedway for the Family Season Passes!

Thursday, May 20th

Jedidiah had fun at school Wednesday with Aunt Julie again and today he drove his remote control truck all around the property. I made it to Cromberg just in time to participate in a cherry seed spitting contest!...;)

Always Remember Me

Grandpa Bobby won! Julie helped Jedidiah stand during his turn and I heard he walked three steps this morning by himself!! He has physical therapy tomorrow at two. He's going to work out in the pool...;) Mom's driving home tomorrow too; it's going to be a good day. =)

Saturday is also going to be fun. It's Jedidiah's Party!! =) Here's what Angie had to say about it: *"Mark your calendars, because Saturday May 22nd is the next Quincy community fund-raiser/party for the Lusk's. It's going to be very fun. First, there's dinner at Pangaea, seating's are at 4:30, 5:30 and 6:30. Tickets are $20, available at Pangaea, Epilog Books and the Natural Foods Store. All the food's being donated and the restaurant employees are working for free that night, so it'll be a generous (and yummy!) donation to the family. Second wave of fun that night is an auction and live music extravaganza at the Quincy Vet's Hall, 5:30 - 9:00. The whole Lusk family is attending, so please come say hello and listen to our local musicians (Quincy has some outstanding talent - youth and adults) Entry and dessert are free."*

Oh, and did you see Jedidiah with the cute cowgirls on the front page of the Feather River Bulletin!?! How cool was that?...;) Thank you to who (whom?) ever submitted that! PLEASE e-mail me that picture, I'd love to use it in the slideshow for Saturday.

Picture of Jedidiah and Grandpa Bobby shooting a BB gun today. =)

He says to himself, "Nothing will shake me; I'll always be happy and never have trouble." Psalm 10:6

Monday, May 24th

Saturday was INCREDIBLE! Thank you to everyone who came and to everyone who made it possible!!! The dinner at Pangaea was Delicious. The staff donated their time to cook, serve and clean for the event! The Vet's Hall was decorated perfectly...:) And the music was Amazing!! The QHS choir all wore blue, Jedidiah's favorite color, and sang their rendition of "Jeremiah was a Bullfrog" in which Jedidiah was a bullfrog who always had a "mighty fine time". Ha ha, it was adorable!...;) They also sang "Stand By Me" very sweetly. Thank you ladies! Then Jedidiah got to play the first three recorder songs with his class!! (The first three songs only use three or four notes and can be played with one hand). His class also turned "When Johnny Comes Marching Home" into a very meaningful sing-a-long that had me crying by the second line! That was So special. Thank you Mrs. Lemnah and her third grade class!!!

Jedidiah asked Dr. Kepple if he could sing his favorite song, "Beautiful Katy", with Natalie and Dr. Kepple said sure! We have the Kepple's CD and Jedidiah loves singing along to that song on the way to school, at the house and in the car, but seeing him sing up front with Natalie turned me into leaky faucet!! Ha ha, it was just so sweet I was crying like a baby! Thank you SO much Natalie. And this was only half of the music!! Johnny McDonald spent Saturday morning writing a new song in honor of Jedidiah that the String Beings played that night! The Scott Arthur Band played and announced the proceeds from their CD sales would go to Jedidiah. Thank you to all of the talented musicians who donated their time and music!!

Oh, and the desserts!! They were delicious. =) And the live auction was great fun! That guy made us all laugh!...:) The entire night was a blast!! I think Jedidiah was the only one who wasn't worn out by the end of the night!...;)

Thank you to everyone!!! It truly is incredible how much support and love there is in this small town!

Pictured: Jedidiah playing the recorder with his classmates.

Jedidiah had fun today at school and at the Cub Scout meeting afterwards. He is looking forward to his class field trip to the Planetarium in Reno on Wednesday and the Blue and Gold Boy Scout night coming up in June. His next physical therapy appointment is tomorrow morning. He continues to get stronger and is constantly pushing his physical limits. Two volunteers from The Make A Wish Foundation stopped by yesterday to ask Jedidiah for his wish which was a Ranger, some sort of utility vehicle. Unfortunately, they do not usually gift motorized vehicles. Jedidiah's plan B and C is an RV trip to Alaska or a Cruise to Hawaii. Jedidiah is also excited for summer. He can't wait to spend a week in Oregon at Robbi's and two weeks in Idaho with the cousins!

Friday, May 28th

So I moved back in with the family last week and my only complaint has been the speed of the Internet. I Love being back and getting to see everyone so much again, but this Internet has made frequent updates a headache. Luckily, it's working right now, so here I go!...:)

Tuesday Jedidiah had his second physical therapy appointment with Corey Felker. Jedidiah uses a hydraulic lift to get into the swimming pool. That's right; Jedidiah does his physical therapy in a swimming pool! Corey makes the lesson enjoyable and you would be impressed with how hard Jedidiah works! At the end of the lesson, Jedidiah gets to dunk Corey! Jedidiah, Mom and I went to lunch at Pangaea with Susan before finishing the day in town, busily running errands.

Wednesday Jedidiah went on a field trip to the Planetarium in Reno with his third grade class!!! Mom drove Jedidiah and used a wheelchair lift to navigate their way through the planetarium. Ha ha, Jedidiah was excited to tell us about using the wheel chair lift...;) Jedidiah brought us home souvenirs- it was Very sweet. =) He got a mood ring for himself and I and bought a "Balance Ball", the pendulum balls that swing back and forth, for his older brother. Jedidiah really is a thoughtful little guy.

Thursday, Mom, Dad and Jedidiah left for the Reno Peppermill and jumped straight into swimming, eating and sleeping. When they met Uncle Rick and cousin Robert Jedidiah hugged Robert with his LEFT arm and said, "I have been waiting for this for three months. Thank you for coming!"

Friday, Aunt Linda and cousins Cole and Carli are flying in. Big Family dinner at the All you can eat seafood buffet! And now Justin and I are leaving for Jedidiah's special "All you can Eat, Swim and Sleep" weekend!!! Woo Hoo =)

Happy Memorial Weekend, have fun and stay safe. I hope everyone's weekend will be as enjoyable and memorable as ours!!!

Tuesday, June 1st

Memorial weekend was a BLAST!! We swam, played tag, freeze tag, Marco polo, red light green light, guess the wrong color and you get dunked game, made races, had group hugs in the pool, ate Tons of sea food and desserts, played in the arcade and watched Beverly Hills "Chi-WOW-wa"!!! ha-ha, it was Great! Jedidiah got all of our attention the first night in the hotel room so we could watch him eat a Nilla Wafer (junk food) with his LEFT hand! He also hugged everyone individually with Both arms and thanked them for coming. =) Jedidiah was SO incredibly mobile and as Dad said, "Look, no body's watching him!" ha-ha! Of course we were watching him, but no one had to constantly stand guard, waiting for him to wobble or fall. It was just FUN for all!

Jedidiah continued getting stronger this morning at his Physical Therapy appointment. His only complaint has been his foot getting stepped on today. ;) He really is working hard and it's showing off. Jedidiah had everyone watch today when he told me to LET GO of him. With reservations, i moved my hands a few inches away from him and watched as he transferred from the car to the wheel chair BY HIMSELF! We were all so excited...;) Mom took Jedidiah on yet another field trip with his class today. =) They walked to the Courthouse to watch a meeting and then walked to Gansner Park to look at a real art studio and then eat lunch and play at the park. I got a cute picture from Mom today of Jedidiah playing catch with a nerf balls at the park with his friends!! =)

Dad was in contact with the Make-A-Wish people today about granting Jedidiah's wish. Our family has reached a little snag. Everyone we talk to from the organization tells Jedidiah to be selfish and wish for what he really wants. Unfortunately he really wants a motorized vehicle and they don't grant motorized vehicles! So Jedidiah's first wish of getting a Polaris Ranger was denied. His second wish of a snowmobile was denied. His clever idea of simply removing the motor from the Ranger before giving it to him was denied! What more does a nine year old boy want than something motorized!? Wanting a trip and a cotton candy machine, or wanting to take a cruise to Alaska were both considered more than one wish. And because I'm 18 they don't consider me part of the family ha-ha, are ya seeing the snag?...;) But after deliberating over the weekend, Jedidiah decided on a trip to The Alaska Smokejumper Base! So after some intense trouble shooting, I think we have reached a suitable compromise. Not quite a Polaris Ranger but Jedidiah still sounds excited. And he doesn't know it yet, but Aunt Linda and Uncle Rick have joined forces to get him his very own cotton candy machine maker! =) Jed's got built in wish granters!!....;)

So I couldn't decide between this picture or the picture of Jedidiah looking so cool and tough riding his dirt bike, but the girl in me won; check out Jedidiah's Adorable baby picture!! ha-ha =)

"Be strong and courageous. Do not be afraid or terrified because of them, for the LORD your God goes with you; he will never leave you nor forsake you." *Deuteronomy 31:6*

Wednesday, June 2nd

Today was the last Wild Wednesday for the school year. So after school, I got to spend the last hour of class with Jedidiah at QES =), Jedidiah went to the public library for the final rehearsal for the Wild Wednesday play. He played the lake and took his role very seriously. He was covered in a blue gauzy material and had his face painted blue with white caps to look like water. The whole family was there for the dinner before they play and for Jedidiah's acting debut...;) When the narrator mentioned the lake Jedidiah raised his hand and smiled, it really was so sweet how proud he was of his role. It was enough to make my heart melt.

Johnny McDonald and the Community Youth Orchestra played "Ode To Jedidiah" today at the Concert at the Green in the QHS gym. Unfortunately Jedidiah, Mom and I were at the play rehearsal but Dad and Justin managed to run over there before the play to listen to the special song Johnny, Jedidiah's violin teacher, wrote and orchestrated just for him. That really is neat. =)

This community truly is amazing! Thank you all. I'm heading to bed now to get recharged for another busy, fun filled day tomorrow. =)

"Trust in the Lord with all your heart and lean not on your own understanding; in all your ways acknowledge him, and he will make your paths straight." *Proverbs 3:5-6*

Thursday, June 3rd

Jedidiah had his physical therapy early this morning followed by a blood draw at the Quincy Hospital. Jedidiah hates needles as bad as I do (a LOT) but he was very brave...;) Luckily, they were able to use a "butterfly" and draw the blood out of his hand, with less pain than regular. Mom and Jedidiah made it out of the Quincy Feed 'N Tack with the truck loaded with grain; without being charged!! I'm not quite sure who is responsible but Thank You!! This phenomenon was repeated when I met Mom and Jedidiah for lunch at Subway. An anonymous donor left Subway gift cards for our family!! Thank you Very much! Subway is one of Jedidiah's favorite restaurants; he Loves the Meatball Marina with pepperoni...;)

I just checked my e-mail finally today and found out from John Sturley that the melodrama the Plumas Christian School produced recently raised over a thousand dollars for Jedidiah!! I was not able to attend but I heard it was very good...:) Thank you to all who organized, participated in, and watched such a great event.

"Be on your guard; stand firm in the faith; be men of courage; be strong." 1 Corinthians 16:13

Friday, June 4th

Phew, what a busy day!! I got to hang out with Jedidiah All day today...:) We left for his PT appointment at seven thirty, almost made it on time too. Lol. I got him there, and outta the pool and showered by myself! It was just him and I the majority of the day! Ha ha, I did not fully appreciate how much thought and energy and planning goes into a navigating an active and inquisitive nine year old boy in wheel chair! It was definitely worth the effort though, Jedidiah and I had fun! We laughed and giggled throughout the day. Jedidiah especially enjoyed the several times I ran over my toes with the wheel chair and bomped my head on the car door. His exasperated voice saying, "Jessicaaaa..." became the soundtrack of the day!!...;) After PT we went to school, made it just in time for morning recess...;) But we did lots of learning throughout the day. I helped Jedidiah with his multiplication tables, science lab and even got to have lunch with him. =) We went to Taco Bell after school, and because some of his school friend's Moms work there, he got a free slushy and kid meal toys!!

Jedidiah has been talking and talking about visiting his old daycare provider Ken, so after school, that's exactly what we did...;) All the kids ran to the window shouting, "Jedidiah's here! Jedidiah's here!" when we pulled up! Ken was excited to see us too and we were excited to be there! One of Jedidiah's "dirt bike buddies" Nano, who also used to go to Ken's came today to be there with Jedidiah. Jedidiah beat Ken at a game of Wii bowling that they played on Ken's Ginormous TV!! It was fun watching Jedidiah play, you could tell he was enjoying it...;)

And as if that wasn't enough for one day, we went and watched Shrek 4!! The whole family (plus Justin's friend and girlfriend) went. =) It was a really cute movie, all about – or at least mostly about- the importance of family, so it was perfect!! =) Barbara, who worked at Pioneer Elementary School throughout my, Justin and Jedidiah's time there got the whole family passes to come back and watch another movie there!....:)

Oh! And yesterday, between the free lunch and Fire Engine ride, Mom and I got our hair cut at Hair It Is, by Lisa, one of Mom's childhood friends and Lisa also refused to take our money!! Our hair does look pretty dang cute, if I don't say so myself...;) I figure with how generous these local businesses have been they deserve a little bit of free advertising! So here goes: If you need a haircut, go to **Hair It Is**. If you're looking for some good food, go to **Pangaea**. Visit **Pet Country Feed 'N Tack** for all of your animal needs. Remember to enjoy a good movie often at the **Town Hall Theatre**. And I can't speak for Taco Bell and Subways everywhere, but the local branches and their employees are amazing as well! And last but not least, I hope to see you all at The **American Valley Speedway** tomorrow night at seven to watch the stock car races!! No doubt Jedidiah will be there...;)

"Therefore encourage one another and build each other up, just as in fact you are doing." 1 Thessalonians 5:11

Thank you all for the supportive messages you leave in the guestbook!! They sure make my job easier!

Cynthia Lusk

Saturday, June 5th

Jedidiah and Dad accompanied me to my horse show at the County Picnic.

Mom and Justin spent the day working on trails.

We met up at the LDS church for Jedidiah's Blue and Gold, Cub Scout celebration!!! We were all very proud of him.:) He plans on entering his pinewood derby truck at fair this year.

Dad, Justin, Jed and I went to the races after Blue and Gold. We stayed out past midnight getting autographs from REAL stock car drivers. =)

Sunday, June 6th

We slept in, finally!!...;)

Jedidiah's friends Nano, JD and Riley came over to play and cook S'More! Nano and JD brought their dirt bikes.

Justin and I ran alongside of Jedidiah while he rode his Go-Kart!!! By the end I was sprinting to keep up!! And I only got ran over once...;

Monday, June 7th

The first day of the last week of school!!! Jedidiah's classmates came to our house for a field trip!...:)

Mom and Jedidiah showed off the chickens and goats, and taught the children which plants in the woods are edible! Jedidiah had a whole conversation with Mom about Miner's Lettuce rehearsed. His joy and excitement is contagious!...;)

Tuesday, June 8th

I took Jedidiah to Physical Therapy and School.

Jedidiah was invited last minute to a school pool party. Fortunately, he had his swim shorts from PT that morning. Unfortunately, I did not have a suit... So I went in with my jeans on!! Ha ha =) Not something I recommend, but it was worth getting soaked to help Jedidiah get in the pool...;)

Jedidiah got Two packages in the mail today from All of the cousins, aunts and uncles, and Bobby and Wawee! It was a COTTON CANDY MACHINE like he's been wanting!!! We tested it out and it works great and tastes delicious!! Jedidiah was So excited. =) Thank you Lusk, Williams and Chavis families!!

I want to again thank everyone for being SO supportive through all of this!! Even the "little" stuff like leaving guestbook messages or giving Jedidiah a pat on the shoulder when you see him really do add up!

Wednesday, June 9,

Phew, it has been an eventful past couple days!! We truly pack more into one weekend than most people do in a week! ...;) It gets stressful at times yes, but it so well worth it. I'll try to stay more current with these updates, so expect shorter ones in the future. But here's just a short recap:

Thursday, June 10th

When I say we do more in a weekend, I guess what I really mean is Jedidiah does more. Ha ha, he's quite the little schemer!! And he's got lots more fun things lined up...;) He's been talking about riding the bus home for at least a month now, and he's going to tomorrow. =) The Alaska trip is also confirmed! The Make-A-Wish foundation is sending Jedidiah to Alaska to tour the Smokejumper Base in Fairbanks. Make-A-Wish also bought tickets for Mom, Dad and Justin! Holly has agreed to feed our horse while we're gone and Mom bought Blue Nanny and I tickets to go too!! We are set! =) Jedidiah says when he grows up he wants to be an Alaskan smokejumper, like his Dad, in the summers and be a professional snowmobile racer in the winters. So Jedidiah gets to go check out the base ahead of time...;) John Gould, Dad's rookie buddy and now head honcho up there, called and asked for down south booster (fire talk for back up) Jedidiah Lusk! Not only has Jedidiah been invited personally by the guy in charge of the Alaska Fire Service, but the Mayor of Fairbanks said we can have the "keys to the city" and invited us to have a BBQ at her cabin...:) This Alaska trip is going to be Great!!

Yesterday Jedidiah went on a field trip to look at the bus barn. Today he played the part of a crocodile in Shell Silverstein's poem, "The Crocodile's Toothache" in his class' Readers Theatre. Mom played the role of the Crocodile jaws and Dad and I were there to watch. =) Both days Jedidiah went to Ken's after school. (Picture of Ken and Jedidiah.) He has been planning and planning the last week of school. He had three items on his must list: going to school all five days, going to Ken's twice, and riding the bus home on the last day of school. And he's doing it all!! =)

Our family has been in contact with another family whose ten year old son also has a GMB. His tumor was also deemed inoperable but they were able to find a doctor who said she could take it out; and she did. His MRI Tuesday came back tumor free. Jedidiah's doctor has been talking to this surgeon, Dr. Gross, to see if she thinks she can operate on Jedidiah as well. We've all been kind of holding our breath waiting on the answer.

And I said I was going to start writing shorter entries. Ha ha! But I think you are completely caught up on the Lusk family doings now...;) Happy last day of school, And to those working: Thank Goodness It's Friday...;) Have a good day. =)

"The earth is full of the goodness of the Lord." Psalm 33:5

Saturday, June 12<u>th</u>

Today, while Dad was fixing Jed's go-kart, Jedidiah used a clipboard and hand wrote a story about his last day of school! So instead of my recapping, I'll just share with you (with his permission of course) Jedidiah's story:

"Today I woke up and went to my swimming PT. Then I went to the last day of school. When I arrived there was an assembly. I thought it was for the older classes so mom and I went to my classroom and guess who was there... nobody! Back to the cafeteria we went. There the principal said oh we have someone who came a bit late. Here is a teacher's award for Jedidiah! Recess will begin in six minutes. Then everyone left. All but me, mom, and mom's friend. And when I say all I mean <u>all!</u>! They talked and talked and talked and talked. (Hey mom the room was empty.) Finally they

stopped talking! Now I had to go to the bathroom then go out to recess. Wait you talked too long! I have to go to the bathroom and then we have to go back to the classroom. Wait it's time for games now? Okay I get this game. You start with a cup and then you fill it full of water and then run or walk down and dump the water into a five-gallon bucket. Then I think we started to go raffle off our group writing. Oops time to go. I am ready but I am going home a special way. "Hey I have to go to the bathroom. Can someone tell the bus to wait? Now to the bathroom mama! Okay now to the bus. Hey Ray can you get me on the bus? Hey Justin I'm here." Then I got on the bus. Mom pushed the wheel chair down to the car. I rode the bus through all the stops. Now it was my stop. Then Justin and Jessica helped me off."

Picture to accompany Jedidiah's story- in the bottom right is Jedidiah's smiling face and in the back ground is his school bus. Sorry for the picture quality, I took it while also hanging onto Jedidiah

I think there might have been more he wanted to write, but we all went to bed shortly after dinner. Jedidiah has also been dictating a story to Justin called, "My Childhood", which begins on the day Jedidiah was diagnosed with his tumor. That will be very interesting to read...

Thank you all for leaving such kind, thoughtful and positive messages in the Guestbook; means so much to me and my family. Jedidiah used his laptop to read some today!

Oh! and I have to say that Jedidiah is very proud of being able to transfer from his wheelchair into the car All by himself now!! His hard work at PT is paying off, he continues to get stronger. =)

Picture of our family- grandparents and cousins too- outside of the Peppermill after the all you can eat, swim and sleep weekend!!

I don't think today's bible verse relates to the last day of school at all, but it sounds positive and I like it...;)

Rise up; this matter is in your hands. We will support you, so take courage and do it. Ezra 10:

Sunday, June 13th

So I wanted to leave Jedidiah's story up for another day, I really do like it...:) I'm just going to add more onto yesterday's post. Today was a fun day though. Mom and Justin ran twenty one miles as a practice run!! Crazy people...;) Jedidiah and Dad picnicked in the shade while I played soccer and then the whole family met up at the Town Hall Theatre to watch "Babies". It was adorable!! =) It's playing again Monday night- I recommend you go watch...;)

I'm going to ask for everyone to extend their thoughts and prayers out to Dozer this Monday as he goes in for treatment for his GBM tumors. He gets a shot that gives him flu like side effects for 48 hours. Does not sound fun, but I've got in on good authority that he is "cowboy tough"! Your prayers for him are greatly appreciated. And if you're thinking your Monday is pretty lousy, just remember it could be worse, so tell yourself to cowboy up!...;)

Tuesday June 15th

Jedidiah got in lots of swimming time today. =) First at his physical therapy appointment in the morning and then later with his brother and friends at the Pioneer Pool! I was lifeguarding so I got to see them all there...:)

Yesterday Mom took us kids to Antelope Lake for a picnic... Justin did a pretty good job driving through the canyon. Jedidiah brought along his Nintendo DSI. Ha ha, he LOVES the polar bear bowling game and has gotten awesome at it. The drive home was a mixture of Mom yelling at Justin to slow down and Jedidiah excitedly yelling, "I got a Strike!" Got to love family road trips...;) Tomorrow, Mom plans on taking us to Bucks Lake- it's a weeklong guided tour of Plumas County...;) Picture of us kids at Antelope Lake.

The earth is full of the goodness of the Lord. Psalm **33:5**

Thursday, June 17th

My hair and eye brows have strings of cotton candy in them! ha-ha, not even kidding...;) Jedidiah seriously loves his new cotton candy machine! We made two batches tonight to wrap up another fun and busy day. =)

After Physical Therapy, Jedidiah had to get his blood drawn again. Much to his dismay, this is something that has to be done every two weeks while he's taking the chemo medication. Davis called back within two hours with the results: his platelet count was low but the rest looked fine. The nurse said Jedidiah just can't do any gymnastics since he'll bruise too easily. Good thing Jedidiah's never liked gymnastics...;)

The road was still too snowy for the Bucks Lake Adventure yesterday, but today Mom took Jedidiah, Justin and I to see Frazier Falls! It was Beautiful! And when we were posing for pictures in front of the waterfall something even more beautiful happened, Jedidiah asked to stand up and wheel the chair away during the photo session. So we have pictures of Jedidiah standing up and hugging us all!! =)

Yesterday Jedidiah took our family and the Pavia Family out to Community Supper where he met his first Nun, he was very excited about that...;) The two women were very polite and pleased by Jedidiah's fascination. They said they too would pray for him.

Picture of us hugging in front of Frazier Falls. =)

"I have said these things to you, that in me you may have peace. In the world you will have tribulation. But take heart; I have overcome the world." John 16:33

Friday, June 18th

Uncle John came up to help watch Jedidiah so Mom could help her friend with the Tevis (a 100 mile horse ride). Dad and Uncle John took Jedidiah to town for Luke's Pool Party!! Jedidiah had fun swimming with his buddies,

Saturday, June 19th

Uncle John stayed while Mom was still gone and Dad and I went on a horse ride campout. Blue Nanny, Uncle John, Justin and Jedidiah's big event for the day was going to Special Sprint Car races at American Valley speed way that night! The Rainbow girls raised $350 in a 50/50 raffle!! Jedidiah got to pick the winning number out of the hat and even received a kiss from the very excited (and inebriated) woman...;) He was VERY excited to hold that huge wad of cash! Thank you all for your support. =)

Sunday, June 20th

Happy (late) Father's Day =) We celebrated outside with a BBQ and LOTS of presents...;) John and Jinx Helmer drove several hours to reach our house on behalf of the National Smokejumper's Association to present Jedidiah with a check for $3,100!! Thank you Mr. and Mrs. Helmer for the incredible smoke jumping photos as well as for driving all the way out here- and thank you to all of the smokejumpers around the country who contributed!

Monday, June 21st

Jedidiah went to town this morning to drop Justin off for the week with the Donald family. After an afternoon of running errands with Mom, the highlight if today was the family watching Stuart Little 2 (given to us by Mrs. Donald) together. =) And now I have to go to bed cause I'm taking Jedidiah to his PT tomorrow morning at eight sharp!

Picture of Jedidiah's shocked face after reading the amount on the check retired Smokejumper, John handed him.

"The Lord bless you and keep you; The Lord make his face shine upon you and be gracious to you; The Lord turn his face toward you and give you peace."
Numbers 6:24-26

Wednesday, June 23rd

Jedidiah had an exciting day today- he had lunch with the SWAT team and then toured the Sherriff Office!...:) Jedidiah has always been very impressed by police, so this was pretty neat for him. =) Unfortunately, he had to get his blood drawn earlier today but he says the butterfly in his hand hurts way less than a needle in the vein by his elbow. Last blood draw his numbers (which how I understand it, mostly mean platelets and white blood cells) were too low to start his second round of Chemo. Those numbers have risen enough since that last draw to continue chemo next week but are still not entirely in the healthy range.

Yesterday Nanny and I had a fun day with Jedidiah while Mom and Dad drove to Medford Oregon to pick up Mom's stallion, Moon Shadow. After Physical Therapy, we went to Dollar Tree and The Hardware store where we found a mini cheese grater that Jedidiah liked so much I had to get it for him...;) We used it to grate string cheese for his sandwich at lunch. Nanny watched Jedidiah while I taught swim lessons and then Jedidiah and I took a lovely nap in the afternoon. =) Jedidiah likes his new mini cheese grater so much he wrote a song about it this morning!...;) It's sung to the tune of "Old Smokey" and is titled "Mini Cheese Grater". Ha ha, you should hear him sing it- it is Great!! Here are the lyrics:

> *Oh, Mini Cheese Grater, you are so small.*
> *You grated cheese for my eggs this morning and all.*
> *It started out from a stick, and then turned into bits.*
>   *Oh you are a good friend,*
>   *When you are not cutting off my fingertips!"*

If you are interested in learning more about GBM tumors, here are two links that Mom shared with the family today. The first is a story written by a man with a GBM tumor called, "Living with a Malignant Brain Tumor- a Patient's Survival Guide". It was written in the late nineties but the information about treatments is still current, as there have been no major advances. It stopped my heart when the first thing I read was the date of the Author's death, but his story is very informative and realistic, yet still positive. http://home.earthlink.net/~sdepesa/ Another print out

Mom gave me came from http://www.childrenshospital.org/az/Site962/mainpageS962P0.html. This is more medically informative site.

Sorry, no picture...:(Jedidiah did wear his official SWAT tactical jacket this afternoon for lunch with the SWAT team though...;)

"So do not fear for I am with you, do not be dismayed, for I am your God. I will strengthen you and help you; I will uphold you with my righteous right hand." Isaiah 41:10

Thursday June 24th

Jedidiah had PT this morning and then an appointment in town with Dr. Kepple. Both Mom and Dad went for that, but because they got home late I haven't really heard much about how that went. They got home late because they drove to Sacramento today to pick up Jedidiah's new, very own, custom deluxe, extremely comfortable, thickly padded, heavy duty, "four wheel drive", stylish blue wheelchair. The one Jedidiah's been using is just a rental. The big wheels on this new one make it easier to maneuver over rocky, rough terrain; which is exactly how I would describe our entire driveway, front yard and back yard! Lol. So to test it out, Dad and I pushed Jedidiah all around our property. We even walked over to the horse corrals to say hi to Mom while she was feeding. Jedidiah is very proud of his new wheel chair. J

Here's a joke Jed made up: *"Have you heard about the wooden car? It's made entirely out of wood. It has a wooden engine, wooden wheels and a wooden axle. The only problem is it wouldn't go."* Haha!!...:)

I can do everything through him who gives me strength. Philippians 4:13

Saturday June 26th

Ok, quick update:

This morning was emotional. We went to the Relay for Life kick off. Nanny pushed Jedidiah around the track for the survivor's lap, Mom gave a speech about care giving and then she, Dad, Justin and I walked around with the other caregivers there. Jedidiah added his hand print and signature to the survivor sheet. He was thrilled to watch the airplane's fly over. =) Yesterday the whole family made it out to Taylorsville to cheer me on during the poles. Hearing Jedidiah's voice sure did make my horse go faster!! =) After that Mom, Justin and Jedidiah went to the Donald's for Susan's special sourdough pizza...:)

Picture of Dad high fiving Jedidiah as Nanny wheels him by on their way around the FRC track for the Relay For Life Survivor's Lap.

And now these three remain: faith, hope and love. But the greatest of these is love. Corinthians 13:13

Wednesday, June 30<u>th</u>

Oh goodness, I really can't ever seem to stay caught up with Jedidiah! I was in Chico for the weekend and the boys just keeping going!!! Mom is working in Oregon this week and Jedidiah has been keeping Dad and Justin busy with swimming at the Pioneer Pool, go-kart rides, trips to Reno, and such!...;) Jedidiah has invented a great new invention- "Firework Cheese". Haha, he grates pepper jack cheese, jalapenos and mixes it with blue food dye!! =)

The Big news today (well BIG enough for all summer too!) happened at 11:15... Dad, Justin and Jedidiah drove into town and were presented with a SILVER MINI VAN WITH A WHEELCHAIR LIFT!!! It's Perfect for Jedidiah's new wheelchair that doesn't fold up. The boys took it for a test drive to Reno today and it worked great!...:) Thank you to Quincy Auto, Quincy High School and Dr. Segura for the van!!!

Dr. Gross called Mom back earlier this week. She was very polite and friendly but operating on Jedidiah's tumor comes with a VERY high risk of permanent paralysis including the need for a feeding tube, and due to the nature of the GMB tumor it would only re-grow. She was able to operate on Dozer's tumor because it was closer to his skull and the size of a dime. (Jedidiah's is deeper inside his skull and about the size of a walnut.) She said surgery or not, the end result will be the same and she told Mom to enjoy every day with Jedidiah. So it was disappointing to hear this, but it isn't anything we didn't already know. So we're sticking with chemo, prayers and enjoying every day!!!

Yesterday, Jedidiah went outside to look at the new goat pen his brother helped make. Jedidiah parked the wheelchair, stood up, balanced on his right leg while shaking his left leg and then balanced on his left leg and shook his right leg- just cause he could!...;) He really is an awesome kid who never gives up!

Before Mom left, Jedidiah took a turn pushing HER in his wheelchair...

"Rise up; this matter is in your hands. We will support you, so take courage and do it." Ezra 10:4

Monday, July 5th

It's been a fun weekend. Mom came back from Oregon, the boys camped at the Taylorsville Rodeo Grounds, we went "crawdadding", watched fireworks, watched the Taylorsville Silver Buckle Rodeo and helped out at the cookhouse during the roping and rodeo. Jedidiah was very proud of his job- taking the hotdogs, hamburgers, and cheeseburgers from out of the oven, to the window for the customer. It was very cute how serious he was.

We are on our way to Alaska now!! A Limo came and picked us up from Cromberg this morning. Jedidiah got the driver's autograph and we watched a movie on the drive to Reno! We just got through airport security: Our flight boards at 2:05 PM. We change planes in Seattle, and then arrive in Fairbanks!! We keep singing, "North To Alaska! North, the rush is on!" This is going to be the Trip of a Lifetime. It already is Awesome!

CaringBridge is an incredible tool, but only holds a limited amount of pictures. I will continue these updates, but am also utilizing Facebook as an avenue to display more pictures of Jedidiah's Alaskan Adventure!!! Jedidiah now has his own Facebook. So, if you have one, add him as a friend!

Tuesday, July 6th

So we made it to Fairbanks last night =) We are staying at Pike's Landing Lodge, only a few minutes' drive from the airport...:) Pike's generously donated the two rooms for our family this week! Us kids and Nanny slept in this morning while Mom and Dad went to the Alaska Smokejumper Base. We had lunch at the Pike's Landing Restaurant before *taking a tour of the Alaska Smokejumper Base!!!* Jedidiah asked everyone he met for their autograph, which everyone was happy to give...;) Jedidiah has his OWN smoke jumping suit, helmet and PG bag, hanging on a peg in the get ready room, made especially for him!!! He tried it on (pictured) and afterwards, practiced throwing a streamer out of the plane he will ride in tomorrow as an official Spotter! We had dinner at the Mess Hall with the other jumpers and Hot Shots. Jedidiah asked questions and cracked jokes the whole day...;) Everyone we met was INCREDIBLE, one guy even gave Jed the hat off of his head! Thank you all! Jedidiah is So excited for his flight tomorrow...:)

I added more pictures from today, check em out...;)

Wednesday, July 7th

Jedidiah says, "Ready to climb to 3,000 feet. Live Jumpers Ready!
I'll have to write up more detailed stories on the flight home, short and sweet tonight though so I can get some sleep...;)
Today's Highlights:

    Breakfast at the Smokejumper Base. Roll Call. Rookie Training. Spotting 101.

    Jump Mock up- Jedidiah practiced throwing streamers and kicking jumpers out from the ground.

    Jedidiah, Mom and Dad flew in the plane and kicked two jumpers out at 3,000 feet!...;)

    Lunch at the Mess Hall on base.

Family watched an eight man practice jump from the ground.
Jedidiah's Rookie Graduation Ceremony and slide show. He got to take off his orange rookie armband and received his wings from the Base

Manager. His Dad, another Alaska Smoke Jumper, awarded him with an Alaska Jumper Belt Buckle!...:) The Alaska Fire Service and Missoula Jumpers were among others who presented Jedidiah with Graduation presents. =)

Dinner at the Chena Pump House- where Dad proposed to Mom twenty-six years ago!!

Today was incredible!!! Thank you to all of the amazing people who contributed and made it possible!!

Thursday, July 8th

The Base Manager, Bill Cramer ordered a mandatory day off for Jedidiah. He set up a rookie camp along the Chena river to celebrate Jedidiah's graduation...:) We rode in a jet boat seven miles up the river and partied on a sand bar till midnight!! We saw two bald eagles and two moose! We fished, took naps, picked wild raspberries, cooked MOOSE steaks and s'mores over the camp fire!!

Jul 12, 2010

Phew. We made it home. This week was incredibly, amazingly fun!!! Mom, Nanny and Jedidiah leave at 6:30 tomorrow for Jedidiah's MRI in Sacramento. Here's a short recap of the past couple days:

Sunday 11th
Jessica and Nanny's birthday! We left the hotel at 4:30 in the morning to make our flight on time!! Limo picked us up at the airport and drove us back to our little house...:)

Saturday 10th
We hung out with the mayor of Fairbanks for the day. She went to college with Dad and invited us all out to her lakeside bungalow! We water skied, jet skied, hot tubbed and paddle boated!!...:) Finished off the great night with ice cream from Hot Licks with the Awesome photographer/jumper Mike!

Friday 9th

We visited Santa Claus's house at the North Pole in the morning, musk oxen at the University of Alaska and the Smokejumper Base in the afternoon and Pioneer Park in the evening for all you can eat Salmon Bake! Yum =)

Thursday 8th

Jedidiah's mandatory day off- for Rookie Campout. We rode a jet boat 7 miles up the Chena river and partied with the jumpers till midnight!! Saw moose, bald eagles, caught fish, picked wild raspberries and cooked Moose steak on a stick over a campfire!...:)

Wednesday 7th

Jedidiah got to throw streamers and jumpers out of the plane both from the ground and then in the air!!! Then he watched another practice jump from the ground before his Rookie graduation ceremony...:) We had dinner at Chena Pump House where Dad proposed to Mom over twenty five years ago!

Added a few more pictures here- and lots on Facebook. Also Mike (the real photographer) will add some to his website soon. spotfireimages.com

Monday, July 19th

Ok, so I hope everyone's learned by now that just because I haven't written anything lately, doesn't mean Jedidiah hasn't been up to anything...;) In fact it's usually the opposite; the more he does the less time I have to write.

But he's been keeping us all busy. =) This weekend the whole family went to Carson City to cheer on Mom and Justin for running the 50 K Tahoe Rim Run!! Tonight I sat between my two brothers at the Town Hall Theatre and we watched Toy Story 3!! That was great fun...:) Back at the house, Jedidiah grated cheese and we all sang the "Cheese Grater Song" he wrote and when he had some ravioli for dessert, we all joined in for the "Ravioli Song" Jedidiah also wrote...;)

I overheard Jedidiah telling Mom something pretty profound before bedtime: "Every living thing, besides trees needs love. Even some trees need love." Jedidiah sure is a sweetheart!

Wednesday, July 21st

Jedidiah is going to the pool tomorrow with his 3rd grade teacher Mrs. Lemnah...:) Everyone else who would like to swim some with Jedidiah is welcome to join. =)

Justin leaves to work a month in the woods for the SCA tomorrow morning. Dad, Mom and Jedidiah depart for the Oregon/Idaho adventure Friday at noon. I will be joining them in Idaho August first. Getting ready for some more very fun and busy times!...:)

I wanted to share this letter Jedidiah wrote yesterday.

Dear Santa,

I just wanted to tell you this because Christmas is one of my favorite seasons. I've already started having dreams about Christmas. Like this one dream I had this morning. My Dad took me to Scheels except that he didn't drive me there. I was looking around and then I saw you. I asked my sister Jessica to wheel me up to you, "Santa I just wanted to see if you were the same Santa, because I got to go to the North Pole for a Make-A-Wish trip and I just wanted to see if you were the same Santa." And then you asked me if I wanted to go upstairs with you. And then I said, "Well I'm kind of in a wheel chair." And then you said, "Yeah, I'm taking you up the elevators. It's not like I'm going to blast you up in a rocket or anything." And then I had to go to the bathroom so I flagged down my sister and I got stuck in the bathroom door. And then I woke up.

The End

P.S. I have a little gift for the reindeer that I included. (A zip lock bag of carrots is stapled to the letter.)

Love,
Jedidiah Lusk

P.P.S.
For this Christmas I would like a blue Nano I-Pod and also a remote controlled helicopter that flies and a 6x6 Polaris Ranger with: reverse, a winch and headlights. And for my Dad, a red 4x4 Diesel.

Jedidiah's Daddy got him a BLUE I-POD NANO with speakers TODAY as an early Christmas present!!...:)

Picture of me and my two Wonderful brothers; Monday morning they jumped on my bed and we grated cheese with Jedidiah's mini cheese grater first thing in the morning!...;)

Sunday, July 25th

Mom, Dad and Jedidiah made it to Redmond Oregon late last night, only a day behind schedule. They camped the night on the Grassland and woke up to a Sherpa dropping 10 smokejumpers, including two Mom knows, only 200 yards from their campsite!!! All the jumpers high fived Jedidiah as he told stories of "When I was spotting in Alaska..."!!! Later Mom, Dad and Jedidiah toured the Redmond Smokejumper base and visited Mom's friend Robbie. Pictured is Jedidiah getting to ride in Robbie's "mule." (Utility vehicle)

Friday, July 30th

Oh man, Jedidiah is having a BLAST in Idaho with his Dad, grandparents, aunts, uncles and cousins!!! They have been biking on all sorts of trails, Jedidiah rides along in a trailer behind Dad's bike...:) They've been eating huckleberry ice cream and smoked rosemary salmon at Aunt Julie's house! Mom and I will be joining them Sunday for even more fun...:)

Tuesday, August 3

Sunday, Mom drove up from Redmond and I flew from Reno, we met in Spokane and then drove together up to Coeur d' Alene!! Mom and I fell asleep hugging the little guy in a Jedidiah sandwich...:)

Yesterday, Monday, we rode the Hiawatha Trail in Montana!! The Hiawatha is a thirteen mile downhill bike trail that goes through several tunnels and over numerous trestle bridges! The longest tunnel is over a mile long!! Every rider is required to wear a helmet and head lamp. We whooped, hollered and howled through every tunnel...;) Jedidiah rode in a wagon behind Dad's bike and did not complain once!! Jedidiah's wagon was nice and padded but I complained about my hind end getting sore, so I was very impressed with Jedidiah! Aunt Linda, Connor, Cole, Dad, Mom, Jedidiah, Mom and I all made it to the end in time to catch the last shuttle...:) We met Aunt Julie and cousin Anna on the way back up to ride through the looong tunnel one more time...:) We then spent the night at Aunt Julie's and Bobby and Wawee's condo in Kellogg, Idaho. The Williams and local Chavis cousins met there for pizza!! We were all tuckered out from such a fun day that we all slept good after filling our tummies with Wildcat pizza. =)

Today we slept in!...:) After checking out of the condo, Dad took us to the Snake Pit for Huckleberry Milkshakes,

It's a wonderful tradition that Grandpa Bobby started! The Snake Pit is a Restaurant/Bar that was established in 1880. It's second floor used to house a brothel. Now it is famous for its huckleberry ice cream and unique history. The owner, Joe Peak, who met Jedidiah during a family dinner there last week, came up to Jedidiah to say hi and showed us the article he wrote about Jedidiah in the local paper!...;) The family met back up at Bobby and Wawee's for Panda Express dinner. We're talking on the deck overlooking the lake now...:) In the morning, we're leaving for a camping trip in Bungalow, where Grandpa Bobby used to work. It's going to be fun!...:)

Don't forget to visit
http://www.smokejumpers.com/nsa_news/item.phpnsa_news_id=480
for more pictures of Jedidiah's Alaskan Adventure

I know I never posted any news about the results from Jedidiah's July MRI. I was shocked by the news and unsure of how to say it "right" for the website... So I'm using Dad's words instead. Here is a note he wrote to Bill Cramer and John Gould, two of the men who made Jedidiah's Alaska trip

SO incredible. Not only does this letter summarize Jedidiah's trip perfectly, but it also discusses the results of the MRI.

"John, I got your phone message today. I'd planned to call you to say, 'Thank You". Yes, we made it home safe and sound! We picked up the envelope at the front desk at Pikes from Lindsay Wyatt. Mike met us at Hot Licks Ice Cream just before we left to give us the photo album and DVDs he made, and gave us a card signed by 13 workers from the Mess Hall. You guys are the greatest!

I've learned these GBM tumors are rare in children, the most aggressive of all brain tumors, with the shortest life expectancies. Your timing was perfect! Jedidiah had a blast! He kept the streamers Jessica and Justin retrieved stumbling across the tussocks and has been demonstrating spotting stories to all who will listen!

He's gained strength back from his biopsy and radiation/chemo treatments and was there physically and mentally for his Alaska Smokejumper trip!!! Putting him in Rookie Training under the Head Rookie Trainer, Loft Foreman, Lead Spotter and PC, letting him eat with the Bros, making him a jump suit with his own PG bag, taking an air tanker/lead plane tour, parachute manipulation and Spotting 101 classes, putting him right at the door with the headphones and letting him talk to the pilots and kick the jumpers, then presenting him his Alaska Smokejumper wings, plague, print, T-shirts and hats in front of all of Alaska Fire Service at the Awards Ceremony, and letting me give him his Alaska Smokejumper belt buckle, followed with the Chena River jet boat grayling fishing moose-on-a-stick eating Rookie Camp! Jedidiah is one of the Best of the Best, the 650th Alaska Smokejumper in 51 years! This is HUGE!!!

Jedidiah went in for his follow-up MRI Monday. Dr Z said he's awful sorry to say, news he knows were not ready to hear, but the MRI shows the tumor's re-grown tentacles and there's nothing else Dr Z can do, except for us to enjoy every day we get with Jedidiah -and to keep making those memories!

I never imagined you and Bill would make Jedidiah's Make-a-Wish this Big, with me and Cynthia in the jump ship, and Jedidiah's brother, sister, and grandma there to participate! From the bottom of my heart, 'Thank You', for making my little boy's dream come true!!!!"

Visit http://www.smokejumpers.com/nsa_news/item.phpnsa_news_id=480 for more pictures of Jedidiah's Alaskan Adventure!!! There is also a link to Jedidiah's article on the homepage of smokejumpers.com!! These photographs were taken by Mike McMillan, an Alaska Smokejumper and accomplished photographer.

Monday, August 16th

Jedidiah is doing good! He has been having a BLAST at fair…:) He entered his pinewood Derby Truck and won an Honorable Mention Ribbon even though we missed the deadline for judging. He was also in the Fair Parade with his Cub Scout Pack. =) The Idaho trip ended wonderfully. One of my highlights was making cotton candy at the Bungalow campground!! (Pictured) We made six different flavors- including warheads!…;) We are spending this week relaxing and winding down after such a whirlwind, amazing summer. Jedidiah is very excited to go back to school next week. He will be in Mrs. Hochrein's 4th grade class!…:) Sorry for the tardiness and brevity of this update; I have been busy with work and soccer practice. More pictures and stories will come. Also, if you have a Facebook, make sure to add Jedidiah to see Lots more pictures of his latest adventures…:)

"We are afflicted in every way, but not crushed. Perplexed but not driven to despair. Persecuted but not forsaken. Struck down but not destroyed." 2 Corinthians 4:8-9

Aug. 26, 2010

Hi, this is Jedidiah's mom. I guess I have been elected to update this website, since Jessica has become extremely busy. We are very proud of the EXCEPTIONAL job Jessica did with this during the first six months of Jedidiah's brain tumor. Jessica jumped right in, feet first, to take on this project. She set the bar HIGH, and it will be a hard act to follow, but I am willing to give it a try!

On Monday of this week Jessica began her sophomore year of college with 21 units, as well as playing on the FRC Women's Soccer Team. To put it mildly, she will be a busy girl this fall.

On Tuesday, Jedidiah went to the first day of 4th grade at Quincy Elementary School, an event he was eagerly looking forward to. His teacher this year is Mrs. Hochrein. Jedidiah was SO excited to be at school! He received his new school books, colored his nametag, and gave a talk about some of the exciting things he got to do this summer.

Jedidiah's energy ran out about lunch time, and he told Mrs. Hochrein that he needed to go home after lunch and take a nap. He said, "I did not get my after breakfast nap today, so I'm kind of tired now. I need to go home and sleep so I don't get mean and grumpy."

He ended up falling asleep around 3 PM at home. He slept all afternoon, and then all through the night without waking up for dinner. Seems that effort at school really tired him out. He sure did enjoy being there, that's for sure!

Jedidiah would like everybody to know that he has a Cotton Candy machine. He is now taking orders for custom made cotton candy flavors, and will ship the product directly to you! His new venture is called, "Cotton Clouds". He is requesting you send him a dollar per bag, and recommends such flavors as Peppermint, Cinnamon, Root Beer Barrel, Lemon, or Sour Warhead, (or a combination of your choice). You may pick any flavor that you can find in a hard candy. You can also mail him 2 hard candy discs of your own, and he will send you the cotton candy back. I tell you, he is quite the enterprising young man!

Today's photo is one of my favorite, taken by photographer & BLM Jumper, Mike McMillian. It depicts Jedidiah getting ready to "kick" an Alaska Smokejumper out the door, for a practice jump. The jumper is leaning back, poised, after Jedidiah's order of "Get Ready!" and is awaiting Jedidiah's final signal to leap out the door....

I will love You, O Lord, my strength. The Lord is my rock and my fortress and my deliverer; my God, my strength, in whom i will trust; my shield and the horn of my salvation, my stronghold. Psalm 18: 1-2, KJV.

Cynthia Lusk

Aug. 28, 2010

 Jedidiah had a Fun Friday. He chose to go on a Four Wheeler adventure with his Dad in the morning, and then went to watch his brother's soccer games in the afternoon at Quincy High School. Jedidiah remains in excellent spirits, it's just his body that gets tired and needs to nap more often. He wants his teacher, Mrs. Hochrein, to know that he did complete ALL his homework from the first day of school!

 I would like to take this opportunity to say THANK YOU to all the wonderful people out there who have given of themselves to support Jedidiah and our family during this tough time with Jedidiah's brain tumor. Friends, relatives, and even strangers have all helped SO much. We cannot say THANKS enough to express our extreme gratitude for all the generosity shown to us. Throughout the 33 days we spent at UC Davis Medical Center hospital, and the following month at the Ronald McDonald House, we were never left feeling alone and without support. From food, visits, money, cards, jokes, & phone calls, to help with fund raisers and work parties at our home, and even continuing on now, the incredible support has been and is always: **GREATLY APPRECIATED!!**

 Thanks to USFS employees who have donated Leave for me!

 Thank you also to those special people who have prayed and continue to pray for Jedidiah and our family. We have FELT those prayers and the power of our wonderful GOD and it has sustained us tremendously, every single day!

 Now here is one more thing, if you are so inclined, that I would like your help with. Would you please think of your favorite Jedidiah story, and write it down on the Guestbook. It doesn't have to be long, just a short note, about something that Jedidiah said or did that you remembered. It could be serious or silly, from school or ski team, or maybe he sold you popcorn? Maybe you have never met Jedidiah, but know his brother or sister, then send a note about them. Please share your story with everybody who enjoys this website, and we all will benefit and be uplifted by the wonderful memories that i know are out there. Thanks again!

*"**Not unto us, O Lord, not unto us, but to Your name give glory, because of Your mercy, because of Your truth.**"* Psalm 115:1 NKJV

Aug. 29, 2010

Yesterday was Soccer Saturday! Between Jessica playing 2 games at Feather River College and Justin having a tournament at Quincy High School, Jedidiah watched 5 games I think! The morning started off cool and damp, so Scott watched Jessica's first game from inside the van, so Jedidiah could stay warm and dry.

Jedidiah did not care about the raindrops outside, he was busy dancing to the "Techno Froggy" on his I-Pod! (Kids these days!) If you have not seen Jedidiah doing his dancing- it is pretty hilarious! When we were in Alaska, Jedidiah started his "Ravioli Dance" by bouncing his hind end on the bed, and almost bounced himself right off the bed! Yesterday, Jedidiah was warming up by Rocking Out in his wheelchair.

Jedidiah makes me laugh, Jedidiah makes me cry! Sometimes Jedidiah makes me laugh so hard that I cry! I will be telling some stories about Jedidiah and filling in some of the gaps from this summer when we were too busy to write about what was going on.

The picture I selected for today was taken with my cell phone, so it is not the best of clarity- not at all like Mike McMillian's photos- Sorry. It was taken at the Redmond Air Tanker Base, after our Alaska trip, but before our Bungalow, Idaho Campout. The three boys and I stopped in and visited at the Tanker Base where I work in the summer. Jedidiah and Justin had spent a week with me in Redmond last summer, so they are familiar with the RDM ATB. Jedidiah LOVES to talk with the pilots, asking them "What does this button do? What happens if your wheel falls off on take-off? How many fires have you fought? Have you ever been struck by lightning?" He seems to NEVER run out of questions!

But this time, HE was the one telling of all his adventures! So, here they are under the wing of Tanker-17, enjoying the shade of the air tanker, in the morning before the tarmac really heats up. Jedidiah is talking to the pilots. One of the pilots said to Jedidiah, "I heard you went up to Alaska?" and that was all it took. Jedidiah was off and running! And every one of his stories started off with, "Now, when I was spotting back in Alaska...."

He told about his jumpers all hitting the spot, he told of his jet boat ride up the Chena River, he told about how good the food was in the AFS Mess Hall in Fairbanks and he told about seeing the CL-214 Air Tanker on the ramp in AK, and asked these pilots, "Now, what do you say when the Duck is coming in?" His answer is, "You'd better duck, the Duck is coming!!"

'And He said to me, "My grace is sufficient for you, for My strength is made perfect in weakness." Therefore most gladly I will rather boast in my infirmities, that the power of Christ may rest upon me.' 2 Corinthians 12:9 NKJV

<u>Aug. 30, 2010</u>

Yesterday was Seafood Sunday! The family drove over to Reno, because Jessica was supposed to have a soccer game and Justin wanted to buy school supplies. Jedidiah was going to stay home with his grandma Nanny, but decided to tag along and go to Reno too.

As it turns out, Jessica's soccer game was cancelled somewhere along the way. So Scott decided it would be a good time to pull into the Atlantis to see what was for lunch.......and, you guessed it! That's where the Seafood comes in! Justin was really hungry from all his soccer games the last few days, so he packed in the calories to catch up on his daily requirements. Jedidiah only went for seconds, instead of fifths- like he did back when he was on a higher dosage of Decadron and we ate seafood at the Peppermill. I won't say how much Scott ate- just suffice to say that he greatly enjoys his seafood, and he got his money's worth!

Everybody got to stop at Wal-Mart for fall school supplies, and Justin also went to "New to You", to pick out some clothes. It was a busy day in Reno. Started raining on the way home, just enough to settle the late summer dust.

The photo I selected today is of Jessica and Jedidiah at Papa's Donut House in Quincy. I took it a couple weeks ago, and it depicts Jessica being what our family calls, "A Promise Keeper".

Jessica had told Jedidiah that she would treat him to a donut at Papa's - sometime down the road. She didn't have time the day he asked, they were running late to get to Jedidiah's PT appointment, and we got to town after Papa's was closed that next day. But when you make a promise in our family, you are held to that promise until you fulfill it. If you say you will do something, you'd better darn well do just that! One of my favorite mottos is, "Say what you do, and do what you say!" Jedidiah, especially, will remember a LONG time, when you promise him something. We sure do appreciate all the people out there who have said they would do something, and then follow up with ACTIONS. Thanks!!

Jedidiah wanted me to remind people if they want to order Cotton Candy, and they send two hard candies, then they owe NO money. Repeat, send NO money if you give him the candy!

"Peace I leave with you, My peace I give to you; not as the world gives, do I give to you. Let not your heart be troubled, neither let it be afraid". John 14:27

Aug. 31, 2010

Yesterday was a Marvelous Monday for Jedidiah to go to school. His Dad took him, and they showed up WAY too early- about 0730. With our family, we are either an hour early to watch them water the arena (set up for the activity)- or else we are just a tad bit late. Jedidiah did enjoy school until 11:00, then he had to go home for his nap.

I'd like to tell you a little about each person in our family over the next several days. That way you will have a better perspective of what formed Jedidiah's life. I will start with Jedidiah's Dad, since he is the oldest (But Shhhh... don't tell him I said that. He thinks he is only 38!)

So, in honor of Jedidiah's Dad, Scott, here is a photo of both of them in Taylorsville, CA going on a crawdad hunting adventure down to Indian Creek.

For all of you that know him, you will certainly agree that Scott is one heck of a wonderful father to all 3 of his children!

Scott may look big, burly, & hairy like a bear on the outside, (and he has been known to growl occasionally at USFS Specialists), but on the inside he has a heart of Gold! Especially when it comes to helping kids. Over the past ten years Scott has been a dedicated Youth Soccer Coach for the Central Plumas Recreation District and a Ski Coach for the Johnsville Junior Ski Team. As a Coach, Scott holds the kids to a higher standard- he tells them to always do their best. He accepts no excuses, and pushes them to try harder.

There is no limit to his love for his children (and his wife of 24 years). He definitely puts the welfare of his family first. He has given unlimited support towards helping our children achieve their goals. He has spent countless hours helping kids at their fiddle lessons, ski team, dance recitals, sports practices and games, 4-H projects, and has taught them lifetime values of leadership, wisdom, and humor.

Thank you Scott, for all you have done!!

"For God has not given us a spirit of fear, but of power and of love, and of a sound mind." 2 Timothy 1:7 NKJV

Sep 1, 2010

On the CaringBridge Website is a photo of Jedidiah's big sister, Jessica, dressed up as a Smokejumper at the Redmond Smokejumper Base a month ago.

Of course, you all know Jessica as she had been the author of this web site for the past 6 months. Ten years older than Jedidiah, Jessica has been the dedicated, loving and ever present and helpful Big Sister throughout Jedidiah's life. She was a bit disappointed when we brought **him** home, as Jessica was REALLY hoping for a little sister! But Jessica fell into the big sister role quite easily, despite the fact that he was a boy. She changed Jedidiah's diapers, gave him a bath, carried him around and gave him his toys when he wanted them. She was, and still is, a wonderful care giver and helps us out a whole lot!

Jessica was born in Missoula, Montana on her grandmother's birthday (AKA "Blue Nanny" & Jessica is the one who coined that term!). Jessica was delivered to this world by Cesarean Section, due to the fact Jessica's mom had an accident and her pelvis was pinned together so a "normal" delivery was not probable. Yes, it was my fault, so sorry Jessica. I was pretty ignorant back then, about the safety of gestating babies. My Doctor told me to "continue to do what your normally do" throughout the pregnancy. (Apparently, he did not believe me when I told him that I liked to jump out of airplanes and ride unbroken horses!) Both Jessica and I got thrown from my Arabian horse, Cheval and we ended up in the Missoula Hospital for a week. But, we both pulled through and everything ended up just fine, though Jessica seemed to develop a dislike of riding bucking horses from a very early age! Wonder why?

Jessica was forced to deal with her own medical crisis just a few years ago, when she was diagnosed with Type 1 Diabetes in November of 2007. She spent a week at Renown Hospital in Reno, learning how to control her body's blood sugar levels by pricking her finger at least 4 times a day, and injecting insulin to make up for her pancreas lack of production. It's a tough go for her. Imagine - knowing you yourself will be responsible for this process continually, every single hour, of every day, every week, every month and every year for the REST of your life. Jessica has developed the tenacity to take good care of herself. As a result as this thrust-upon-her medical condition, she has had an increasing interest in the medical field as a future career. She succeeded in passing the Emergency Medical Technician semester long class at Feather River College, AND passed the National EMT Registry Test with flying colors! GREAT JOB JESSICA!

Now she is attending FRC full time, completing General Ed requirements in order to transfer to another college to peruse a Nursing Degree. We are behind you 100% Jessica, and wish you all the best!

"Trust in the Lord with all your heart and lean not on your own understanding. In all your ways acknowledge Him, and He will direct your paths." Proverbs 3:5-6

Sep 2, 2010

Yesterday was a Wonderful Wednesday for Jedidiah to stay home and rest. He did not go to school. He showed his Dad how to use the Cotton Candy Machine, and now Scott is one of only 4 people who are "Certified" to operate Jedidiah's Cotton Candy Machine! Don't forget- they will be at tonight's Farmers Market- selling "Cotton Clouds" Cotton Candy in a rainbow of flavors! It will be a Fund Raiser for the Quincy History Club.

Jedidiah was thrilled yesterday when his Dad also learned how to play the Bowling Game on his DS. He loves to share that toy with us. Mrs. O'Massey came over to our house and read Jedidiah some stories. She also made a balloon bouquet for Jessica!

Jedidiah's Dad is learning to play the cello. Most of you know Jedidiah is very musically inclined, and he did NOT get that from his mother! So Scott was upstairs trying to eke out a few songs, when Jedidiah hollered up at him, "Hey Dad! Could you maybe wait and play that thing AFTER I get my nap?" We are glad to know that Jedidiah has not lost his sense of music tone, or his sense of humor!

Today's photo is of brother Justin, hugging Jedidiah. Justin has GOT to be the sweetest big brother in the world! He is always loving on Jedidiah, kissing and hugging him every day. Jedidiah gets annoyed, and says, "Stop that Justin!" as he wipes the kisses off. They are always being brothers, despite their 7 year age difference- constantly poking at each other, wrestling around, egging each other on, trying to get the other in trouble. We've always admonished Justin, "You better watch what you are doing, your little brother is watching you!" But there was little for us as parents to worry about, Justin has been an excellent role model for Jedidiah. In fact Justin has been so good, he earned the nickname, "Mr. Perfect"! (Of course we know the only human who was ever perfect was Jesus Christ). I think the one who first started calling Justin that was his big sister. Since she was the oldest, she was the first one to get corrected for testing the limits. And Jedidiah, being the little guy, was always getting himself into trouble just by being a young BOY. Here was poor Justin, stuck as the ignored middle child! He was quiet, optimistic, and enjoyed school- As long as he arrived ON TIME! Justin hates being LATE!

Justin was born in Prineville, Oregon on his Mom & Dad's Wedding Anniversary! What a nice present we received! He has grown into a wonderful, 16 year old, nice young man. We are very proud of him and his success in school and sports. He is a "Scholar Athlete", maintaining good grades while competing in a multitude of sports and activities both in and out of school. He plays Soccer, Basketball, and runs Track. Justin displays a very mature sense of responsibility, emerging leadership, and of course, loves his family very much! Justin- Thanks for being YOURSELF! WE LOVE YOU!!

"For He Himself has said, 'I will never leave you nor forsake you'. So we may boldly say: 'The Lord is my helper; I will not fear. What can man do to me?' Hebrews 13:5-6 NKJV

Sep 3, 2010

Yesterday was a busy Thursday for Jedidiah. He went to a doctor's appointment at Dr. Kepple's office at 0900, then he went to school for a while. Back home for a rest before the evening Farmer's Market in Quincy. Photo shows Scott making Cotton Candy with Jedidiah's Famous Cotton Candy Machine, Jedidiah supervising in the background AND giving his "Sales Pitch"! It was a resounding success!! They added $50 to the History Club profit, and received orders for another $20. worth of Cotton Candy!!

This week I received a phone call from Dr. Z, who was Jedidiah's Oncologist at U.C. Davis Medical Center. The last time he saw Jedidiah was for his last MRI on July 13th. He inquired on how Jedidiah was doing, and i told him about Jedidiah's activities, his determination to go to school, his high level of focus and concentration, and Jedidiah's spirit of happiness and steadfastness. The doctor admitted that Jedidiah has done so much better, for much longer than he ever expected.

My response is, "Well, yeah. He has a ton of people praying for him!!" And I thank ALL OF YOU who made a difference in our lives. I know only God determines the length of our lives.

We can determine the Quality of LIFE and LOVE we put into this life and how much we share with others. Thank all of you for sharing with us. It is greatly appreciated!

"Do not lay up for yourself treasures on earth, where moth and rust destroy and where thieves break in and steal. But lay up for yourself treasures in heaven where neither moth nor rust destroy and where thieves do not break in and steal. For where your treasure is, there your heart will be also." Matthew 6:19-20. NKJV

Sep 6, 2010

Jedidiah has three incredible grandparents, that are alive & well, and quite active in his life: Scott's mom & dad, Bob and Betty Lusk, whom recently celebrated their 55th Wedding Anniversary (**Congratulations**!) live in Coeur d' Alene, Idaho, and my mother, Donnal Nichols whom lives with us in Cromberg, CA (my father died in 1987). As grandkids often do, they made nicknames for their grandparents. Jessica called my mother, "Blue Nanny" from a very early age. Bob and Betty became, "Bobby and Wawee" named by Conner Williams, one of Jedidiah's cousins.

As everyone already knows, Grandparents are oh so important in a child's life, as ALL family really is. But there is still something very special about a grandparent who takes an interest and an active part in their grandchildren's lives. Jedidiah, and all of us, have been very blessed in this department by his grandparents.

Blue Nanny has lived with us at various times over the years, to help out with our children, from Montana where Jessica was born, to Oregon where Justin was born, then back to Quincy where Jedidiah was born, (and where i grew up). She does way more than her share around the house, from outdoor chores like tending to baby goats born in a snowstorm, to wiping snotty noses on the human variety of kids. She is physically active as a rider, trainer and owner of her special Appaloosa horses. As a Registered Nurse for most of her life, she was the first one to notice potentially dangerous signs and symptoms in both Jessica and Jedidiah.

We appreciate ALL your wonderful help! Thank you so much Blue Nanny!

When a person is first married to an individual, do they REALLY know they are marrying into the WHOLE family, and not just to that person? When I selected Scott as my lifetime mate, I didn't realize how lucky I would become, to gain his side of the family. I was and am, greatly blessed by the Lusks, (Williams, and Chavis included!) Bob and Betty are quite remarkable people. From folks who have know them for 50 years, or someone who has just met them, ALL will agree, they are very special people! Their most enduring quality is their outward expression of love for their family. It is no secret that they love each and every one of their grandchildren, as well as each other. They have passed that quality on to all of their four children; Julie, Rick, Scott and Linda- who have in turn, passed that quality on to their children.

Thank you Bobby & Wawee- You are the GREATEST!

"If we live in the Spirit, let us also walk in the Spirit."
Galatians 5:25, NKJV

Always Remember Me

Bob and Betty Lusk with a tiny baby Jedidiah in 2001, joined by big sister, Jessica, and middle brother, Justin.

Sep 4, 2010

Here is a photo of Jedidiah and I at Antelope Lake on the Plumas National Forest in July. Just a week before, Jedidiah was with me to see one of my most embarrassing moments. It happened the evening of July 13th, as we were heading home from Jed's last MRI in Sacramento. We FINALLY got out of that crazy city, and into the foothills above Auburn, traveling up I-80. It was a hot summer afternoon, we were frazzled, the car needed gas, and Jedidiah had announced that he needed to use the restroom.

So I turned off at the Dutch Flat Exit, where I knew there would be both gas and a restroom. After fueling up the car, I pulled it over to the side to get out Jedidiah's folding wheelchair from the back, set it up, and get Jedidiah loaded into it. I wheeled him towards the convenience store with hopes they had a nice large wheelchair accessible bathroom inside.

I was already feeling shook up and unsettled by the results of the MRI earlier that day. Dr. Z's voice was still ringing in my ears saying, "I am sorry, the tumor has grown larger. There is nothing else we can do for Jedidiah...." So, I wasn't really focusing on the task at hand. (And HOW many times have I told the kids NOT to do that? Thinking about one thing, while you are doing another...) As I approached the door with the wheelchair I decide the best way to get in would be to push the door open with my back and pull the wheelchair inside. (I am still NOT too good at driving those things- a fact Jedidiah readily tells people!)

So, this is how it went:

I am backing, backing, backing thru the door and pulling Jedidiah in the wheelchair with me. I feel a nudge at my shoulder. Turning to look, I see a four foot tall, four sided display rack, plumb FULL of fancy sunglasses tipping over and falling towards the floor. "NNNnnnnooooo!!" Too late!

Do you know what noise 80 pair of sunglasses make when they hit the floor? It kind of sounds like, "Skitter, scatter, crash!" and then a final, "!BANG!" as the display rack crashes to the floor- on top of some of the sunglasses.

It was a VERY LOUD noise! Only to be followed by a deafening silence. Then the sound of a loud voice of a 9 year old boy:

"It wasn't me! I did NOT do that! It was NOT my fault, it was HERS!!" and he points to his mother.

What could I say? It WAS all my fault! If I had followed my own advice of not thinking one thing while doing another. If I had just focused on the task at hand, this would NOT have happened. But I did not, and it HAD happened. There was nothing left to do but pick up the sunglasses and apologize.

So I mumbled, "I'm sorry. I am very sorry." I up righted the rack, and began the slow process of replacing the very scattered sunglasses back to their proper place on the display rack, while a multitude of stunned onlookers stared at me.

Halfway thru, Jedidiah piped up, "Oh, uh ... Mom....I still have to go to the bathroom..."

"Oh, yeah." I said to myself, "There is one more thing to do... make that two. I still have to get us back home in one piece!"

There ARE embarrassing moments in life! But we know God STILL loves us ! And life goes on.....

"But the fruit of the Spirit is; Love, joy, peace, long suffering, kindness, goodness, faithfulness, gentleness, self-control. Against such there is no law." Galatians 5:25

Sep 5, 2010

    Yesterday Jedidiah went for a ride in the woods with Corky Lazzarino in her Jeep. They had a great time! Thank you so much, Corky! (And keep up the good work with Sierra Access Coalition.)

    Jedidiah has always loved machines with motors. Speaking of motors- Thank you also to Andy Feinblum at Sierra Cycles in Quincy for working on Jedidiah's 4-wheeler, and for Dee Vagart for saying Jedidiah could use his. We appreciate you guys!!

    I remember when Jedidiah was a little boy, before he could even walk or talk- he used to push his matchbox cars on the floor and make that BBbbrrrrmmm, bbrrrmmm noise. As he grew, he wanted bigger and louder toys. He absolutely enjoyed remote control cars, monster trucks, snowmobiles, and jet skis. It wasn't long after he learned to walk, he learned to snow ski, and then it was on to dirt bikes! Yes, I learned, mini dirt bikes can and **DO** come with training wheels! A bicycle wasn't fast enough, Jedidiah wanted it with a motor!

    When Jedidiah was one and a half years old, we lived in Lakeview, Oregon for a short while. We had a backhoe come over to work on the septic. Jedidiah stared thru the sliding glass door, spellbound, as the heavy machine dug thru the dirt in our back yard. He would point and say, "BIG!" with such excitement. The equipment owner and operator, an old timer named Dorwin Padget, watched Jedidiah watching him. When he shut down for a break he came over to talk to me. "Hey, would you mind if the little guy came out side? I could use some help in the cab with the controls." Jedidiah came out of the house wriggling' with excitement! As he sat on Dorwin's lap, with the backhoe controls in his hands, you never saw a more excited little boy in your life!

    In the winter, it's the snowmobiles that entrance Jedidiah, and always have. A few years ago, when I'd come home after riding snowmobiles at Bucks Lake for Recreation Patrol, I'd get peppered with questions, how far did i ride? How fast did i go? How many horsepower were the engines?

Did i need to change the oil? Were the machines two stroke or four stroke? Jedidiah just had to know all the details. It wasn't long after when he started begging his parents to get him a snowmobile. He used all kinds of persuasive speech to prove his point. What would happen if it snowed 12 feet at home, and we couldn't get out of driveway? Just think about how much he could help out with the chores in the winter, if only he had a snowmobile....Why, he would even take the trash out, using the snowmobile to transport the garbage bag!

We finally found a suitable snowmobile for him, that Alexis Decoe had outgrown, and her mother offered it for sale. But Jedidiah's dad would not **give** him one- just because. By golly, Jedidiah had to EARN that snowmobile. His Dad made a deal with Jedidiah that if he would memorize and play a fiddle tune he had been working on, then he could get the snowmobile. Jed was pretty reluctant at first, but the more he wanted that snowmobile, the more he started to practice O'Keefe's Slide on his fiddle. One month later, there was Jedidiah with his fiddle, out on a misty day in December, playing that song as he sat on the seat of that snowmobile!!

"Restore to me the joy of your salvation, and uphold me by your generous spirit." Psalm 51:11 NKJV

Sep 10, 2010

Tuesday Jedidiah got to help build the Spanish Creek Bridge on Hwy 70. He got to operate CCMyer's big Cat 475 excavator. He also got to watch them drive the steel bridge I-beams pillars with a diesel cannon attached to the World's biggest crane! Thank you CCMyers, Caltrans, John Hughes, Ron Collins, and Crew for letting Jedidiah help, and for giving him his own hard hat, vest, and signed T-shirt!

Speaking of cranes, Mrs. Hochrein's 4th Grade Class is building 1,000 Origami Cranes for Jedidiah, each with a kind thought. Mrs. Hochrein said it takes a lot of focus for her 4th graders to make that many folds, but It's working! Thursday after school, Jedidiah brought home the first 60 cranes. On Thursday night Jedidiah walked from his brown chair all the way down the hall and back, with his Dad holding his belt loop just in case he stumbled, which he didn't!

Sep 11, 2010

Jedidiah rode his new blue 4-Wheeler all by himself today!

He's only taking 0.25mg of Decadron, down from 8.0 mg a while ago. The reduced amount of Decadron is allowing the water retention, face swelling, and voracious appetite to start to subside. Jedidiah is starting to look more like himself every day!

Jessica played Center D with FRC's trounce of Lassen College today, 5 to 0. Cynthia and Blue Nanny are helping with Kassandra's Patriots Day Endurance ride over the weekend. The three boys are going to go play a round a golf at Mt Huff Golf Course from Randy Beck's Wellness Fund Raiser Sunday morning 0 dark thirty!

The Redding Smokejumpers called today and invited Jedidiah to their end of season BBQ next Friday!

Written Sep 12, 2010 7:29pm- by Scott Lusk

The boys played a round a round of golf today at Mt Huff Golf Course. It was fun! We were high bidders at Randy Beck's Fund Raiser and thought we'd give golf a try. The Plumas County Sheriff's Office had a fund raiser here for Jedidiah. We didn't attempt to play a round then.

Jedidiah drove the golf cart today! Justin and Dad kept striking out. Dad got a golf ball stuck in a tree! Justin had the farthest hit. It went way high straight up, then came straight back down and landed on top of the golf cart, which we thought we had parked in a safe spot.

We thought 10 holes was almost as much as 18 so we went to the Pro Shop for cheeseburgers and to tell of our adventures, They laughed 'cause they thought we were making it up!

At the end of the day nothing was broke or bent so we called it a very successful day, with Pizza and handpicked Blackberry pie for dinner!

"This is the day the Lord has made; we will rejoice and be glad in it." Psalm 118:24

Sep 15, 2010

Mike Taborski donated a scenic flight of Plumas County to Randy Beck's Fundraiser. Jedidiah was high bidder and invited Justin and Jessica! There was even room for dad!

Jedidiah wanted to see his house, his friends at Quincy Elementary, The 'Q', American Valley Speedway, FRC Soccer field, and QHS. Mike took the time to fly over Buck's Lake. Jedidiah wanted to see the view from 1,500 (streamers) and at 3,000 (square jumpers). Jedidiah proudly yelled, 'Jumper's Away!' when we hit 3,000! What a spectacular view of Plumas County! It is Beautiful!

Mike let Jedidiah fly when we went over our house. Jedidiah took right to it and wiggled the wings at his mama who was filming from below!

"For by grace you have been saved through faith, and that not of yourselves; it is a gift of God, not of works, lest anyone should boast." Ephesians 2: 8-9 NJKV

Sep 16, 2010

Yesterday Jedidiah and his mom went to lunch with Deputy Shawn Webb and Sgt. Todd Johns. Jedidiah asked Shawn what it felt like to wear handcuffs. He asked the deputy, "Hey, can I try them out?"

Jedidiah said to tell you he got handcuffed because he did not eat all his lunch! Maybe next time he'll eat his food when he is supposed to!

After that Jedidiah went to meet his 4th grade class as they headed back from their hike up to the Quincy "Q". Jedidiah brought them all a snack. He handed out what he called "Cheese Head" cheese sticks to replenish his classmate's energy.

Then we picked up Justin at Quincy High School and drove to Loyalton to watch the boys Soccer game. QHS won!

Jedidiah is still making "Cotton Clouds" cotton candy. We made a supply of Root Beer flavor yesterday, and will be manufacturing more soon!! So keep those orders rolling in!

"We love Him because He first loved us." 1 John 4:19 NJKV

Sep 19, 2010

The Redding Smokejumpers invited Jedidiah to tour their base and their end of season BBQ Friday. They presented Jedidiah with a California Smoke Jumper belt buckle, belt, PG bag, helmet, and 'Jumping for Jedidiah' cash! Jedidiah got to try smokejumper spam- spam flavored with Gatorade mix and hot sauce! He described it politely as, "Not something I'd want to eat for breakfast, lunch and dinner for the rest of my life" Ha ha...;) He got a tour of the base, got to watch grown men ride around on a go-kart like little boys, tell jokes over the base intercom, look at the planes, talk to some pilots and tell spotter stories!! Jedidiah told jokes the whole time, and the jumpers listened the whole time! They laughed, joked and talked with him! It was so special. He also autographed one of his "jumper bro's" helmet! His wheelchair is sporting three new stickers, including his official jump weight and name. Make sure to ask him about them- he's very proud...;) Redding Jumpers, you guys are amazing! THANK YOU!!

Here's a picture of Jedidiah telling jokes to his captive audience of Jumpers!

Saturday we watched Justin play two awesome games of soccer at U-Prep tournament and ended Saturday with a family dinner at Golden King in Quincy. Sunday morning we all got dressed up and went to Church where Jedidiah and Justin are going to get baptized in a few weeks...:)

It was a wonderful family weekend! <3

"Being confident of this very thing, that He who has begun a good work in you will complete it until the day of Jesus Christ."
Philippians 1:6

Sep 22, 2010

WOW! Jedidiah got a NEW puppy! It's a Chihuahua! We brought her home last night. It was love at first sight for both Jedidiah and "Pep". Jedidiah has been SO EXCITED, he is literally bouncing with happiness. He has been enjoying his puppy ALL DAY today!!

Jedidiah dictated his story of picking up Pep, to his grandma Nanny today. I will copy it down tonight, so i can add it to Jed's Caring bridge soon. (Hopefully tomorrow.)

Watching Jedidiah interact with his new puppy today, and helping him learn to care for her, reminded me of 1 Corinthians, Chapter 13 in the Bible, where it describes real love:

"Love suffers long and is kind, love does not envy; love does not parade itself, is not puffed up. Does not behave rudely, does not seek its own, is not provoked, thinks no evil; does not rejoice in iniquity, but rejoices in the truth, bears all things, hopes all things, endures all things. Love never fails. But whether there are prophecies, they will fail; whether there are tongues, they will cease, whether there is knowledge, it will vanish away."
1Corinthians 13:4-8 NKJV

Sep 23, 2010

Jedidiah's New Puppy

This is the story, in Jedidiah's own words, of him getting his puppy. He dictated the story to his grandma, Donnal (AKA: Blue Nanny). So, I am writing it down for Jedidiah's CaringBridge Website, with some slight edits and grammar corrections (by his mother).

Wednesday September 22, 2010 – Three days ago I was thinking back about getting Life Flighted to U.C. Davis and it made me sad. I was thinking about what could make me happy. I wanted something to play with. I have my three black cats at home, but I can't take them to town with me. Everyone else in the family has had a dog, but me….. Blue Nanny, Mom, Dad, Justin and Jessica…. Hey, where is my name on that list?

I really like Nano's dog, "Chucky". He is a Che-wennie, and they can be expensive! But, I also really like Chihuahuas. Hey! I could get a Chihuahua! So, yesterday (Tuesday) my parents took me over to Greenville to someone's house, who had Chihuahua puppies for sale.

I got to pick one out! Except, I did not pick her….I looked at her, and I knew she was picking ME out! She was saying, "Jedidiah, pick me!"

Time for my checklist: Brown…Check! Chihuahua….Check! Puppy…. Check! Female…..Check!

Before I could look at any of the other pups, I said, "THAT ONE!"

On the way home I put her in my green tote Chihuahua carrier. As we drove away I felt sorry for her. She started to whine and cry. I thought she had to go to the bathroom (but she didn't poop until the next day). My Mom said she would miss her family of brother and sister, mom and dad. I felt sorry for her. I did not want her to be homesick.

The next morning I woke up and asked, "Where is my CHIHUAHUA?"

"Here she is", said Blue Nanny.

"I want her!"

Blue Nanny put her on my bed. I started playing with her and saying, "Who is a good girl? Who is a good girl?" She got all excited and it made her happy! She was jumping up and down. I sat up in the bed and looked at Pep. Pep jumped up to lick my face and knocked me back down.

"Ha Ha, Ha!" I laughed. "You are SUCH a good dog, Pep!" I said.

Then, I laid back down and Pep came up to my ear, snuggled up, and fell asleep on my shoulder.

Your dictator, writer and Pep say, "Thank you for reading Jedidiah's story of getting Pep!" - By Jedidiah Lusk- 9/22/10

"*Whether therefore ye eat, or drink, or whatsoever ye do, do all to the glory of God*." 1 Corinthians 10:31

Sep 24, 2010

Here is Jedidiah's continued story about his new Chihuahua puppy, "Pep".

Chapter 2- Introducing Pep to cats:

"The first cat I introduced Pep to was Emerald. Emerald is my Grandmother's cat. She is old, fat and gray. I was sitting in my brown chair with Pep in my lap, hugging her. Emerald walked up towards me in the living room and my mom said, "Emerald, we have a CHIHUAHUA now!" Emerald look up at us, turned around and left, with a disgusted look on her face. I think she heard the word, "Chihuahua", and said, "I am OUT of here!"

Then, Pep got to meet my cat, Black Lightning. Plus the other two black cats, Midnight and Baby Cakes. They were more fun than Emerald. They were all very curious of Pep. They sniffed and sniffed her cage, and tried to put their paws through the wire openings in Pep's kennel cage. I think the cats think Pep is a squirrel or rat or something."

Jedidiah will continue to add chapters to his book about Pep every day. Jessica promised she will take more photos of Pep and Jedidiah for me.

Today's photo was taken last week, when I took Jedidiah to his school. He wore his hard hat and visible safety vest from his trip to Spanish Creek Bridge, to show his classmates. Mrs. Hochrein let him give a little talk about his day spent working on the bridge.

Jesus said to him, "I am the way, the truth and the life. No man comes to the Father except through me." John 14:6 NKJV

Sep 25, 2010

CHAPTER 3- A School Day-9/23/10

Today we had to leave Pep at the house in her kennel crate while I had to go to a Dr. Kepple appointment and to school. When we got home I laid down and mom let Pep out of her kennel. Pep came tearing over to me and licked my face all over. Also today she did her 3rd bark. It kind of sounded like a human trying to bark!

I brought a box of paper crane origami's home from school today. Two were made from tissue paper. Pep found the box and she liked the tissue cranes best. Mom had to move them really quick so Pep did not eat them. We didn't do that much with Pep today because I was in school.

Black Lightning was also very happy to see me when I came home from school. She wanted lots of attention. I had to take turns with puppy kisses and kitten love so they were both happy and not jealous.

CHAPTER 4- Playful Pep Pup- 9/24/10

Today I woke up in bed and said "Where is my Chihuahua?"

Mom said, "She is upstairs in her crate." Mom brought her down and put her on my bed. Again, she ran over and tried to licked my face all over. We played around on the bed for a little while. Then I got up and in to my brown chair with Pep. She started nibbling on me very gently, so I knew she wanted her chew toy. I asked mom to bring over her stuffed llama toy. I squeezed the squeaker inside the llama and it made a high-pitched sound. I had to squeeze it for her because her jaws are too small to squeak it herself. Pep turned around and barked at the llama. Surprised, I squeaked the llama again. This time Pep turned around and bit the chew toy. I squeaked the toy one more time to see what Pep would do. This time she bit the chew toy harder and pulled back on the chew toy. I could tell she was having fun by the little doggie smile on her face. The next time I squeezed the llama, Pep ran over to it, bit it, pulled back, and growled!

I kept squeaking the toy to make her happy, until she got tired of the game. Then we both took a nap.

When Pep woke up, she started chewing on the fly swatter. She likes to play with a lot of things. She even was chasing and biting her own tail!

I bet she was thinking, "Hey what IS this thing that WAGS when I get happy? Hey, it's kind of fun to chase it! But it moves when I try to chase it"

Here is a joke for you: Q-) If lights run on electricity, and cars run on gas, what do Chihuahuas run on?

A-) They run on their little paws!

That's All for today!

In Him we have redemption through His blood, the forgiveness of sins, according to the riches of His grace. Ephesians 1:7 NKJV

Sep 27, 2010

CHAPTER 5- Camping with Pep- 9/26/10

Pep and I went camping this weekend for my Dad's Birthday. Yesterday when we got to the camping spot, Pep got cold and started shivering. Mom had to put Pep under her sweatshirt to warm her up. I sure did not want Pep to get frozen stiff!

Last night I had a dream that mom came up to me and said, "Pep's dead!"

I asked, "What happened?"

Mom said, "We did not keep her warm enough."

But this morning when I woke up and said, "Where is my Chihuahua?"

Mom had her under her sweatshirt again, keeping her warm!

Mom handed me a pop tart to eat. I was sitting in the truck with Justin so we could stay warm too. I didn't feel like eating the pop tart just yet, so I told mom to put it on the truck seat. I needed to scoot myself up. While I was trying to scoot up, Justin asked, "Do you want your pop tart now?"

I said, "Not yet!" But Justin tried to make me eat it anyway! He shoved it into my mouth, which hit my lip, which jammed into my teeth. That hurt!

"Hey, Justin, STOP!" I tried to mumble!

Then Mom came to get us out and said it was time for breakfast.

We ate breakfast, and the sun came up higher, and it finally warmed up. Mom said she kept Pep under the sleeping bag with her ALL night so she would not freeze.

I sat in my wheelchair and hugged Pep. Then she nibbled on my finger and I could tell she wanted another chew toy. Justin got out her pacifier squeaker chew toy and handed it to me. I squeaked the binky and Pep growled at it. That's not the only chew toy she has growled at. I squeaked the binky again and Pep attacked it more and more.

That afternoon, Mom tried to get me to eat a plum. I promised her I would eat it later. About an hour later, I looked at it, I thought, "mmm, it looks delicious!" My mouth started to water. So I quickly took a bite. Then I pulled the plum away and spit it out in a hurry!

"Bbleck! Something is wrong with this plum! It is NOT normal!"

"What's wrong?" Mom asked. She took the plum and took a bite. "Yuck!" she said, "It is rotten!" Then she threw it away.

Question for the day: What happens when you say my dog's name, then say "yes" in Spanish?

Answer: Pepsi !

"Therefore if there is any consolation in Christ, if any comfort of love, if any fellowship of the Spirit, if any affection and mercy. Fulfill my joy by being like-minded, having the same love, being of one accord, of one mind. Let nothing be done through selfish ambition or conceit, but in lowliness of mind let each esteem others better than himself." Philippians 2:1-3

<u>Sep 28, 2010</u>

Jedidiah is doing great! He is enjoying his puppy, feeling good, and staying busy with lots of fun activities.

Yesterday he went to 4th grade for the afternoon. Then he went to the first Cub Scouts meeting of the school year.

He got weighed at his doctor appointment last week. He has lost 3 pounds in the last 3 weeks. From the slow decrease of the steroid Dexamethasone, his appetite is decreasing, and he is able to lose some of the weight he rapidly gained while on large dosage of the steroid.

The only medication Jedidiah remains on is .25 mg of the dexamethasone every other day.

Jedidiah's hair is even growing back where he was bald from the chemotherapy and radiation he received to shrink his brain tumor.

Sometimes he has occasional pain in the end of his fingertips of his left hand. (That was the hand that was temporarily paralyzed after his biopsy.)

He wants you to know that he is happy and feeling great!

Jedidiah has a tongue twister he wants to share with you.

Say this three times really fast:

"I want to play with and pet my pet pup, Pep".

Jedidiah is going to be making some more cotton candy today, then going to school. This afternoon we will be watching Jessica play soccer at an FRC home game!

"Praise the Lord! Praise, O servants of the Lord, praise the name of the Lord! Blessed be the name of the Lord from this time forth and forevermore! From the rising of the sun to its going down the Lord's name is to be praised." Psalm 113:1-3, NKJV

Sep 29, 2010

Chapter 6- Cleaning with Pep- 9/29/10-by Jedidiah Lusk

Last night Pep, me and my Mom slept together in my bed. Pep snuggled and curled up next to my neck then went right to sleep. She sure is warm! It made me sleepy and I fell asleep next. My mom said it looked so sweet watching both of us sleep peacefully together.

Yesterday afternoon Pep ran down the hallway and didn't come out for a while. Mom sniffed the air and said, "Jedidiah... I think the poopy pupped. No wait a minute, I mean the puppy pooped!"

I laughed and laughed at her until she got mad at me. She had to clean up Poopy's pup, wait, I mean Pep's poop. Ha! Ha!

Later that day my mom was sweeping the house and Pep was chasing the broom. When Mom was done, she set the broom down. The bristles were showing and Pep ran over to it and bit it and pulled back. She started wrestling with the broom. I think Pep was thinking, "Hey, it's my turn to sweep the house now!!" Then Mom started mopping the floor and Pep really went crazy chasing the mop back and forth, and barking. She thought it was all play and no work!

At breakfast today, Pep took a nap. She must have been having a weird dream because she was whimpering and barking in her sleep!

Joke of the Day- Q: What do you when a Chihuahua sneezes?

A. You hand her a teeny, tiny handkerchief!

One I thought of: Q- What do you get when you cross Pep with a lollipop?

A- You get a pep-a-pop!

"I will lift up my eyes to the hills- from whence comes my help? My help comes from the Lord, who made heaven and earth."
Psalm 121:1-2

Oct 1, 2010

Yesterday was a busy, hectic day for Jedidiah and his Mom. We had an appointment to get all three of the kittens fixed at the vet office in

Beckwourth, and needed to get them there between 0800-0830. As if we needed another crisis to deal with- sometime during the night, my Appaloosa yearling, Elijah, acquired a laceration on his face- a wound that needed stitches.

So, after we got Scott off to work at 0630 and Justin off to the bus stop at 0710, I hooked up the stock trailer, caught the kittens and stuffed them in pet carrier, put the carrier inside the pickup, and went back to the house to get Jedidiah.

As I was pushing and shoving the wheelchair (with Jed in it) down our very bumpy, rough and rocky driveway to the truck, Jedidiah said, "On three! One,.... two,... Wheee!!!...Augggh!

"MOM!" Jedidiah yelled. "This wheelchair is NOT a dump truck! Please quit trying to dump me out of my wheelchair!"

We had hit one of the larger rocks in the driveway with the smaller front wheels of the wheelchair. It made the chair come to an unintended, quick stop! Whoops! Sorry, Jedidiah.

While I was catching Elijah to put him in the trailer, Jedidiah was amusing himself with the cats inside the pet carrier in the back seat of our crew cab pickup. Jedidiah thought up this pre-Halloween story. He called it, "Kitties From the Dead".

KITTIES FROM THE DEAD
By Jedidiah Lusk

"I was in the truck, All alone, one very dark and stormy night. We were parked near a Pet Cemetery. I was waiting for my mom to show up. Suddenly, I heard a noise from behind me, which made me turn around. The hairs on the back of my neck stood straight up! Before I could blink, a small, black, tail creeped out from under the seat and tried to grab me! I saw two blazing yellow eyes, glowing in the dark and glaring at me!

"YYYEEEOOOWWW!" something screamed. It sounded like a kitty being murdered!

I looked back and saw something black, ooozzzzing out from a crate in the back. Was that Black Cat's Blood?

Uh, what was happening?....The crate started quivering, then rattling, and finally was SHAKING madly!!! Then more kitty screams. It sounded like there was a dozen of them being murdered, all at once!

I was getting frightened! What on earth was going on? Was there an earthquake??? Or was I just imagining it? It is not even Halloween yet!

Then there was two, black, furry things, sticking out from the crate. "What are those?" you may be asking. "Oh, those are cat paws...." With claws! EEccckkkk! Are they going to attack me? I feel like I am going to die!

Slowly, oh so slowly, the truck door creaked open....right then a voice spoke...out of the eerie pre-dawn darkness...

"Ok, Jedidiah. Are you ready to go?"

We did get all three kittens to the vet on time, and dropped them off to get spayed and neutered. We got Elijah to the Large Animal vet in Chilcoot, and he got 12 stitches in the side of his face. We got home at noon, just in time for Jedidiah to take a couple hour nap before heading back to pick up the fixed cats.

Jedidiah has been reading and remembering some more funny things....

The teacher said to the student, "Please give me a sentence with these four words; defeat, deduct, defense, detail."

Students answer: "Defeat of deduct went over defense before detail".

(Jedidiah really got a kick out of this one when he figured it out- you read it like this: The feet of the duck went over the fence before the tail.)

Joke of the Day: Q- What kind of pizza is Jedidiah's puppy's favorite flavor?

A- Pep-o-roni!

Thanks to the Williams Family in Idaho for that one!

"Oh come, let us sing to the Lord! Let us shout joyfully to the Rock of our salvation. Let us come before His presence with thanksgiving; let us shout joyfully to Him with psalm." Psalm 95:1-2

Oct 4, 2010

It's been a fun, busy weekend! I will write more tomorrow when I am not in a hurry to take Jedidiah to school. This morning we already made 10 bundles of cotton candy, and played with Pep.

Today Jedidiah wants to go to school, Cub Scouts afterward, then Justin has a soccer game against Squaw Valley at the Quincy High School.

Here is a short update: On Saturday we took Jedidiah to the Fall Fest at the Forest Service, Mt. Hough Ranger Station. He has been going every year and greatly enjoys ALL the activities.

Here is a photo of Jedidiah after a Secret Admirer at the Fall Fest left a lip stick kiss on Jedidiah's cheek!

On Sunday, Justin and Jedidiah got baptized at the First Baptist Church of Quincy. It is very exciting that both boys wanted to publicly show their commitment to follow Jesus Christ in their personal lives.

I will put more new photos on tomorrow!

"Whoever confesses that Jesus is the Son of God, God abides in him, and he in God. And we have known and believed the love that God has for us. God is love, and he who abides in love, abides in God, and God in him." 1 John 4: 15-16. NJKV

Oct 5, 2010

Photo of Jedidiah getting baptized on Sunday by Pastor George Tarleton at the First Baptist church of Quincy!

Today Jedidiah wrote a new chapter on his book about Pep:

CHAPTER 7- Training Pep- 10/5/10- By Jedidiah Lusk

Now I just have to train Pep! What should I train her to do? She already knows how to come to me when called. She even does backflips and front flips! You should have seen her- I was shaking her new soft rope toy above her head and she leaped up to get it and I moved it behind her. She did a backflip to grab it! She is very quick and agile.

She always gets SO excited in the mornings when I say, "Where's my Chihuahua?!" and Mom puts her on the bed. Then I say, "Who's a good girl? Who's a good girl?" This morning she got WAY TOO excited and was zipping around on my bed going faster and faster. Then she zipped off the edge of the bed and Mom tried to catch her, but she went flying thru the air like Underdog! Except she wopped her head on the dresser about 6 feet away. I got really scared and thought she died. She did not move for a minute, then she slowly stood up and shook her head and walked off. Mom scooped her up and put her in the crate so she could calm down and rest up.

My cousin Anna wrote me a letter and suggested that I "train Pep to: Sit, Stay, Roll Over, High Five, Potty Outside, Hula Hoop, Sing Karaoke, Push Wheelchair, Keep Kitties in Line, and Make Cotton Candy." Ha! Ha! I think Pep already likes to eat cotton candy. She was trying to clean up the floor with her little tongue after mom made cotton candy yesterday and it went flying all over the place.

Yesterday Pep got to go to town with us. She stayed in her crate in the car while I went in to my school classroom for a little bit. I had Cub Scouts after school. We went with the scouts on a walk to the Plumas County Museum. Afterwards we took Pep out to show her to the Cub Scouts. Then we drove to the feed store and Mom showed her to the ladies at Pet Country.

Justin had a soccer game at the High School yesterday afternoon, and it started to rain. I got sleepy and stayed in the car to take a nap. Maybe later I can train Pep how to walk on a leash.

"Therefore we were buried with Him through baptism into death, that just as Christ was raised from the dead by the glory of the Father, even so we also should walk in the newness of life." Romans 6:4, NKJV

Oct 6, 2010

Today, Scott, Jedidiah, Pep and I will be leaving to go camping at Lava Beds National Monument near Tulelake, CA. Scott will be attending the Regional Range Meeting for three days. So, I won't be updating this website for a little while. Don't worry, i will eventually catch you up again on the adventures of Jedidiah and Pep. Maybe by Sunday, I will get back to a computer and have time.

Jedidiah has been thinking a lot about Halloween. He is planning his costume. It gives him a huge event to look forward to. He really enjoys the Community Trick-Or-Treat that is held in Downtown Quincy. As Jedidiah proudly says, "I attend every year!" (He must have said that twenty times at the Forest Service Fall Fest.)

Another thing Jedidiah is planning and scheming, is he wants to host a Halloween Campfire Party at our house on Saturday night, October 30th. He plans to invite ALL his friends that want to come! We will be sitting around the campfire drinking hot apple cider, roasting marshmallows and telling scary Ghost Stories. So, get your stories together and write the date on your calendars! It will be a fun time.

"I love the Lord, because He has heard my voice and my supplications. Because He has inclined His ear to me, therefore I will call upon Him as long as I live." Psalm 116:1-2 NJKV

Oct 10, 2010

We have returned from our campout at the Lava Beds National Monument! Here is a photo of Pep on a lava rock. We had to keep her close at hand, with her tiny leash and collar. She is no bigger than the ground squirrels that ran around in the park! We did not want her to be mistaken as prey and dined upon by the red tail hawks or golden eagles who circled the sky looking for breakfast, lunch and dinner.

Jedidiah wasn't too excited about exploring Captain Jack's Stronghold, learning about the Modoc Indian Wars, or hearing about the Fire Ecology and range grass studies while we were at the Lava Beds. Those were programs that Scott enjoyed with the Society of Range Management, OR/WA, Cal/Pac Meeting.

What Jedidiah REALLY enjoyed was camping in his van, getting all warm and cozy under the sleeping bags while watching the cool fall wind blowing the stormy clouds outside, and being read to. We had the wonderful privilege of reading, "Hank the Cowdog". Volumes one, two and three appeared in the mail, just as we were departing to drive to Tulelake.

Perfect timing, THANKS so much to Nancy Quigley and family!! Jedidiah loved the stories. We whipped through those books in 2 and 1/2 days. In between reading, while Mom was resting her voice, Jedidiah got creative and dictated 3 stories of his own.

Don't ask me where these stories came from! Jedidiah is still preoccupied with thoughts of upcoming Halloween, so has been writing Ghost Stories. So, here is where Jedidiah starts off:

It was Thursday. We were camping out! Me and Mom were sitting in the van. We watched three deer sneak past our van. They did not even know we were in the van watching them. There was two does and one buck. He had the antlers! I counted them on the "Cow Counter Clicker" my Dad let me borrow. After deer passed, Mom turned on her cell phone to check for messages from home. The phone suddenly squawked in a funny voice, "Please say a command!" Mom yelled back at it, "Oh you be quiet!" and the phone obeyed Mom's command!

It was a cold, gray and kind of rainy day. We wrote stories and read books. Mom took Pep outside to go potty. When they came back, I asked Mom to write a story. But Pep grabbed Mom's writing pen in her mouth and carried it away. Mom had to get it back from her. It gave me the idea for my next story. I call it: "Chihuahuas of The Dead".

CHIHUAUAS OF THE DEAD
By Jedidiah Lusk

One gray day, me and Mom and Pep went camping. Pep got hungry. My Mom asked, "Do you want to eat, Pep?"

Jedidiah said, "Why should we eat Pep?"

Mom said, "Because she is from the 'Chihuahuas of the Dead'
That's why."

"No she is NOT!" Jedidiah yelled.

Mom asked, "Then why do you think she has those long fangs and great, long, sharp toenails? What are those for?"

Jedidiah finally agreed and said, "Mom, will you please put Pep in her kennel?" Which she did.

Then Pep went to the back of her kennel, turned around, and came launching straight at me! She busted thru the kennel door, missed me, slammed into the window, slid down, and stopped at the bottom of the door. Pep stood up, licked the window, and said, "Sorry about that window. I was trying to get Jedidiah. But, ooohhh...he is too hard a target. I'm not going to waste my energy on him. His mom looks a little easier."

On her way to attack Mom, Pep flew right under my chin, and whipped me with her wagging tail. I tried stopping it with my hand, but her powerful tail pushed my hand into my face. Ouch, that hurt! Then she ran over to Mom and grabbed the pen she was trying to write this story you are reading now.

Pep was trying to mess up the story! She took the pen and ran back to her secret lair. She ran back to Mom, without the pen, and tried to run up Mom's shirt. Mom screamed and pulled her shirt down. Pep ran back to the back of her kennel and pushed a red button. An elevator door opened and Pep ran in. Inside the elevator Pep licked a button and put her paw print on it. The elevator door closed and Pep went back to THE CHIHUAHUAS OF THE DEAD. The End!

"Finally brethren, whatever things are true, whatever things are noble, whatever things are just, whatever things are lovely, whatever things are of good report, if there is any virtue and if there is anything praiseworthy- meditate on these things." Philippians 4:8 NKJV

Oct 11, 2010

Today I would like to go back in time for a few minutes, to say a huge **THANK YOU** to Jedidiah's Uncle John and Aunt Stevie!

My one and only sibling, (He is the <u>older</u> one!), is my brother, John Nichols. He and his wonderful wife, Stevie Kobus, live in Sacramento.

Pictured in todays' photo is Jedidiah and his Auntie Stevie, on the very first day that Jedidiah was allowed to go outside of his hospital room- since being admitted to UC Davis Medical Center for his brain tumor, some 3 weeks earlier. It was so great to see the sunshine that day!

I used to jokingly call my brother, "The City Kid of the Family", since he departed Plumas County for the Sacramento Valley, living in Davis, then West Sacramento. But, boy oh boy, was I SO GLAD to have him down there- back in February and March of this year.

I called John from the Emergency Room at the Plumas District Hospital, as soon as we knew that Jedidiah was being flown to UC Davis Medical Center. I knew that my brother lived somewhere down near there. He answered my call and said he would be there, and do whatever needed to be done to help.

And true to his word, my brother was there! At Jedidiah's bedside, bearing gifts of food, bringing news from the outside world, and quietly lending support, love, help, companionship, and last but not least, joking with the nurses! (Oh! So that is where Jedidiah got his great love of joking!)

Stevie came to the hospital too, in the evenings after a long day at work, to lend a hand. She would sit with Jedidiah so Scott and I could grab a bite of dinner together.

I remember when John & Stevie took me to their home to get a break & even let me sleep in their bed! I had been sitting with Jedidiah at the hospital for two days and two nights, without much sleep. Wow, was i ever grateful for that soft bed!!

I really **don't** like to recall those memories of the early days of Jedidiah's brain tumor at UCDMC. It is all a foggy blur of shock, pain, grief, fear, anger, doctors, hospital, anxiety, surgery, emergency radiation, and finally, after 33 long days and nights, RELEASE!

Then another month spent at the Ronald McDonald House, just a few blocks from UCDMC, to finish up the next 4 weeks of Jedidiah's five day a week Radiation. My brother was there to help the whole time! He was either there in person, or just a phone call and a ten minute drive away. I am so very thankful for that! THANK YOU JOHN AND STEVIE!

Because, if you know me, you may know i don't function too well in the City. Too many cars, people, buildings, pavement and stoplights! I missed my mountains, trees, horses, and the lovely small rural town where I knew who the people were. I was very homesick, and longed for my immediate close-knit family, which I knew would never again be the same as I knew it in the past.

How would I have survived 2 months in Sacramento without my brother being a local guide to help me out? I am glad that I did not have to!

I did not forget about Jedidiah's Ghost Stories, but it was a good sidetrack. Will continue on with Halloween theme tomorrow....

"Blessed be the God and Father of our Lord Jesus Christ, who according to His abundant mercy has begotten us again to a living hope through the resurrection of Jesus Christ from the dead." 1 Peter 1:3 NKJV.

Oct 12, 2010

Jessica came over on Sunday and surprised Jedidiah with a large orange pumpkin to carve! Jedidiah was just wriggling with excitement! He really enjoys the festive atmosphere around Halloween and all the fun of preparing for it. He loved spending time with Jessica and carving out the pumpkin. He has talked more about his Halloween costume and he has decided he wants to be the "Headless Horseman". He said it was important to him that his wheelchair fits right in with his costume, and now his wheelchair can be the horse!

So, as promised, here is one more of Jedidiah's SCARY stories that he wanted me to write down... .... It's called: "GHOST"

GHOST
By Jedidiah Lusk

Once upon a time there was a family who adopted a little girl. She was their only child. She slept in their upstairs bedroom. The little girl was very lonely and wanted a friend. One day while she was playing by herself in the upstairs bedroom, she spotted a foggy white image floating in the air. The image took on the shape of a small girl. The white figure came closer to the little girl. She was afraid at first, but then made friends with the ghostly figurine. The adopted girl was happy because she now had a new best friend. The girl and the ghost became inseparable. They played games together like chess and tag.

One day, one of the family members heard the noise of kids playing upstairs. She creped quietly up the stairs to see where the noise was coming from. She cracked open the bedroom door and saw the little girl playing and having so much fun with a ghostly figure. That member told the rest of the family. They all told the little girl she would have to stop playing with the ghost. Her family did NOT like it one bit. But the little girl did not want to stop. So, she continued on, even though she was disobeying her adoptive parents.

Then one day while the little girl and the ghost were playing, the ghost came up to the girl, reached out and touched her on the shoulder. "Tag" it said. "It's your turn!"

The girl suddenly got cold. She slowly sat down on the floor and started shivering. She was very, very cold! Her family took her downstairs that night, because she did not come down for dinner. They placed her in front of the fireplace. But she did not warm up. They wrapped thick wool blankets around her, but she didn't warm up. They tried everything they could think of to get her warm, but with no success.

So, the parents took her to the doctor to try and find out what was wrong with the little girl. The doctors all said, "We've never seen anything like it! We don't know what to do to help her.

The very next day, the girl got the coldest she had ever been. She went upstairs. She laid down on the hard, cold floor. And she died. The End

Well, there you have it kids. Pay attention to your parents when they tell you not to play with ghosts!

Thanks to Adam Donald, from whom Jedidiah said he first heard of this wonderfully scary Halloween story.

"Because 'all flesh is as grass, and all the glory of man as the flower of the grass. The grass withers, and its flower falls away, but the word of the LORD endures forever!' Now this is the word which by the gospel was preached to you." 1 Peter 1: 24-25.

Oct 17, 2010

Ok, are you ready for an update? Sorry for the delay. I can blame it all on computer problems!

We have all been doing great! I really don't know where the time goes, and why it goes by so quickly.

Yesterday we spent a couple hours unloading the stock trailer, with supplies to build a small deck in the front of the house. Jedidiah supervised while sitting in his wheelchair nearby.

Justin had a soccer game Friday afternoon. QHS lost to Whitell, but Justin played a very good game and we are proud of him.

Pep the puppy remains as charming as ever. She is actually sitting on my lap right now! She thinks it's her duty to keep me company, when Jedidiah does not want to hold her. He is listening to his iPod this morning, so he does not want Pep to chew his iPod cord with her sharp little teeth.

Today's photo shows Jedidiah's Uncle Tim and Aunt Julie with Jedidiah near their home in Newport, Washington. I think the photo was taken in July or August. We spent a very special Christmas at Tim & Julie's last December. The whole family was there and we had a blast!!

Jedidiah has always been such a good little traveler. He loves going to see his relatives in ID, OR & WA. He also likes it when they come to see us! We have high hopes of seeing Julie, Bob & Betty the first week of November, if they make it down to see one of Jessica's FRC Women's soccer games.

"Confess your trespasses to one another and pray for one another, that you may be healed. The effective, feverent prayer of a righteous man avails much." James

Oct 18, 2010

Jedidiah has a new game. It's a Wii! (That's a word i had never even heard of until one week ago!)

Ok, so I admit that i am NOT up on all the electronic games that this younger generation plays with. But the youth of today, including my

3 children, think this is the GREATEST thing since sliced bread. (Even though they were not around when bread was made and sold unsliced.)

Many thanks to the contributions from the Snow Witch and the Redmond Smokejumpers that made the purchase of this item possible!!

We have several games for the Wii, including a Cabala's Big Game Hunt, a 4 Wheel Drive Truck Race, Winter Sports Game, and Summer Resort Games.

Well, Jedidiah is waiting for me at the door. He is saying, "Hurry Up Mom!!" We are heading to town as soon as i sign off this computer. We are going to 4th Grade to hand out cotton candy to his WHOLE class, and bringing Pep for Show and Tell. Then after school, is the Cub Scout Meeting.

Ok, got to go! More updates tomorrow....

"I will praise you, O Lord, with my whole heart; I will tell of all your marvelous works. I will be glad and rejoice in You; I will sing praise to Your name, O Most High." Psalm 9:1-2

Oct 19, 2010

Jedidiah had a great day yesterday! He took Pep to school and did 2 separate "Show & Tells" at Quincy Elementary School. One for Mrs. Hochrein's 4th grade (Jedidiah's class) and one for Mrs. Lemnah's class (whom Jedidiah had for a teacher last year in 3rd grade.)

Today's photo shows Jedidiah and Pep with Mrs. Lemnah!

After school Jedidiah went to the Cub Scout meeting and enjoyed that as well. After that he was tuckered out! But happily tired, and ready to go home. But first we had to pick up Justin after soccer practice.

This morning Jedidiah and I went with Justin to the DMV. It was time for Justin's Driver's License Test!! and... HE PASSED!! So, congratulations to Justin for being the newest licensed Lusk! Now he can drive himself to town. Wow, how did that happen? Best wishes to Justin and DRIVE SAFE!!

Here is Jedidiah's Question of the Day:

"How do you make a casserole?"

(Answer coming tomorrow)

"But God forbid that I should boast except in the cross of our Lord Jesus Christ, by whom the world has been crucified to me, and I to the world." Galatians 6:14

<u>Oct 21, 2010</u>

Yesterday was another busy day in town, so I did not even turn on the computer at home. Jedidiah had an appointment at the clinic in town in the morning, (great news- Jedidiah has lost 10 pounds within the past 6 weeks!) then I had a bunch of errands to accomplish. Jedidiah and I ate lunch at Express Café with the Plumas County SWAT Team. That really made Jedidiah happy!! In the afternoon, while we were waiting for Justin's soccer game to begin at QHS, I had to get my new cell phone working, which meant calling Verizon and pushing an endless cycle of buttons to try to get to a real person to talk to! It was frustrating- but the good news is, I eventually got the phone working correctly and Quincy won the soccer game against Squaw Valley! This means the boys go on to play the Championship game at Portola on Saturday at 2:00 PM! Go Quincy Trojans!!

So, did you figure out the answer from Jedidiah's Question on Tuesday, "How do you make a Casserole?"

His answer is: "You put it on a Skateboard!" Ha! Ha! …..and to think that I was actually trying to explain my famous recipe to him, the first time he asked me that question…!

Jedidiah has some pretty good jokes and he really enjoys his "Jokester" reputation. Pastor George at First Baptist Church is known for telling jokes, too. But last Sunday at church, George forgot to print off his joke of the day, so he turned to Jedidiah and said, "Folks, this morning I am going to ask Jedidiah to tell one of his jokes." Of course, Jedidiah's mom and dad were holding their breath, wondering just which joke Jedidiah would tell. But without hesitation, he took the microphone and confidently launched into one of his personal favorites, called: **"Meals on Wheels"**. Here is how it goes:

One day there was this cat, and he died of natural causes. He went to heaven. There he was met by St. Peter at the Pearly Gates. St. Peter greeted him with this offer, "Cat, you have lived a wonderful life. If there is ANYTHING we can do to make your stay in heaven more comfortable, just let me know."

The cat looked at St. Peter, thought a little bit, and then said, "Well, all my life I have had to sleep on a hard wooden floor with a poor family..."

"Say no more," said St. Peter.

And "POOF! Right then a nice, soft, fluffy pillow popped up in front of the cat.

A few days later, some mice were killed in a tragic farming accident. They went to heaven. They were met at the Pearly Gates by St. Peter, and greeted with the same offer, "If there is ANYTHING I can do to make your stay in heaven more comfortable, please let me know."

The mice looked at St. Peter and said, "Well, all our lives we have been chased by cats and dogs, and even women with brooms! Maybe could we have roller skates so we won't have to run anymore?"

And right then, each mouse was fitted with a PERFECT pair of red roller skates!

The next day, while St. Peter was checking on everybody, he saw the cat sleeping on his soft pillow. He gently shook the cat to wake him and asked, "How has your stay in heaven been going?"

The cat replied, "OH, even BETTER than I expected! Especially those MEALS ON WHEELS you have been sending by!! The End

"Being confident of this very thing, that He who has begun a good work in you will complete it until the day of Jesus Christ."
Philippians 1:6 NKJV

Oct 25, 2010

OK, ...for an update now... Jedidiah and family have been WAY TOO BUSY!! But Life continues to be GOOD, so what do i have to complain about? Absolutely nothing!

Getting ready to take Jedidiah to school now. Its Monday! Jedidiah is awake and ready to go. It's just his Mom that is so slow to get ready. And Jedidiah is W...A...I...T...I...N...G!! (Not very Patiently)

Jedidiah is sitting in the Brown Chair and sipping Egg Nog. It's his new favorite food! Now he has an "Egg Nog Song" he sings when he wants to have some.

So, here is what we have been doing: On Friday morning we drove to Sierra Valley to pick up some hay. The Roberti Ranch generously donated a stock trailer load of hay for Jedidiah's horses, Adam and Monique. THANK YOU very much!! So Jedidiah came with his Mom and Dad to supervise the loading and unloading of the hay. We got back home just in time to change our clothes, then rush off to FRC to catch Jessica's afternoon soccer game against College of the Redwoods. Which we lost, but it was sure fun to see Jessica play. Boy, she can run fast!

The highlight of Saturday was watching Justin play soccer in the Quincy Boys' Soccer Team, and they beat Portola, to WIN the League Championship!! Way to go QHS! Next game will be against Tulelake on Tuesday, for North Section Championship.

On Sunday, Jedidiah was invited to the St. John's Catholic Church, for the Breakfast Club, sponsored by the 3rd/4th grade Faith Formation Class. The children made and brought breakfast for our whole family! We had a great time!! Thank you very much Michele and class. We are grateful for your kindness.

"That the genuineness of your faith, being much more precious than gold that perishes, though it is tested by fire, may be found to praise, honor and glory at the revelation of Jesus Christ." 1 Peter 1:7

<u>Oct 27, 2010</u>

Jedidiah had a music lesson with Johny McDonald last night. Here is a photo of him playing his recorder with Johny. They worked on writing a song that Jedidiah had thought up yesterday. Jedidiah even had several of the notes figured out while he was composing his song. Thank you so much for working with him, Johny. Jedidiah really likes music, and i am so glad that he gets to continue with that.

This morning we made Jedidiah's Halloween costume of "The Headless Horseman". He will be ready to make his debut at the Community Trick or Treat in Quincy on Friday afternoon.

This afternoon we go to school for the cutting of the pumpkins in Mrs. Hochrein's classroom.

Jedidiah's puppy, Pep is doing well. The whole family enjoys holding, loving, and cuddling with her. Of course, she is spoiled! We even took her to get her photograph made, with Jedidiah and his fancy wheelchair. We also had photographs taken of Jedidiah with his brother and sister, Jedidiah with his whole family, and a boy's picture, of Jedidiah with his brother and his father.

Jedidiah has some jokes for you today: (But, he says, "Please DO NOT try this at home!")

Q. What do you have after you put your cat in the freezer?

A. The "Coolest Cat" in town!

Q. What do you call your cat after you put it in the dryer and it's never seen again?

A. "Socks"

"For I am convinced that neither death nor life, neither angels nor demons, neither the present nor the future, nor any other powers, neither height nor depth, nor anything else in all creation, will be able to separate us from the Love of God that is in Christ Jesus our Lord." Romans 8:38-39 NKJV

Oct 28, 2010

It's been another busy and fun couple of days for Jedidiah! Yesterday's pumpkin carving at Mrs. Hochrein's classroom was very educational. The students each got a worksheet and divided up into small groups. Each group with a large pumpkin and an adult. The students had to write down several estimates about the pumpkin; how much it weighed, how many lines it had, how thick was the rind, how many seeds it had inside, and if the pumpkin floats when placed in a tub water. Then we had to measure, count, and carry out various experiments with the pumpkin. And, oh, the pumpkins all had names, too! The pumpkin in our group was named, "Mr. Snicket".

And in case you have been wondering; Yes, pumpkins DO float!

Mr. Snicket had 261 seeds inside!

Today's photo is of Jessica, after her FRC Soccer game on Tuesday. They lost to Shasta College. She plays another home game next week. Better luck next game, Jessica!

Justin's team lost to Tulelake, 1 to 3. So the QHS boys are done playing soccer for the season.

Yes, Jedidiah is still planning on having his Halloween Party on Saturday night October 30th, from 5 to 7. Bring your ghost stories and come on out!! It will be an outdoor bonfire, so bring your coats! and No, we don't need any more goats. Bring your coats, but leave your goats (and dogs) at home. Thanks!

Here are a couple jokes from Jedidiah:

Knock, Knock.

Who's there?

Alaska

Alaska who?

I'll ask another person if you don't know!

"Since, then, you have been raised with Christ, set your hearts on things above, where Christ is seated at the right hand of God. Set your minds on things above, not on earthly things." Colossians 3:1

Jedidiah the Soccer Player, on a frosty, fall morning. Photo by Leslie Froggatt.

Oct 30, 2010

Jessica, Justin and "The Headless Horseman" at Quincy's Downtown Halloween Trick or Treat. Mama made the costume! We have enough candy till Christmas!

Written Oct 29, 2010 9:34am

Yesterday Jedidiah attended the Retirement Party for his grandma, "Nanny" at the Mt. Hough Ranger Station. We ate pizza and salad! It was a very nice event. Today is Nanny's very last day of working for the Forest Service! We wish her the very best, relaxing, happy, and enjoyable Retirement!!

Today's photo was taken a few weeks ago when our family went to dinner at William Jack's house in Meadow Valley. We had such a blast, and ended up laughing for most of the evening. We ate a really nice meal prepared by Jessica and William, then played a board game called, "Cranium". The "Girls' Team" including Cynthia, Jessica and Scott, beat the "Boys' Team" of Justin, Jedidiah and William.

Tonight is the Community Trick or Treat in downtown Quincy. Jedidiah is getting ready! This morning he said he wants to wear his SWAT jacket under his Headless Horseman costume. He is so excited to be able to be going out to town tonight.

And we are so very happy and GRATEFUL to be able to take him downtown. We are very fortunate and VERY BLESSED to still have him here with us. I know it is nothing less than a miracle that Jedidiah has done so well, for so long. He is doing GREAT! He feels good, looks good, and it's almost like we have our little Jedidiah back!

Jedidiah is happy, in excellent spirits, and displays incredible, positive attitude each and every day. When he awakes in the morning, he does his stretch, and a big, "Daddy Yawn". Then, just to remind us, he shouts out, "I'M STILL ALIVE!!"

Jedidiah's Jokes for the Day:

Q. What do you get when you cross a tornado and a mouth?
A. *A Tongue Twister!!*

Me: Just by looking, i can tell where you got your shoes.
You: ......where?
Me: On your feet!

"I eagerly expect and hope that I will in no way be ashamed, but will have sufficient courage so that now as always Christ will be exalted, whether by life or death. For me, to live is Christ and to die is gain." Philippians 1:20-21 NKJV

Oct 31, 2010

Jedidiah had a great time at his Halloween Party! Thank You to all his friends who made the trip out to Cromberg! Jedidiah got up at 0630 to start stuffing goody bags in anticipation of his friends coming over. The rain held off mostly and he had his Alaska Smokejumper parachute hootch set up just in case. After hotdogs when it got dark, it was time for S'mores around the campfire and Ghost Stories. Jedidiah led off with two scary ones to start the round robin off, followed by a true scary story from his brother! Caleb played the guitar for background music as the stories got scarier. Everybody had a turn who wanted to tell a story. Then Jedidiah handed out the goodie bags and said, 'Thanks for coming, and Good Night everybody!'

<u>Nov 5, 2010- AM</u>

Well, I wrote this update on Monday, then the computer stopped working before I could post it. But at least i had saved it on a word document. But now it's Friday, and the computer decided to start working again! Yippee!

It's been a busy week here with Jedidiah, but i don't remember where it all went to!

We have been doing a lot of reading lately. Jedidiah loved those first three "Hank the Cowdog" books so well, I went ahead and ordered the next 7 in the series. And we have already read 3 of those this week! They are LOTS of fun!!

Jedidiah's Lusk Grandparents are here now!! They flew down from Idaho to watch Jessica's last FRC home soccer game which was today. The women lost their game, darn. But it sure was fun watching Jessica play, and having her grandparents here, and Aunt Julie, made it EXTRA Special!!

Well, hope your calendars have been changed by now! It's almost time to change the clocks back too.

Here is what I wrote Monday:

Wow, it is November today! Don't forget to turn your calendars!

Jedidiah told me he had a "Terrifically FUN" weekend! Thanks to everyone who made the effort to come out to our place in Cromberg for Jedidiah's Bonfire Party!

Many Thanks to Jedidiah's Dad, who held the fort down this weekend so i could take my 6 year old mare, Rose, to the Patriot's Day at Lake Almanor Endurance Ride. She completed her first 25 Mile LD Ride!!

Scott also did a great job on updating Jed's Web Site, thanks!

Today Jedidiah wants to go to school, then to Cub Scouts. That's his usual Monday schedule. He also likes to transfer himself from his chair, to the wheelchair, to the car, ALL BY HIMSELF! He tells me to stand and watch. I usually try to jump in and help assist him. But he is so proud to accomplish this task alone.

Here is a Sponge Bob joke that Jed likes to tell:

Q. What is the difference between Sponge Bob and a gold chain?
A. One is yellow and neck-less, and the other is yellow and a neck-lace!

"For the grace of God that brings salvation has appeared to all men, teaching us that, denying ungodliness and worldly lusts, we should live soberly, righteously, and godly in the present age." Titus 2: 11-12, NKJV.

Nov 5, 2010 –PM, by Scott Lusk

The whole family got to watch Jessica play soccer today; Bobbie, Wawee, Aunt Julie, Blue Nanny, Mom, Dad, and Jedidiah! Justin was in school.

Jedidiah looks more like himself everyday as he continues to lose weight. He doesn't eat near as much as he used to. He's in good spirits, has his sense of humor, and still wants to do a lot of stuff.

Coach Richard Daun and his son, Robin, are building us a deck. It's looking great! We'll soon be having BBQs on it. Tonight Julie and I set up boards across the framing and sat in chairs to watch the stars. We'll have morning coffee on the deck with my mom, Wawee, as we do when we visit Camp Grandma in Coeur 'd Alene.

About two days ago Jedidiah got a headache. His left leg is unstable and shakes when he stands. So now we do, 'Flying Baby Cake Transfers' where we carry him from his chair to his van or bed. Yesterday he threw up 3 times. Today he only threw up once. Those were the symptoms he had back in February. Jedidiah says not to worry he's feeling good and he's not seeing double!

Keep him in your prayers!

Nov 7, 2010

Your prayers are working! Jedidiah woke up this morning with a big stretch and his 'Daddy Yawn' and said he feels "Great!" He's over his throwing up and did his own transfers today. Jedidiah said not to worry, he'll let us know when he feels bad and it's time to worry.

Jedidiah did all his own transfers today, except for the one in the parking lot at the Town Hall Movie Theater this evening before we watched 'Secretariat' when Justin picked him up and spun him around 9 times before he set him down in his wheelchair with Jedidiah squealing the whole time. Big Brothers!

Today's picture is 'Morning Coffee on the Deck' with Bobbie and Wawee, who flew down from Coeur 'D Alene with Aunt Julie to watch Jessica's FRC Soccer game on Friday, play Wii with Jedidiah Saturday morning then take Scott out for his Birthday supper Saturday evening. The whole family went! Jedidiah got to pick the restaurant and choose Mi Casita on top of the hill. It was great! B&B thought they were coming for a short vacation, but when there's work to do, they are right in the middle of it. They grabbed hammers and nails and put up all the blocks in the deck Coach Richard's building!

Because you have made the Lord, who is my refuge, even the Most High, your dwelling place. No evil shall befall you, nor shall any plague come near your dwelling; For He shall give His angels charge over you, to keep you in all your ways. Psalms 91.9-11.

Nov 8, 2010 by Scott Lusk

Our emotional roller coaster ride continues. Jedidiah woke up early and insisted he be the first one to put a footprint in the first snow of the year because he always does. He also made me put a handful of snow in the freezer from off his snowmobile in a zip lock bag because he always puts the first handful of snow from the first snow in the freezer then makes a snow cone with it in August during the fair. Then he sang and wiggled all morning about riding his snowmobile as soon as the snow gets deeper!

Then at about 1:00 he had a headache and threw up 4 times.

Then about 5:00, he said he feels Great and he's back to telling stories about when he was little, petting Pep and telling jokes!

Here's a picture of Jedidiah getting the 1st footprint in the 1st snow of the year.

"Yeah, though I walk through the valley of the shadow of death, I shall fear no evil; for You art with me; Your rod and Your staff they comfort me." Psalms 23:4 NJKV

Nov 9, 2010

Jedidiah is feeling pretty good again today! He has not thrown up, so i think he will go to his Recorder Lesson with Johny McDonald tonight. He did take an afternoon nap, and is all refreshed!

He did not go to school on Monday, because he got a headache, and then he slept most of the day. I think he wore himself out over the weekend, but he sure did enjoy having his Grandparents and Aunt Julie here!! Thanks so much for coming down all the way from Idaho.

I am re-using the photo of Justin carrying his brother, it was taken last Christmas vacation in December in Oregon, on our way up to Idaho. Justin takes such good care of his little brother. He is a GREAT big brother! Thanks, Justin!!

"Trust in the Lord with all your heart, and lean not on your own understanding; In all your ways acknowledge Him, and He will direct your paths." Proverbs 3:5-6, NJKV

Nov 11, 2010 by Scott Lusk

Jedidiah went to see Dr. Kepple for his three week checkup yesterday. He's lost 22 pounds and is almost down to his fighting weight. Jedidiah weighed 122 pounds yesterday! We're going to give him Zophran to keep him from throwing up and an arm patch for his headaches. Keeping fluids down will keep him from getting dehydrated and life will be a whole lot more fun without a headache. The flip side of the medicines are they will make him lethargic and he'll sleep even more.

Jedidiah likes to have visitors. Jedidiah asks Please make a point to stop by and visit with him.

When Jedidiah's awake he's still happy, bright, alert, telling stories and wanting to do stuff! He got a headache and threw up just as he was heading out the door Tuesday night to go play his recorder with Johny McDonald so he didn't go. His mama had the van pulled around and he was already to be loaded up. Johny had a surprise for Jedidiah, an instrument that he can play using just his right hand and that has more notes than his recorder, -a Harp! Johny let me bring it home for Jedidiah and I showed him how to play, 'Hot Cross Buns'. At first he was concerned because he thought he'd have to give up playing his recorder. I told him no, he just gets to add another instrument that he can play! Jedidiah smiled and beamed! Now we have the soothing angelic sounds of a harp being strummed. I sure hope Jedidiah feels good enough to go to his next lesson in two weeks to show off the songs he's learning to play!

Here's a picture of Jedidiah playing his new harp! Thanks Johny!

Nov 13, 2010 by Scott Lusk

Jessica is going to help her dad coach the Snow Leopards this year! Jessica raced on Johnsville Jr. Ski Team when she was little. It'll be great having Jessica help coach this year! She has an exceptional way of working with little people. Snow Leopards is the developmental team where the really young kids learn the basics of skiing. Johnsville Jr. Ski Team is a really fun group with excellent coaches, supportive parents, and winning racers. This is JJST's 25th season. Many Plumas Countians have either raced or coached on the team. Signups are occurring now so if your child hasn't signed up yet, do so on Monday at the Parks and Rec!

They went to Bobo's to get Jessica a ski coat and pants yesterday. Afterwards, Jessica thought she'd broaden her dad's horizons and took him to the Sushi place across the street.

They had the all you can eat lunch buffet. They ate everything that wiggled, including; octopus, salmon, salmon roe, tuna, crab, mussels, and flying fish eggs. They got full before they could try it all and will have to go back again. Coach Scott said Sushi was, really, good! Jessica looks great in her new snow gear! Yesterday was a fun day!

Jedidiah stayed home to rest and his mama read him the 8th 'Hank the Cowdog' book. Jedidiah plans to go to Noah's birthday party today!

Nov 14, 2010

Jedidiah's grandmother Donnal, the much loved, AKA: "Blue Nanny" watched Jedidiah on Saturday so Jedidiah's Mom & Dad could go riding horses together on a trail ride. It was good for Mom & Dad to do something fun together! Jedidiah had a good time, asking Nanny about the "Old Days" when she was younger. She enjoyed telling him story after story! We are so blessed to have her living with us, and giving us so much help. Thank you Nanny!! We appreciate you!

Jedidiah is getting more tired and needs to rest more, but he is still happy and loves to tell jokes still! He is taking Zophran medicine now, and has not thrown up or had a bad headache since starting to take that medicine Thursday. That makes us all happy! Jedidiah does not have much of an appetite anymore, and we have to continually remind him to sip his juice and have a bite of something to eat.

"But if we walk in the light as He is in the light, we will have fellowship with one another, and the blood of Jesus Christ His son cleanses us from all sin." 1 John 1:7 NKJV

Nov 15, 2010

Here's a picture of Jedidiah dressed up as a Mummy at Noah's Birthday Party on Saturday.

Jedidiah's newest joke: 'Dad, I didn't know you went to Egypt.'

'I didn't.'

'Then where'd you get my Mummy?'

Sunday Jedidiah rested and played Wii Bowling with his dad while his mama, Jessica and Blue Nanny went on a trail ride. Justin played soccer. Chloe and Mrs. Donald stopped by to visit with Jedidiah. Friends and Family!

Monday Jedidiah plans to go to school, then Cub Scouts!

Nov 16, 2010- AM

The McCall Smoke Jumpers sent Jedidiah a HUMONGUS check today! Thank You! In true Jedidiah spirit, Jedidiah said he wants to use the money to buy something for all his family for Christmas, -instead of thinking of himself!

Some more good news is the truck didn't need a new alternator; the battery cable was just loose. Thanks Quincy Tow!

Nov 16, 2010- PM

Yesterday turned out to be more of a rest day instead of going to school and Cub Scouts. Jedidiah did not want to take Zophran and did not have a headache or through up at all yesterday!

Jedidiah did make it into town and had a late lunch with his friend Mikey at the Taco Bell yesterday as planned.

Last night, for family's entertainment, Blue Nanny and Mama each tried, and took right to, playing Jingle Bells on the Harp from Johny's computer harp lesson. They are ready for more songs! Jedidiah was happy just to sing along then strum it to feel the vibrations, when it was, finally, his turn to play!

"Praise the Lord with the harp; Sing to Him a new song; play skillfully with a shout of joy". Psalms 33:2-3.

Nov 17, 2010

Jedidiah wanted to tell his cousins in Idaho that Pep enjoyed one of her "Pep-O-Roni" dog snacks this morning, (the ones they sent down to Pep with Bobby and Wawee). Jedidiah says, "Thanks!" and "Pep says Thank You, Too!" She also likes the cute dog sweaters they sent. I will have to get a photo of her wearing one. It's really hard to get her to hold still to pose for a photo. Just ask Aunt Julie! Maybe she got some good pictures of Pep when she was here?

I asked Jedidiah if he had any turkey or Thanksgiving jokes, and he already came up with this one, just off the top of his head.

Q. Why did the turkey cross the road?
A. To scare the kid!

Q. Why was the little boy afraid of the turkey?
A. He heard it was a Goblin!

Jedidiah continues to enjoy his pets. He just loves his Chihuahua puppy and the kittens, (now cats, I believe!) still curl up in his lap and make him smile! Even though Jedidiah's body is beginning to tire easily, he remains in great spirit. Right now he is watching, "Beverly Hills Chihuahua" and laughing at the humorous scenes. We are still reading, "Hank the Cowdog" and are on volume 10. I also checked out, "Smokey the Cowhorse" by Will James, but have not started reading it to Jedidiah yet.

Tonight is Justin's "Soccer Awards" ceremony at the Quincy High School cafeteria. We hope Jedidiah feels good enough to attend with us.

"They that wait upon the Lord shall renew their strength; they shall mount up with wings as eagles; they shall run, and not be weary; and they shall walk, and not faint." Isiah 40:31 KJV

Nov 18, 2010

Jedidiah decided to stay home last night with his grandma "Nanny" instead of going to the Soccer Awards at Quincy High School. Justin was voted the "Best Defensive Player" by his team, and earned the "Scholar Athlete Award".

Today Jedidiah rested up on his bed, with Pep keeping him company. See the new photo! Jedidiah took a good nap for a couple hours.

When Justin gets home from school, we are going to take his Subaru and our pickup truck down to Les Schwab to get the studded snow tires put on. Getting ready for the expected, predicted: "First Big Snowstorm of the Season!" that is supposed to arrive this weekend. When Jedidiah heard that on the news this morning, he got all excited. He really wants to ride his snowmobile by Sunday! We shall see if we get the foot of white stuff!

Here are some "musical jokes" that Jedidiah told today:

Q. What do you get when you drop a piano on an army base?
A. A Major B-flat.

Q. What happens when you drop a piano down a mine shaft?
A. A Minor B-flat.

Q. Why was the opera singer afraid to get a job on the cruise ship?
A. She didn't like the High C's

Q. When is a tire a bad singer?
A. When its flat!!

"Oh magnify the Lord with me, and let us exalt His name together." Psalms 34:3

Nov 20, 2010

Jedidiah went to school yesterday to see his friends and for the "Hawaii Lula Party" Mrs. Hochrein put on just before the big snow storm! It was fun! Jedidiah had a great time. He made pineapple, marshmallow, banana shiskabobs! His classmates wrote Haiku poems for Jedidiah about the 1,000 Origami cranes they have been making for him and complied all the poems into a book of poems they gave Jedidiah.

It snowed 8" last night at our house, just barely enough, so after breakfast Jedidiah is going to take his snowmobile for a ride! Jedidiah has a poster on his door of a guy in an Arctic Cat snowmobile suit in the summer stomping on a sand castle that says, 'Stomp Out Summer!'

Jedidiah didn't get to ride his snowmobile much last winter. He's been looking forward to riding all year -and he has made it here!

Here is a picture of Jedidiah at the Hawaii Lula Party.

Q. Why did the Thanksgiving Turkey cross the road?
A. To prove he was not a Chicken!

"The heavens declare the glory of God; and the firmament shows His handiwork." Psalms 19.1

Nov 23, 2010

Here is a photo of Jedidiah making a snow angel!

Jedidiah enjoyed having 4 visitors who stopped by to see him today!

Chloe with her father, Ron and Deputy Shawn Webb and Sargent Johns. Thanks for stopping by!! Jedidiah says he looks forward to seeing more friends.

We are all still enjoying the snow out here in Cromberg. Today was the last day of school for Jessica and Justin. Now they have 5 days of Vacation, including Thanksgiving Day. We are looking forward to Jedidiah's Uncle John and Aunt Stevie joining us for Thanksgiving and Jedidiah's cousin Christy Chavis visiting us too!

Some more Thanksgiving jokes:

Q. Why was the turkey wearing pink sneakers?
A. Because his boots were being repaired!

Q. Why is a couch like a turkey?
A. They are both full of stuffing!

More jokes tomorrow! Jedidiah is feeling pretty good. He had a nice long nap yesterday (Monday) and got all rested up, after riding snowmobiles the day before (Sunday). He is looking forward to lots of family togetherness this week!

"Looking unto Jesus, the author and finisher of our faith, who for the joy that was set before Him endured the cross, despising the shame, and has sat down at the right hand of the throne of God." Hebrews 12:2, NJKV

Nov 22, 2010

Jedidiah took a couple laps around the house on his snowmobile yesterday! He was excited. There's two feet of snow on the ground and 8 inches to a foot more expected tonight! All before Thanksgiving!

After snowmobile riding, Jedidiah made a "Snow Chair" and sat comfortably in the deep snow in the yard, watching his brother and Dad zip around on the snowmobiles. his sister laid down beside Jedidiah and they both made "snow angels"!

Jedidiah's friend, Mrs. Donald, let Jedidiah borrow a book called, "101 Thanksgiving Jokes". He was thrilled with that! Here are two of his favorites so far:

Q. If April showers bring May flowers, what do May Flowers bring?
A. Pilgrims!

Grandma: What would you like for dessert, Joey?

Joey: Pumpkin Pie!

Grandma: Pumpkin pie, what, dear? Say the magic word....

Joey: I'm sorry, Grandma- Pumpkin Pie, Abracadabra!

"But seek first the kingdom of God and His righteousness, and all these things shall be added to you." Matthew 6:33

Nov 27, 2010

Jedidiah is enjoying the winter! Yesterday he asked his brother to go outside and bring him back an icicle. He loves to lick them! It's been a tradition that both the brothers have shared for years.

This morning Jedidiah awoke at 0430. He asked us to move him to his brown chair. He threw up a couple times, then we gave him some medicine. He stayed awake, and was able to drink and keep down a glass of milk and a glass of water. When he was feeling better he preceded to sing us several songs! These are very special songs he wrote and composed all by himself. Jedidiah's singing voice is so very sweet! Even at 0600 AM in the morning. His song goes, "I love you Mom, I love you Dad, no matter what happens, no matter what happens."

He has several verses and variations, all so very special to us!

We plan on staying home to enjoy the family togetherness for the weekend. We had a wonderful Thanksgiving. Thank you for all the thoughtful prayers and good wishes you all have sent our way. We really appreciate them!!

"That at the name of Jesus every knee should bow, of those in heaven, and of those on earth, and of those under the earth. And that every tongue should confess that Jesus Christ in Lord, to the glory of God the Father." Philippians 2:10-11 NKJV

Written Nov 27, 2010 by Scott Lusk

Cousin Christy and her friend Steve drove up from Santa Barbara to spend Thanksgiving with Jedidiah. Uncle John and Aunt Stevie drove up from Sacramento for smoked turkey. It was fun to see you guys. Cynthia's endurance rider friend Tara, and her two boys, are driving over tomorrow on their way back to Boise!

Jedidiah's had a rough couple days. For Thanksgiving all he ate was two spoonfuls of dry Top-a-Roma and he's thrown up most of the past two days. Even with all that, Jedidiah woke up this morning and the first thing he asked was, -Why is there no expiration date on sour cream? And then he went with Cousin Christy, and family, to watch Mega Mind tonight at the Town Hall Theater! Jedidiah's hanging tuff and keeping his unbelievable happy positive attitude! He says he's in no pain, just doesn't like to throw up.

Our computer's been down, off and on, the past two weeks. We called Dr. Mac today to see if he can fix our Apple so we can keep the updates timely.

Here's a picture of Cousin Christy, Jessica, and Justin at the Chicken Tree, from our afternoon hike today. The Chicken Tree is kind of special to us!

Cynthia Lusk

Nov 28, 2010

We had such a wonderful Thanksgiving weekend! Jedidiah was here with us! He rode his snowmobile, made Snow Angels in the snow and smiled! Uncle John and Aunt Stevie came. Cousin Christy and her friend Steve came. We ate Hickory smoked turkey, ginger cheese cake, pumpkin pie and pecan pie! Blue Nanny played the harp and dad played his fiddle while Mama broke ice, fed the horses, and chopped wood! Tara and her two sons stopped by Saturday!

Jedidiah spent a sleepless night Saturday night with a steady stream monolog of rambling thoughts and dreams. This was his first restless night since leaving the Ronald McDonald house back on April 19th. Jedidiah has such a sweet voice, even late at night while he's rambling. Then around 0630 Sunday morning he finally fell asleep.

Jessica took Justin Christmas shopping in Chico on Sunday and got Justin all decked out for his basketball tournaments, which start this weekend with the Quincy Classic Tip Off. Justin's looking sharp in his new pre-game shirts, ties, and pants!!

Blue Nanny watched Jedidiah after church while he slept, so Mama and Dad could take a quick ride on Jedidiah's and Justin's snowmobiles up past 'the Elbow'. It was fun breaking trail! Thanks Blue Nanny!

Jedidiah did wake up at noon Sunday, said, "Good Morning!", then went back to sleep.

On July 13th, after his last MRI, Dr. Z said as his tumor re-grows larger, Jedidiah would sleep more and more until one time, he just won't wake up.

At midnight, Jedidiah did his, 'Big Daddy Man Yawn', winked at Dad and said, 'I'm Still Here', then went back to sleep.

Dr. Mac is going to work on our computer tomorrow, so it may be a couple days before our computer's back up and running and we can update Jedidiah's web page again.

Here's a photo of 'Jedidiah Flying' back last year when he felt better!

'And he took a child, and set him in the midst of them: and when he had taken him in his arms, he said unto them, Whosoever shall receive one of such children in my name, receiveth me:

Always Remember Me

and whosoever shall receive me, receiveth not me, but him that sent me. 'Mark 9:36-37

Dec 1, 2010

Jedidiah's feeling much better today! He sat in his brown chair, had a few bites and drank some juice. When the kids got home from school, Jedidiah danced and wiggled to his new favorite Christmas song, 'The Hat I Got for Christmas is too Beeg!'.

Jedidiah scared his brother with a huge remote controlled Tarantula that his Grandpa sent. Justin doesn't like spiders. This one is huge! It's about 8" with 8" legs. He hid it under Justin's chair and when Justin sat down to eat, Jedidiah made it start walking towards him. Justin jumped 3' straight up and screeched like a girl! Jedidiah laughed at his big brave brother. He got him good!

Mrs. Barker sent a funny 'Are you thinking of me' card that had Jedidiah played and laughed at all afternoon. Thank you!

Jedidiah's going to rest up tomorrow and try to go to Quincy Main Street Sparkle Friday night to watch the lighting of the Christmas tree, see his friends sing and dance, watch the Lighted Lights Parade, and sit on Santa's lap to ask him to bring his Cousins and friends some very special Christmas presents!

We hope to see you there!

Dec 5, 2010 by Scott Lusk

Jedidiah enjoyed the Quincy Sparkle Lights Parade! He sat in the front seat of his mini-van that Quincy Auto and QHS "S" Club got for him. We had front row seats in front of Plumas Bank. Jedidiah's eyelids were too heavy to open so his dad described each entry for him as they drove past. Dad has been spending a lot of time at work lately so it was fun just to sit and talk with Jedidiah. They talked and talked! Jedidiah tricked his dad into telling him what he got him for Christmas, just in case he's not here for Christmas.

Dr. Mac called and said our motherboard was fried, a problem with that year's make and model and our 3 year warranty expired last year so we'll have to get a new computer. William, Jessica's friend, volunteered to go with Dad to Chico to explain how to select and use a lap top. In the meantime we'll borrow Jessica's lap top and update the web page off and on.

Give Hope Foundation is funding a portion of the labor costs to build Jedidiah a permanent ramp/deck for his wheelchair access to our home. QHS Ski Coach, Coach Justin Barker, built Jedidiah a temporary ramp in April. Coach Richard Daun, Jedidiah's Ski Team Coach, is donating half of his design and labor costs to Jedidiah. Thank You!

The Boise Smokejumpers just sent Jedidiah a huge Christmas check from their '2010 Jumping for Jedidiah' campaign. It was fun to have been a part of that outfit when we waved the Jolly Rodger on the ramp!

Jedidiah spends most of his day sleeping. But when he is awake he still has his sense of humor and loves to hear and tell stories with his friends and family. Chloe has been spending lots of time visiting Jedidiah. Mrs. Lemnah stopped by today to play the recorder with Jedidiah. Jedidiah sips juice and milk occasionally. He hasn't had a headache or thrown up in over two weeks! Without eating too much Jedidiah continues to lose the weight he put on with the Decadron. Jedidiah says he's in no pain!

Our plans for Christmas include seeing what Santa brings us here at home then visiting all the Cousins in CDA and having a huge bon fire at Aunt Julies New Year's Eve!

"Lord, You have been our dwelling place in all generations. Before the mountains were brought forth, or ever You have formed the earth and the world, even from everlasting to everlasting, You are God". Psalm 90:1-2

Dec 7, 2010

We had a busy weekend with Justin's Basketball Tournament, The "Quincy Tip-Off Classic". Next weekend we have another tourney in Portola, and the weekend after we travel to Hamilton City in the valley, for another three day Basketball tournament. On Game Days, Justin is required to dress-up in button-down shirts and a TIE! We think he looks handsome, don't you?

Jedidiah has had a busy few days with lots of visitors stopping by:

Pastor George spent some time telling Jedidiah stories of his colorful past.

Mrs. Lemnah stopped by on her way to Reno to play her recorder and sing Christmas songs to Jedidiah.

Coach Hannah and his family stopped by on their way back from a basketball game in Reno to say hi to Jedidiah.

Mrs. Hochrein and her husband brought out a whole box of wonderful cards for Jedidiah, handmade by his classmates. Thank you! She also has some great news:

Jedidiah's friends have worked very hard and accomplished their goal of completing 1,000 paper origami cranes! WOW!

Thank You Quincy Elementary School!!

Mrs. Hochrein delivered some very tasty cookies also. THANKS they were yummy and have all been gobbled up and appreciated!

Jedidiah spends most of his time sleeping during the day and night, but wakes up for a couple hours and displays his unfailing sense of humor! Will have to tell some of his funny stories that continue to crack us up:

Last month, after the big snowstorm, Jedidiah woke up, looked out the window and asked, "Mom, what month is it?" I answered, "Jedidiah, its November! Remember, we are having Thanksgiving in a couple days?" Jedidiah said, "No, it is NOT November, Mom, it is SNO-Vember!"

Jedidiah watched closely as his father was preparing the Thanksgiving Turkey, and as he opened the door to take it outside to the smoker, Jedidiah quips, "Dad, YOU are cooking the turkey? Better check and see if it's a Burn Day first!"

Then yesterday as Jedidiah was waking up, he asked his father, "Dad-what kind of cheese can't you eat?" His Dad thought a moment, and said, "I don't know Jedidiah, what kind of cheese can't I eat?" Jedidiah yelled, "Nacho Cheese! It's Not Yo Cheese, get it?"

Jedidiah also has received some nice mail. Thanks to Dennis and Karen Barker for sending Jedidiah a "talking card"! He continues to open and listen to that talking card every day. Each time it makes us laugh!!

Jedidiah can't see very well, due to the tumor putting so much pressure on his optic nerve. He describes it as, "My eyelids are SO heavy, i can't open them". But he relies on his sense of hearing and touch to discern his surroundings. He can even tell each family member by the feel of their hands. Justin is continually trying to fool him by hugging Jedidiah and telling him its Mom. Jedidiah grabs his hand, and yells, JUSTIN! I know it's YOU. Get off!"

"Blessed is the man who endures temptation; for when he has been approved, he will receive the crown of life which the Lord has promised to those who love Him." James 1:12

Dec 9, 2010

Hope you don't mind a few "re-run" photos of Jedidiah. Here he is at the "Dirt Bike Birthday Party" with his friends, JD and Nano.

Seems like it was just the other day that Jedidiah was zipping around the house on his dirt bike. He would GO & GO, until we physically went outside to STOP the bike and pull him off, or his bike's gas tank ran out of gas, whichever came first. It seemed like Jedidiah's tank of enthusiasm for speed & movement and humor & life would never run low.

Well, the days continue to fly by. The snow has relented and changed to rain, which is helping to erase the existing snowpack we had. Looks like we won't be able to ride snowmobiles from the house until the next snowstorm.

We are updating Jed's website with Jessica's laptop. Looks like we will have to get a new computer since our 4 year old Apple Mac has become "Non-Operational!

Jed is sleeping comfortably in the couch-turned-bed in the middle of the living room, with all of Life's activities & family business constantly going on around him. During the day we have been playing audio tapes of "Hank The Cowdog, and lots of CD's of Christmas Songs! I've been getting Christmas cards addressed, Jedidiah's Dad has been wrapping Christmas presents, and plenty of visitors have been stopping by, which we have enjoyed. Of course, from both friends and family, Jedidiah receives lots of LOVE in the form of HUGS & KISSES from everybody!! He gets lots of hands-on comfort and cheer.

Jedidiah's cats still want to snuggle with him too. But the two snuggly, fluffy males have grown so large, that they almost squish Jedidiah's chest when they lay on top of him. But Jedidiah's pup, Pep is just the right size to cuddle with him. She likes to give him kisses, then builds a nest under his blankets.

Hans Holtz stopped by yesterday, bringing a big bag of goodies for Jedidiah. Thank you Hans and Michele! Your fresh avocados are a delicious Treat!

Tuesday afternoon, Mrs. Beer-Secretary Extraordinaire- from QES, stopped by to see Jedidiah, and brought another box of cards and gifts from his classmates. Also, a special gift from Mr. Beer- A fellow Smokejumper ! Mr. Beer gave Jedidiah a hand carved Loon, signed on the bottom- "Jedidiah Lusk- FBX '10, from Milt Beer- RDD '65". Wow, Thanks!

On Tuesday night, Mrs. Donald and Mrs. Rahmeyer stopped by. Susan provided the Hank The Cowdog tapes, and Cathy brought another soft, stuffed critter to snuggle with Jedidiah. Thanks to both of you!

Wednesday is "Paper Day". Quincy's weekly newspaper, the "Feather River Bulletin" came out yesterday. There is a very special message on the front page of the latest issue.:

WE LOVE YOU JEDIDIAH

It is spelled out in large letters being held by students in Quincy Elementary School, along with four large red hearts between the words. The photo includes a large gathering of people- The ENTIRE student body- everybody in the school, teachers, kids, and staff! Next to the people is a tall Christmas Tree, decorated with 200 of the 1,000 folded paper origami cranes. WOW! What support for Jedidiah. It made us all cry with overwhelming gratitude to know Jedidiah is SO LOVED. Thank you very much!

A big Thanks goes out to Delaine Fragnoli for giving Jedidiah the first newspaper copy- Hot Off The Press!! We appreciate that, Delaine.

"Be anxious for nothing, but in everything by prayer and supplication, with thanksgiving, let your requests be made known to God: And the peace of God, which surpasses all understanding, will guard your hearts and minds through Christ Jesus." Philippians 4:6-7 NKJV

Dec 10, 2010

Here is a photo of Jedidiah and I from a sunny, summer day in July at Antelope Lake. Myself and the three kids all took a trip together up to Antelope to play and explore. It was a fun day! I remember letting Justin drive up the winding road past Genesse Valley, with Jedidiah hollering corrections from the back seat, "Justin, don't drive so fast! Justin, watch out for that corner, ok, speed up now!"

Jessica was trying to sleep in the back seat next to Jedidiah,(She is definitely NOT a morning person, and we woke her up WAY TOO early that morning!) and every time we'd turn a corner, she would bang her head on the window, and mumble something about Justin's driving. He just had his Learner's Permit, and we were trying to get him some miles. I had always wanted to take the kids up to see the places I had worked in the Forest Service, to share some of my adventures with them. So, I remember it being one of those wonderful, perfect days, when every moment was cherished and enjoyed.

Today Jedidiah is again sleeping peacefully on his bed in the living room. And, like yesterday we are listening to Christmas Songs on a CD. I think Christmas music HAS GOT to be my most favorite kind of music. i never get tired of listening to them. Especially the old classics: Away in a Manger, What Child Is This, Angels we have Heard On High, and Silent Night. Those are my most favorite. I hope they are Jedidiah's, too, because I keep playing them over and over for him!

Last night was Justin's first game in a series of three at the Portola Basketball Tournament. Quincy won against Loyalton. Tonight QHS plays Portola. Should be a challenging, exciting game. Jedidiah stayed home with Nanny last night. He got to listen to the re-play of the game when we put the video tape on TV (that I recorded at the game.) He drifted off to sleep about halfway thru. Then Jedidiah woke me up at 11:00 PM, saying that he wanted me to "Fly him to his Brown Chair" to drink some water.

That is Jedidiah code for: Pick me up and carry me to my favorite sitting spot on the leather recliner. So I did! He drank almost a full glass of water, sat up in the brown chair, and spoke with me. But around midnight, he threw up all the water he drank. He did not want any of the Zophran anti-nauseas medicine, explaining, "I don't feel bad, I just throw up. Now, can i go back and lay down on the bed?"

I carried him back to bed, and we cuddled and talked about the day's activities until around 1:30 AM. Then we both went to sleep!

"For unto us a child is born, unto us a son is given: and the government shall be upon his shoulder: and his name shall be called Wonderful, Counselor, The Mighty God, The everlasting Father, the Prince of Peace." Isaiah 9:6 KJV

Dec 11, 2010

Jedidiah always wanted to have a trailer to help move hay for the horses and to do chores.

Dad got him one for Christmas.

Jedidiah said he'd rather use it now then to wait until Christmas.

Here is a picture of Jedidiah and his brand new trailer.

The snow is all melted so we can do chores with the four wheeler. Today mom and Dad rode horses up Oxygen hill and up Oak Trail.

Dec 14, 2010 by Scott Lusk

When I was a little boy growing up, my Dad used to say he didn't want anything for his Birthday, just having the family together is all he needs. -Now I know what he means!

Jedidiah slept through 3 visitors on Monday. Chloe stopped by. William Ross, with his little brother and their dad, Steve, stopped by. They brought Jedidiah an electronic bed bug, that vibrates and crawls all over the bed when you turn it on. (Jedidiah loved to turn it off and on when he finally woke up.) Sarah, Jedidiah's friend who plays in the Orchestra, stopped by also. Jedidiah slept through it all.

Then at 0022 he woke up, stretched, did his 'Big Daddy Man Yawn, and sang 'Happy Birthday' to his mama, whose birthday is today, December 14th! Cynthia said Jedidiah singing was her best Birthday present ever!

Today is the Community Orchestra's Christmas performance at noon at the Quincy Courthouse, conducted by Johny McDonald. It's free! The Orchestra always sounds so good in the Courthouse as the music reverberates off the 4 stories of marble. The acoustics is great! Cynthia plans to bring Jedidiah in to listen if he's not too tired from playing with his bed bug!

Then at 6:30, QHS basketball plays their first home game! That'll be fun to watch. Cynthia is a big fan of basketball having played at QHS herself, ...some ought years ago!

Yesterday Blue Nanny watched Jedidiah so Cynthia could take her horses on an early Birthday trail ride. She rode Rose and led a colt up the steep canyon trail. There were a lot of trees down across the trail. PNF needs a trail crew just to keep the downfall bucked out! A stealth fighter made its way up the canyon over the trail while Cynthia was riding. It was a great learning experience for her young colt!

Jessica has a FRC final late tonight so at about 11:00 Cynthia will eat crab, open presents, blow out candles on her lemon cake, that Jessica made, with lemon ice cream!

Birthdays are Celebration Days and Cynthia has certainly worked unselfishly the past 10 months to celebrate a day of family fun!

Happy Birthday Cynthia!

Dec 15, 2010

Jedidiah is sitting up in his Brown Chair today! Yay!!
(This is something he has not asked to do for 3 or 4 days.)

Jedidiah decided he did not want to go all the way to town yesterday to hear the Community Orchestra play at the Courthouse at noon. He was too tired and just wanted to stay home with his Grandma Nanny. So i went and recorded his Dad playing his fiddle, so Jedidiah could hear all the wonderful songs, conducted by Johny McDonald. It did sound very beautiful!! Great job to all you musicians who played yesterday!

Right now Jedidiah and I are listening to the Christmas CD which Hans and Michele sent. It is a really good one, thank you so much!

Jedidiah's eyes remain closed, even when he is awake, and he does not speak out loud very much. But he does maintain communication with us, and lets us know he is still here. Like just a few minutes ago, when a song with pretty Harp music came on. I looked over at Jedidiah in his brown chair, and he was making the movements of plucking on the harp strings in time to the music on the Christmas CD!

He also enjoys holding things in his hand and feeling them. A favorite toy of his these last few days has been his new "Buggy Wuggy" as he calls it. It's a small little creature that fits in the palm of his hand and buzzes when he turns it on with a switch. It was a gift from Steve and Leslie's sons. THANK YOU! Jedidiah won't let go of it!

Jedidiah's body is getting weaker and it is hard for him to sit up by himself. We support him when he sits up to drink water, then he asks to lay back down. He also communicates by wiggling his eyebrows, which is a sign that he means, "Yes" to the questions we ask. For "No" he shakes his head.

Jedidiah does speak when he has something to say. Sometimes it comes out in a mumble. This morning he was trying to tell me something. I leaned closer and listened carefully. He had this annoyed look on his face. I knew he wanted to tell me something. I moved in closer still and waited patiently for him to form the words. My ear was inches from his lips. Still i listened.

Finally, Jedidiah said very distinctly, "I said...Get....Your head...... OUT ....of my.... FACE! I need room to breathe!"

Jedidiah told a joke last week, that I forgot to put on the website. So, here goes:

"A young man was on one of those game shows, where you earn a lot of money for answering questions. He had done well and had the potential to double his money and WIN, if he could answer ONE remaining Question. The very last question was: 'Name three of Santa's Reindeer.' The man said, "Oh, this is too easy! Three reindeer's names are: Prancer, Dancer and Olive!"

The Host said, "Whoa, wait a minute! I know Prancer and Dancer, but who is this Olive?' The man turned red and looked embarrassed. "You know, in the song about Rudolf. It goes, "Olive the other reindeer....."

"Therefore the Lord himself shall give you a sign; Behold, a virgin shall conceive, and bear a son, and shall call his name Immanuel." Isaiah 7:14 KJV

Dec 16, 2010

We have decided that Jedidiah must be a nocturnal creature. Like his sister, Jessica, Jedidiah seems to like being awake best at night. Even during this sleepy period the past 5 or 6 days, he still wakes up at night, and stays awake 2 to 3 hours. His Dad and I have started taking turns sleeping with him, so one parent can enjoy talking with Jedidiah when he is most awake, and the other parent can sleep, to be prepared for watching Jed the next day, or being awake at work.

Sometimes on weekends, we all sleep with Jedidiah, and he lays in the middle of us and we call that a, "Jedidiah Sandwich!"

Last night was my night to sleep with Jedidiah. Around 2 AM, I awoke and thought i heard a Yodel. Hmmmm...? I turned over to Jedidiah and asked sleepily, "Hey, were you yodeling?"

"YO-D-Lay-D-O!" Came the answer. I awoke up just a little bit more. "Jedidiah, what are you saying?" I got curious.

"Just answer the question, Mom!"

"What, Jedidiah?'

"Knock, Knock"

"Who's There?"

"Yodel"

"Yodel who?"

"You Old Lady U!"

"Hey, Jed, No Remarks about my birthday, ok? That was so two days ago!"

"But Mom, It's NOT about your birthday, I am Yodeling~! Now, can you carry me to the Brown Chair?

And so began a couple hours of spending wonderful time with my son!

"Brethren, I do not count myself to have apprehended; but one thing I do, forgetting those things which are behind and reaching forward to those things are ahead. I press toward the goal for the upward call of God in Christ Jesus." Philippians 4:13-14 NKJV

Dec 19, 2010 by Scott Lusk

I got to watch Jedidiah this weekend with Jessica and Blue Nanny while Cynthia went to Hamilton City to watch Justin play basketball!

Our Ski Team Coaches Clinic on Saturday was postponed -due to too much snow!

Friday night I slept with Jedidiah. I was rubbing his hand when he squeezed my hand back, then started pulling my hand to his chest. Jedidiah wanted to arm wrestle me! We used to arm wrestle all the time. Jedidiah beat me 4 out of 5 times! He stayed awake from 0100 to 0400! While he was awake we talked about fears: Justin's fear of Spiders, my fear of Heights, and Jedidiah's fear of going slow! We also talked about name person present's, but I can't tell whose names until after Christmas! Our family is so big we draw names out of a hat each year so we only get our 'Name Person' a really big present.

Last night Jedidiah was awake for a only a short a time. I was listening to Cowboy Christmas. on the radio. Jedidiah woke up and we sang, 'Silent Night' together, or Jedidiah did. I was silently crying too much listening to Jedidiah sing with his sweet voice in tune!

Today Mrs. Lemnah stopped by to play the recorder for Jedidiah. Cynthia taped the Orchestra's Christmas performance on Thursday so we watched that. Then Mrs. Lemnah played the recorder. Jedidiah was awake but didn't say anything. He was conducting with his right arm. Jedidiah requested Jingle Bells but we didn't know which song he wanted till he smiled and nodded his head that that was the song! Then just as Mrs. Lemnah had left, Jedidiah said, 'That was nice of Mrs. Lemnah!' Mrs. Lemnah was Jedidiah's third grade teacher and taught Jedidiah to play the recorder.

Jedidiah is sleeping now, with Pep curled up on his lap, sleeping too. I tried to move Pep but she looked up at me, curled her lip and seemed to say, "I'm staying right here!"

Cynthia Lusk

<u>Dec 20, 2010 -by Cynthia</u>

Justin and I are back from the weekend basketball tournament in Hamilton City. The Quincy High School Trojan Varsity Boys Team won First Place in the Tournament! It was a really fun time all the way around and I enjoyed the time spent with Justin.

It was good to get home and see Jedidiah again. I gave him lots of big hugs and cuddles and slept curled up with him all night. Of course he awoke at around 0130 in the morning, and he "talked" to me with his hands. We practiced the "Secret Lusk Family Handshake" and then the Boy Scout Handshake. Then we played with the Buzzing Buggy Wuggy, and the Wiggly Squiggly bracelet thingy. I told Jedidiah all about the three basketball games that his brother played in. Then I told Jedidiah how pretty the canyon looked with all the beautiful waterfalls streaming whitewater from the tops of the mountains all the way down to empty into the river.

This morning Jedidiah's Grandma Nanny gave Jedidiah one of the strips of large sleigh bells we had hanging on the door. He has them wrapped around his wrist and shakes them to play Jingle Bells and they make a lovely Christmas sound. Plus, we know that Jedidiah is awake & talking to us!!

Right now, Nanny is playing Jingle Bells on the Harp, and Jedidiah is shaking his bells! Justin ran to get his camera and made a short recording!

Jedidiah has received some very nice letters and cards. Thanks to people who have taken the time to write to him. We all appreciate it very much! Thank you Curt, for your wonderful letter! (And compliments to your Photographer/Artist in WA)

Jedidiah received his Christmas "Name Person Present" in the mail today! We learned that Jedidiah's Uncle Tim had his name! He gave Jedidiah a "IXP3" or in plain words, it is an internet message clock! We are utilizing big brother Justin's "Techy-ness" to get it all set up and working. Thanks Uncle Tim!!!

"And she brought forth her first-born son, and wrapped him in swaddling clothes, and laid him in a manger; because there was no room for them in the inn." Luke 2:7 KJV

Dec 21, 2010- AM, by Scott Lusk

You know it's going to be a Great day when the first thing you hear at 0500 in the morning when you squeeze Jedidiah's hand and whisper, "I love you", is to hear Jedidiah say loud and clear, "I Love You Too Dad!"

Then we sat up and sipped some water, clear, cold Cromberg well water, and cut off the Christmas paper loop for December 21st together, making Christmas be just 4 days away! Jedidiah made his first Christmas loop in the 1st grade and that's a tradition we've carried forward. We have red and green paper loops with each day in December written on one. Each day Jedidiah cuts off a loop and we can track how many days left till Christmas!

Today I'm taking Justin and Jessica to Reno to help me buy a new computer, so we can give Jessica's back. Thanks for letting us borrow yours Jessica so we could keep updating the web page. 'I Love Making Decisions' lap top vs. desk top; Apple vs. non-apple; seeable screen vs. tiny screen; inexpensive vs. way too expensive; email vs. Excel analysis; I've been left way behind.... Then I'm going to treat my computer chooser helpers to Sushi! I can't wait to see Justin try the eel and the quail egg!

Then Blue Nanny's going to go to fiddle lesson with me this afternoon and bring the Harp! Johny's going to let me try her viola!

"Make a joyful noise unto the LORD, all the earth: make a loud noise, and rejoice, and sing praise." Psalm 98:4 KJV

Dec 21, 2010–PM, By Scott Lusk

We had fun in Reno today! First we went to Best Buy to get us a computer. Justin and I had it all figured out. We had a 8.6 megabyte tower that could run a 55 inch TV as our monitor while we played World of War Craft! Shawn was our helper. He left twice to go get aspirins. Jessica was our sense of reason, she pointed out that for all we use a computer for, the $400 Dell desk top, with Microsoft 2007, is all we'd need to write a term paper, update Jedidiah's web page, and store photographs -and that we didn't even know what World of War Craft was! Jessica prevailed. We bought the $400 Dell desk top. I have to go back tomorrow to pick it up because we choose to have them install the Windows and back it up with a Restore CD, instead of me trying it.

Then we went to eat Sushi. We really started it off with the raw quail egg followed by the eel! Jessica had been before so she suggested the octopus. It was a real octopus leg. Jessica's was sliced thin. Justin followed suit. His was thick and had the suction cups. Justin got a suction cup stuck to his tongue and I had to pry it off! It was quite a commotion! Undaunted, Justin tried the flying fish eggs next. It was an all you can eat smorgasbord and we got our money's worth! It was good!

Then Blue Nanny went to fiddle lesson with me late in the afternoon and impressed Johny with her harp playing. I played my cello. Johny gave us both new music to go home and practice with. Johny let me try her viola. We're getting to be quite a band, we have the instruments to be a good one!

Cynthia is good at starting colts and trimming mule's feet but she doesn't spend much time in the house baking. So yesterday when it was snowing hard, Cynthia baked all our favorite cookies. It was great to smell fresh hot cookies baking in the oven while watching the snow fall outside with a fire crackling in the woodstove! Cynthia spent most of today delivering cookies she had baked yesterday. Except at every friend's house she stopped at to give cookies to, she came home with more cookies from them!

When we got home Jedidiah greeted us by ringing his Christmas bells he has on his wrist. He raised his eyebrows and smiled. Mama flew him to his bed from his brown chair. I had to chuckle when Justin went to kiss Jedidiah good night and stayed too close for too long, Jedidiah wrinkled his nose and frowned his eyebrows at Justin. Their still the same boys that Justin filmed on the porch last summer on a tripod with Justin jumping over Jedidiah sitting on the steps just barely missing each time. We saw that video last week! Justin is a Great Big Brother! Justin's going to sleep with Jedidiah tonight, snuggled together like in the back of the truck at the Taylorsville Silver Buckle Rodeo two years ago.

"And there were in the same country shepherds abiding in the field, keeping watch over their flock at night. And lo, the angel of the Lord came upon them, and the glory of the Lord shone round about them: and they were sore afraid." Luke 2:8-9 KJV

Dec 22, 2010

Scott headed out to Reno this morning, driving the van, to go pick up the computer. He came back about 5 minutes later to trade the 2 wheel drive van, for the 4 wheel drive pickup. It was snowing pretty hard, and the sign at Hwy 70 said, "Chains Required or 4 wheel drive with snow tires- OK'.

Last year at this time Jedidiah was gearing up for ski racing- as shown in this photo of him in the racing starting gate!! His Dad sure enjoyed helping him. This year, Scott has volunteered to help on the Snow Leopards, which is the young, developmental team, with daughter Jessica as his Assistant Coach.

Today, the precipitation has since changed to rain, and now all the snow is sliding off the roof with loud thumps.

Jedidiah is sleeping peacefully in his brown chair, and Nanny is practicing the harp. Every so often Jedidiah will wake up and shake his jingle bells and add to the music.

Justin slept in the living room bed with Jedidiah last night, to keep him company and help out. Jedidiah squeezed Justin's hand a couple times, but did not fully wake up to talk to him at 0200 AM in the morning. Jedidiah's wake up periods are getting less often and he sleeps more now.

Jedidiah's kitties love to curl up with him and take long naps. It's good to see Jedidiah's fingers reach out to stroke the long, soft feline fur! When the cats get down, then Jedidiah's puppy, Pep wants to take her turn to curl up and hug Jedidiah.

A box arrived to Jedidiah from the Paiva family! They sent lots of goodies. Thank you very much! Justin opened the box and immediately was reading from the book, "Moses' favorite Travel Jokes". I read a few of the jokes to Jedidiah and he wrinkled his eyebrows for me. I like the animal jokes best, so here are a few short ones for ya'll:

Q. Why don't ducks tell jokes while they are flying?
A. The might Quack up!

Q. Why do birds fly south?
A. It's too far to walk!

Q. Why did the gum cross the road?
A. It was stuck to the chicken's foot!

and for one last joke today......
Q. How many animals did Moses take on the ark?
A. Moses did not take any....Noah did!

"And the angel said unto them, Fear not: For, behold, I bring you good tidings of great joy, which shall be for all people." Luke 2: 10, KJV

Dec 23, 2010

Last night Jedidiah was awake and very active! His Mom & Dad spent the night in Jedidiah's bed with him. We did not get much sleep, but it was sure worth it.

Jedidiah was shaking his jingle bells off and on from 11PM to 1AM, in time to the Country Music Radio Station that Scott turned on! Then he switched to thumb wrestling his mother at 2AM!

Then we arm wrestled a few times, and i was surprised by his strength! He beat me twice, then i could feel that he "let me win" for the third and final arm wrestling match!

He kept squeezing my hand, so I could tell he wanted something. I propped him up in the bed with lots of pillows behind him, and got him a drink of water. He drained a whole cup of cold water thru his straw!

He was still wanting something else, so I got him a drinkable yogurt, and he drained that too!

Then he was back to jingling the bells and wriggling his legs, like he was dancing. He was making so much music, that his brother came out to the living room at 0300 AM to see what was going on!

Scott could not sleep so he turned on the new computer to get it working. It said the time was 0500. Scott thought it was time to get up anyway. It wasn't until 3 hours later that he figured out that the computer was set to Central Time, and NOT Pacific Time. So, it really was 0300 AM, when Scott got up and thought it was 0500 AM.

Jedidiah still had plenty of energy and obviously was NOT sleepy, so he was still ringing away the bells, when he woke up his grandma Nanny at 0600. We all laughed and talked awhile, then decided to turn on the Channel 3 News.

Guess where the Newsman was standing? He was at the North Pole!! We recognized the Santa Claus House right away!! We were right there with Jedidiah in July- at THE Santa Clause House at THE North Pole. We even recognized the EXACT same Santa Claus! The only thing different was that it was pitch dark in Alaska at 0700 this morning. And another thing- the newsman was holding up a large outdoor thermometer, and today it read -40! That's 40 degrees **BELOW zero!** Thank goodness it was more like 78 degrees when we were there in July! So, Steve, Terry, Linda, and Mom, oh- & Noodle!- Hope you all are keeping warm!!

Now, we got the computer set to the correct time, and Scott is drifting off to sleep in Jedidiah's bed. Meanwhile, Jedidiah is sitting up in his brown chair, joyfully ringing his jingle bells some more!! Justin is adding more pretty ornaments to our beautiful Christmas Tree, while Jessica is busy adding wrapped presents under the tree!! CHRISTMAS IS COMING in a few more days!!!

"For unto you is born this day in the city of David a Savior, which is Christ the Lord!" Luke 2:11 KJV

Dec 24, 2010

Happy Christmas Eve!

You may send Jedidiah email messages to message@myixp3.com (I forgot to add .com last time so if you tried and it didn't work it was probably because of that) with the subject Jedidiah and it will pop up on his new e-mail clock that he recently received from his name person Uncle Tim.

This picture is Jedidiah's whole school lined up holding signs that say 'We Love You Jedidiah'. Notice the 1,000 origami hanging on the Christmas Tree. This picture was on the front page of the Feather River Bulletin.

Thank you Fascination Toys and Gifts for the speedy Fed-Ex iXP3 free Replacement!

Cynthia Lusk

<u>Dec 25, 2010</u>

12/25/10- Merry Christmas! This was the BEST Christmas EVER!!!! We had a wonderful day together! A Very Special Christmas for Scott, Cynthia, Jessica, Justin, Jedidiah, and Blue Nanny.

Jedidiah was here with us.

Need I say more? You know, Life all boils down to Love, appreciating what you have, and thanking the Lord God for your friends and family. Enjoy and hold close those you have. Hold tight for now, but be prepared to let go when you have to.

We enjoyed every minute of the day today; from slowly opening and appreciating every gift under the Christmas Tree to watching family videos from this past year, that Justin downloaded onto our new computer!

Jedidiah wriggled his legs and wrinkled his eyebrows in appreciation of the gifts his friends and relatives sent to him. Jessica and Justin took turns opening presents for Jedidiah, while describing the gifts and letting Jedidiah touch and feel them. Thanks SO much to all who gave to him!

The videos made us laugh and cry. Beginning at the Fair in August 2009- Jessica and Justin showed their Shorthorn 4-H steers, while Jedidiah showed his Naked-Neck chicken in Primary 4-H. Then Jedidiah was playing Basketball in December, building a Boy Scout Pine Wood Derby truck in January and racing it in February, then reciting his chosen poem : "The Cremation of Sam McGee" at the QES Talent Show- all before being diagnosed with his Glioblastoma multiformes brain tumor on Feb. 14, 2010.

The videos continued after Jedidiah's treatment began- his 9th Birthday Party at home in Cromberg, when all his wonderful cousins came to share it with us. Scott's 38th Birthday Party Camp-Out, when we took Jedidiah camping in the woods- wheelchair and all! Plus- 4 wheeler, dirt bike, horses, and his new puppy, Pep! Then Justin's basketball season started… bringing us back to the present.

We enjoyed reading messages today on Jedidiah's new IXP3, that was fun! Thank You, Friends, for sending those neat notes! From Reindeer resting on back porches in Washington, to the chilly temperatures in Fairbanks, and lots of Merry Christmas wishes in between, much thanks!

Last night, for Christmas Eve, Jedidiah's Dad read the book, "Twas The Night Before Christmas" that Santa Claus signed and gave Jedidiah when we visited the North Pole in July. Then I read the Bible, Luke Chapter 2, about Jesus' birth. Then Scott proceeded to tell the story of how I scared Santa away our first Christmas in Terrebonne. After the laughter faded away, Jessica and Justin turned on "A Christmas Story" on TV, the one about the Leg Lamp and Don't Shoot Your Eye Out!

The night before last we had a pleasant surprise of a large group of Christmas Carolers, who arrived at our doorstep in Cromberg. They all had such wonderful singing voices and sang beautiful songs! I know Jedidiah appreciated them, as much as we did, as they filed inside to wish Jedidiah well. Thank you so very much!!

"But while he thought on these things, behold, the angel of the Lord appeared unto him in a dream, saying, Joseph, thou son of David, fear not to take unto thee Mary thy wife: for that which is conceived in her is of the Holy Ghost. And she shall bring forth a son, and thou shalt call his name JESUS: for he shall save his people from their sins." Matthew 1: 20-21 KJV

Dec 27, 2010

Where have the last couple of days gone?

We have been cleaning up the house after a carefree Christmas Day. Today i took down the Christmas Tree. Didn't really want to do that, but needed the room for Jedidiah's Brown Chair & room to work around the house once again.

Jedidiah has been pretty quiet at night these last two nights. mostly sleeping, but also quiet because he hasn't been able to talk at all anymore. He can't walk, can't talk, can't see and can't eat. But he does still have that spark of life, and he does ring his jingle bells!

This morning Jedidiah was sleeping with his Dad so I could get some much needed sleep between midnight and 0400 AM. I got up at 0500 and went to check on Jedidiah. Scott said they both had been awake for the past hour, and Jedidiah had constantly been using sign language to spell out, "M.. O.. M.."

As Ii sat down next to him, he reached out for my arm and pulled me close. With his eyes closed, he opened his mouth and squeaked out, "Ma...ma....Mama!"

I hugged my little guy with my heart full of joy.

Who needs sleep, anyway?!!

"And he sent them to Bethlehem, and said, Go and search diligently for the young child; and when ye have found him, bring me word again, that I may come and worship him also. When they heard the king, they departed; and, lo, the star, which they saw in the east, went before them, till it came and stood over where the young child was. When they saw the star, they rejoiced with exceeding great joy." Matthew 2: 8-10, KJV

<u>Dec 28, 2010</u>

Here is a photo of my two big kidlets, wearing their new clothes they got for Christmas! Jessica is holding a photo frame that Justin customized for her with lots of shiny "Bling" and some really nice photos.

Justin was supposed to have a basketball game tonight against Whitell (near Lake Tahoe) but it was cancelled due to the expected big snowstorm tonight. The sky has been darkening all afternoon, as heavy clouds move in.

I am very proud of my two oldest children! They have helped so much these past 10 months. Jessica is 19 years old and Justin is 16, but they both display such a high level of maturity and wisdom, far beyond their years.

All throughout the crisis of Jedidiah being diagnosed with a brain tumor, extended treatments and hospital stay, Mom & Dad coming & going in a blur and all stressed out, their little and much loved younger brother finally coming home after 62 days, but immobile and in a wheelchair, Jessica and Justin persevered.

They continued on in school, making VERY good grades, playing sports and completing their chores at home, plus helping out with Jedidiah to give Mom and Dad a break. They demonstrated their love for Jedidiah on a daily basis, making sure he felt included in all family activities, asking him what they could do to help him. And Jedidiah was not shy when it came time to tell them! He was a bit bossy at times, (or should I say he was A LOT bossy?) But Jessica and Justin tolerated it well and humored Jedidiah. I know just how much they LOVE their little brother!! Or, as Jedidiah would say, "IT IS WUV!"

One thing about Jedidiah, despite his young age, he knew what was important to him, how to organize what he wanted, and how to enact or enforce those things with his siblings. Not to mention his SALESmanship.... when it came time for fundraising. Never one to turn away or shrink back from asking people for money- Ha, Ha! Last year at this time Jedidiah was awarded the highly coveted "Bow & Mallow" for bringing in the MOST money for selling Cub Scout Popcorn!

Today Jedidiah is in his Brown Chair, sleeping away. He drank some nutrition drink earlier, got his fingernails trimmed, had a foot message, got his clothes changed, teeth brushed, face washed, hair brushed, then sipped some more water.

Now we are listening to a Celtic Music CD, and it's starting to rain! Well, maybe the snow will come a little later. It's almost time to go out and feed the horses...

"And when they were come into the house, they saw the young child with Mary his mother, and fell down, and worshiped him: and when they had opened their treasures, they presented unto him gifts; gold, and frankincense, and myrrh." Matthew 2:11 KJV

<u>Dec 29, 2010</u>

Here is a photo of Jedidiah and his Grandma Nanny taken this week. Nanny's REAL name is Donnal Nichols. My daughter Jessica coined the term, "Blue Nanny" for her grandmother more than 18 years ago. It has stuck ever since!

Nanny recently retired from her second career (or was it the third?). She left the U.S. Forest Service in Quincy, CA the end of October. Nanny was the Front Desk Receptionist for the Mt. Hough Ranger District. Although she was only "Part-Time", she worked ALL the time! She does not have to worry anymore about driving back and forth to Quincy, especially now that its winter.

Nanny lives with us in the two story home we had built in Cromberg. She has been home, helping with Jedidiah for the last two months. Well, I could not ask for a better helper and caregiver than my very own mother! She is a Registered Nurse, and even better: she loves her youngest grandchild very much!! An excellent Role Model for me and for Jessica-(who has hopes and plans for becoming a Nurse also) on being a great mother AND for caring SO much for others.

To say that I greatly appreciate her help is SUCH an understatement! Extreme Gratitude is a better way to put it I guess. Many THANKS to you, Nanny!!

Jedidiah has remained pretty quiet last night and today. He has not been ringing his bells much, preferring instead to communicate with his thumb. It's been "Thumbs Up" for yes and "Thumbs Down" for no. He wanted to stay in his bed today, instead of flying to his Brown Chair. So he is propped up in bed with pillows behind his back so he can drink his fluids. Much to his embarrassment, Jedidiah has to wear "Hospital Pants" at this stage in his life. We are NOT to use the "Diaper" word in our household- a rule Jedidiah made VERY plain to us last spring when he was at UCDMC, recovering from his biopsy surgery.

We had some snow flurries this morning and it came down hard for about an hour, so I was telling Jedidiah how pretty the snow looked all swirling around in the sky, and how even the trees were being tossed about by the wind. He nodded and squeezed my hand.

My friend, Nancy Quigley sent a beautiful Bible Verse that I would like to share today:

"Yet I am always with You;
You hold me by my right hand.
You guide me with Your counsel'
And afterward You will take me into Glory.
Whom have I in Heaven but You?
And earth has nothing I desire besides You.
My flesh and my heart may fail,
But God is the strength of my heart
And my portion forever!"
Psalm 73: 23-26

Dec 30, 2010

    I was able to get outdoors for an hour and a half hike thru the woods yesterday, while Nanny watched Jedidiah. I try to do that at least every few days, but sometimes it's hard to get away. One of the things I really enjoy about going for a walk by myself, is it allows me time just to think. I have the freedom to reflect on whatever subject I choose, or to just let my mind wander. Of course, as you might suspect, Jedidiah has been the main thing on my mind for the past 10 ½ months.

    If you would have asked me one year ago, I would not have any thoughts on what would happen if one on my children developed a life threatening or terminal illness. I would have given you a blank stare. It truly was the furthest thing from my mind. My thoughts on raising kids : they are born, you raise them, they grow up, go to college, and move away. Lots of little details in between alright, but you get the picture. A good parent makes sure the child gets all the required vaccinations to protect them from childhood diseases, you keep a handy supply of Scooby Doo Band-Aids, cough syrup, and fever reducer/pain medicine, combined with lots of love, education, support and encouragement. You base all your thoughts for the future, that your child will out- live you.

    While raising children, you plan for the occasional skinned knee, the bump on the head, maybe a bike wreck, or two. Or, as Jedidiah did the first week we lived in our new house- getting stitches! He was running away from his brother- up the stairs, and fell on the hard oak surface of the top stair. He sliced his chin open, requiring a late evening trip to the Emergency Room! Thirteen stitches later, I brought him home and he recovered just fine!

    When you get married you pledge, "For Better or Worse, In Sickness or in Health" to your spouse. You go into the partnership knowing, most probably, there WILL be sickness, things that may happen for the worse-as you do hope to grow old together- and all the problems that come with a lifetime shared together. But with children, you may not anticipate problems on that scale. Well, at least I did not. Most kids are young and healthy. They bounce right back,... right?

    How do you prepare yourself to deal with your child's brain cancer? What do you do when the neurosurgeon tells you that your young son has the deadliest form of brain tumor, in an inoperable location and says he is very sorry, but there is nothing he can do? How do you prepare yourself and your child, for a journey of this magnitude?

I still don't know the answers. All I can do is turn the whole situation over to God, and trust in Him.

What I do know is we love our little Jedidiah! We love him the whole world's worth!!

I am so grateful for the love of our community, too. With community, I don't just mean the local county, (which has been unbelievably generous!) but also in a broader sense- an emotional web with connections that reach from Alaska to Virginia, and all the way in between. A heartfelt thank you to each and every one of you who have supported us and given your love to Jedidiah. All of of you have shown your love to us in many, many ways and we are grateful for all. Your love is all encompassing and wraps us in a warm cocoon! THANK YOU !!

"Trust in the Lord with all your heart and lean not on your own understanding. In all your ways acknowledge Him, and He shall direct your paths." Proverbs 3: 5-6

Dec 31, 2010

Very Sad to say- and tougher yet to see- but Jedidiah is pretty much unresponsive now. He had trouble swallowing yesterday and was not able to get down much fluids. We have been using a small bulb syringe to trickle water into his mouth a few drops at a time. He does not ring his jingle bells anymore. He has not been able to move his thumb much. He does, however, wriggle his right foot!

Jedidiah's Uncle John and Aunt Stevie drove up from Sacramento yesterday to visit with us. They brought Jedidiah a toy "stretch shark" to play with. It's a fun- feeling rubber and it really
S T R E T C H E S when you pull on it. Super cool!! I had fun playing with it!! Then I remembered that it was really for Jedidiah, so I put it in his hand. Jedidiah wriggled his foot to say Thank You to John & Stevie!

Jedidiah had some more visitors yesterday. Dee Stowe and her son Alex stopped by, and Steve Ross with his son William came over. Thank you for your gifts and your presence. Jedidiah's friends just being here with him is the BEST gift of all. Thank You!!

I remember when Jessica and Justin were little kids, some years ago, they used to pout and say, "That's NOT FAIR..." Maybe it was that Justin got more pushes on the swing, or Jessica got to sit in the front seat of the car longer...something was unjust, somehow. They would voice their opinions and look to me to correct it. I would shake my head and say, "You know kids, this whole life is going to be unfair to you. You better just get used to it now!" That was my mantra, repeated often as the kids were growing up. I thought they might as well know the truth, right out of the gate, that life was not going to treat them fairly at all times. Lots of things are unequal, unjust, not fair, or whatever you want to call it. No matter how hard you try, those scales just won't always balance out.

What I meant was that some things will be out of your control, and not to waste time fretting about the things you couldn't control. Do the best you could, whatever the circumstances, but don't let the circumstances rule you.

Pretty quick, the kids figured this out, the pouting stopped, and they were able to shrug off the minor disappointments in life and push on. No, things did NOT always go your way, but that's OK. Life goes on...

It seems Jedidiah was born already knowing this. Or maybe it was his brother and sister that taught him early on? But Jedidiah was all about the "Pushing On" part. "Just Get Out of My Way" was his motto.

His Mom and Dad, big sister and big brother all tried to shield Jedidiah from the bumps and bruises of growing up. Jedidiah wanted NO part of coddling.... But his Mom did. She explicitly told Dad, "Now, DO NOT teach Jedidiah how to shift his mini dirt bike from first to second gear!! He could hurt himself!"

But the next time I looked outside, he was already in third gear...and reaching for fourth...

"I returned, and saw under the sun, that the race is not to the swift, nor the battle to the strong, neither yet bread to the wise, nor yet riches to men of understanding, nor yet favor to men of skill; but time and chance happen to them all." Ecclesiastes 9:11 KJV

Jan 3, 2011

I changed the oil in our truck this morning. It brought out a LOT of memories of Jedidiah!

Jedidiah is the only one in our immediate family with an interest in mechanical things. He developed that interest early on. Of course, most little boys like to take things apart. "Ya got to find out what makes 'em work, don't ya?" But I knew he was special, when he'd TRY to put some of them back together! He LOVED to help me change the oil in the cars and trucks since he could walk. I would crawl under the vehicle with the socket wrench and he would wait with the socket set in hand, fingering all the different sizes with curiosity.

"What do you need Mom, a 5/8 or 9/16?" Jedidiah would ask. He would always hand me the one I needed. He especially enjoyed pouring the new oil in! When he was tiny, I hoisted him up to perch on the edge of the engine compartment, so he could reach. Then he graduated to standing on the front bumper. But anytime a hood was open on a vehicle, you would soon find Jedidiah scrambling up next to you, peering in.

"What should we check, Mom? Transmission fluid? Brake fluid? Coolant? Clutch fluid? Power steering fluid? What do you need help with, huh? And, OH, Have you checked the air pressure in the tires lately, Mom?" He was such a HELPFUL guy!

Jedidiah loved to look under the snowmobile hoods also. He was so proud when he could teach his big brother, Justin, a thing or two about snowmobiles. "Justin, see this red switch here? That's how you turn the gas on or off. Your machine doesn't have it, but mine does. And I think your sled is water cooled but mine is air cooled…see, yours uses radiator fluid, but mine doesn't." he'd proudly say. He had so much fun with that. He was learning ALL the time! When we were in town together, he would beg me to stop by the Forest Service office to show him the snowmobiles I rode at work. And we could NOT, EVER, drive by DuPont's without Jedidiah screaming, "S T O P!!" I would try many things to distract him just before we got there. But it would never work. So, I would stop and try to be patient, while Jed looked over any and all vehicles that were outside in the parking lot. If the store was open, he'd beg to go inside to look and ask questions.

Jedidiah was especially impressed with his Uncle John, because he could help Jedidiah work on his mini dirt bike. Uncle John knew ALL about motorcycles! He even helped Jedidiah's Dad with his Yamaha. "Oh, that was easy to fix," said Scott. "Why didn't I think of that?" Then he would elaborate on his mechanical knowledge. "I know where the gas goes, and where the oil goes," Dad would laugh. "And I've only mixed up those two things once!"

Jedidiah started collecting tools, from who knows where, and USING them! One nice fall weekend a couple years ago it was quiet inside the house, so I knew Jedidiah must be outside. I peeked out the window, to see him bent over our old lawnmower. He appeared to be "Working" on it! I just let him, 'cause the old lawnmower did not work anymore. In fact I often wondered to myself why we even bothered to lug it around with us after 20 years.

Soon Jedidiah came traipsing inside the house, hands dirty and greasy, but a big smile on his face. "So, Mom...can you tell me ...is this the carburetor?"

"No, honey," I had to say. "That is the air filter. See, it has a rubber gasket on the outside with this paper looking stuff on the inside."

"OK, I will go look some more. Don't worry Mom," Jedidiah said with confidence, "I will get it running again in no time!"

But, alas, it did not run again! However, Jedidiah did succeed in taking off the push handle, and re-installing in on the other side of the mower!!

"When thou liest down, thou shall not be afraid: yea, thou shalt lie down and thy sleep shall be sweet. Be not afraid of sudden fear, neither of the desolation of the wicked, when it cometh. For the Lord shall be thy confidence." Proverbs 3: 24-25 KJV

January 2, 2011, by Scott Lusk

We're back! Justin, Jessica and I spent the week after Christmas in CDA with the Cousins! We were all here for Christmas. Jedidiah actively participated on Christmas Day! Jedidiah would feel presents with his fingers when we gave them to him and ring his bells, smile with his eyebrows and wiggle his legs to show he liked the presents! When we left, we all kissed Jedidiah and said we'll see you in a week! I sat on his foot and he said, 'Ouch'! Jedidiah kissed Jessica back on her cheek, -and he aimed a right round house at Justin!

Our plan was for all of us to go to CDA, but as it turned out, Jedidiah was too sleepy to travel that far, so Cynthia said she would stay home with Jedidiah. We had a blast shooting skeet off the deck at Tim's Cabin; skiing powder at Silver Mountain; spending the night in the Condo; surfing at the water park; playing several games of pick-up basketball at the Krog; bouncing off the walls at the trampoline park; watching Carli step in to play after her ACL surgery as her team won the Championship tournament game; and spending quality family together time driving 18 hours up and back!

I read Cynthia's updates. She wrote Jedidiah was unresponsive. To me, an unresponsive Jedidiah means when you tell him not to get his good school shoes wet in the creek the day before Valentine's Day, 2010, he jumps in to his knees and sends mud splattering all over his brother, grinning ear to ear! I was not ready for this kind of 'unresponsive' when I got back and saw Jedidiah last night. I knew it was coming and have had a while to prepare. But I'm not ready for it. Cynthia has been doing the daily physical hands on part the past few days of rolling Jedidiah to change his hospital pants, holding his head to brush his teeth, and lifting him to change his clothes. But that's not what I wanted to write about. I want to write about Jedidiah's unconquerable spirit! My little guy who rides snow mobiles fast, stands up on dirt bikes, floors 4-wheelers, wore the #21 bib in ski races, plays the fiddle, and -who does not like homework!

Throughout this entire 10 month ordeal Jedidiah has remained his sweet, caring, funny guy. He never once said, "Oh why me" or "Oh pity me" or even be ashamed of how huge he had gotten, from 67 pounds to 142 pounds! When he went back to school at the end of the third grade last year some kids said you don't look like Jedidiah, he said it's because the Decadron made my face swell and gain weight. When asked why he had no hair, Jedidiah explained because he had had radiation and chemo for a brain tumor. When asked why he's in a wheel chair, Jedidiah said it's because they nicked my brain stem doing the biopsy. His friends and schoolmates have been very supportive and kind. No one made fun of Jedidiah!

Jedidiah wanted to do all the activities we wrote about in his journal. He wanted to be an Alaska Smoke Jumper, so the Bros did it! Jedidiah told jokes to the Smoke Jumpers from his book of jokes he memorized while at the Ronald McDonald House. He wanted to be baptized and understands why. He told jokes at Church on the microphone when Pastor George forgot his for the sermon. He wanted to ride the school bus home the last day of 3rd grade! He wanted to go on the Hiawatha Trail with the Cousins, so we found a bike trailer and he did, and took pictures of moose on the trail! Jedidiah loved to swim because he had unlimited mobility again and could do all the things he used to do on land in the water. At the pool this summer a little girl said, 'Oh, you're the little boy with brain cancer who's going to die.' Jedidiah replied, 'Yes, we are all going to die at some time, live life now'. He wanted to make "Cotton Cloud" Cotton Candy free for his friends and only charge $1 for the others, but if you didn't have a dollar, he said just mail him two hard candies and he'd mail you yours. He donated all the money he made at the Farmer's Market selling Cotton Clouds for the Quincy History Club's trip to Greece this year. He loved going to school this year and being in the 4th grade because he got to see all his friends and he didn't have to do any homework! He would raise his hand and answer questions at the start of the 4th grade this year.

Jedidiah made a list of things he wanted to do when he left the hospital and he has crossed most of the things off of his list. His list is amazing for a 9 year old! Thank You to all of you who have made it possible!

Jedidiah asked me a couple months ago that when after he dies, he wants to be cremated, like Sam McGee, and to give half his ashes to Justin and Jessica and to spread the other half under the Chicken Tree.

Jedidiah asked me not to forgot him! I said, "I never will" !

After breakfast, we gave Jedidiah the Christmas presents his Cousins made for him. He's wearing the Whitworth Football shirt Connor gave him. We passed around the jar of hot peppers Robert and Sarah gave him. Jedidiah spread his fingers to help when Justin put on the bracelet Cole made for him out of turquoise, white, and black duct tape and he squeezed the day-time-blue water bottle with the smiley face sticker Carli made that says:

"Always be Positive for Jedidiah".

Cynthia Lusk

Jan 1, 2011

HAPPY NEW YEAR!

Jedidiah had a peaceful New Year's Eve. Jedidiah's friend Mikey Bruce and his mother stopped by to visit yesterday. They sang songs to Jedidiah out of a book called, "Take Me Out of the Bathtub and other Silly Dilly songs", by Alan Katz. They are silly songs that are sang to the tune of other classic childhood songs. One song called, "Go Go Go to Bed" is sang to the tune of "Row, Row, Row Your Boat", and "Cranky Poodle" is sang to "Yankee Doodle" tune. The Title song, "Take Me Out of the Bathtub" is sang like "Take Me Out to the Ball Park". It was fun!!! Thank you Mikey and Mary! Jedidiah enjoyed it, I am sure.

Jedidiah and I watched the New Year's Day Parade on TV this morning. The horse entries in the parade are my favorite! I described in detail the breed and color of the horses to Jedidiah, plus told him about the pretty costumes, fancy tack or other special features about it. We saw Arabians, Quarter Horses, The Buffalo Soldiers, Peruvian Pasos, and I think Jedidiah's favorite was the incredible team of Budweiser Clydesdales!

One of the TV commercials today said many people spend New Year's Day reflecting upon the past year. For our family, this has been one heck of a crazy year. It would take a lot of time to go thru this past year's events in reflection! Mostly, I have been thinking back on fond memories of our family and time spent with Jedidiah. Our Alaska trip was remarkable, and we had SO much fun. It was the most perfect adventure with the whole family together! Thank you Make-A-Wish Foundation. Thank You Pikes Landing and Santa Clause House. Thank you Alaska Smokejumpers, Alaska Fire Service, and Thank you Fairbanks Mayor & family!

This afternoon Mrs. Lemnah came over and spent time with Jedidiah. She read him Bible verses, then played the recorder for him. When she was leaving, Jedidiah moved his hand like he wanted to wave good-bye to Mrs. Lemnah.

Photo of Jedidiah & Mrs. Lemnah taken in October, at Quincy Elementary School in Mrs. Lemnah's class. Jedidiah brought Pep in for a special Show &Tell in her class.

Here is a joke Jessica came up with today:

Q. Why is the frog never annoyed?
A. Because he eats everything that bugs him!

"Let us hear the conclusion of the whole matter: Fear God, and keep his commandments: for this is the whole duty of man."
Ecclesiastes 12: 13 KJV

<u>Jan 4, 2011</u>

Wanted to let you all know that Jedidiah died last night, Monday January 3, at 8:58 PM, PST, surrounded by his loving family at his earthly home in Cromberg, California.

<u>Jan 5, 2011</u>

Jedidiah's death leaves a huge, gaping hole in our home, hearts and lives. We miss him fiercely already! We find ourselves talking to him, telling him what activities are in store for the day, or wanting to pass on a tidbit of information that he would be interested in. He is constantly in our thoughts, as he has been for the past 10 1/2 months. (As well as he has been my baby, and always with me the for the last 9 years.)

The passing of his spirit, I consider a victory over cancer. Though the terrible disease, and a part of the treatment, ravaged his little body, he NEVER, ever let the presence of a brain tumor overwhelm his incredible life character, or his love of life, family and God.

We ask that no food or flowers be brought to our house. We appreciate your thoughts, but our freezer is already overflowing. Save your flower money to provide goodies for your own family. If you feel you must give money, please direct it to either of Jedidiah's favorite organizations: Johnsville Junior Ski Team or Sierra Access Coalition.

Jedidiah was a member of JJST before he could walk! He spent every winter since he could walk, racing with the Johnsville Junior Ski Team. It is an excellent youth program, under the Central Plumas Recreation District. It isn't just about skiing, though children will learn the fundamentals of the sport of downhill skiing, as well as strength, balance and other great physical fitness attributes. Kids also gain a greater sense of responsibility and self confidence as they grow and mature into young adults. The program serves children up to the eighth grade.

The Sierra Access Coalition is a locally founded organization, working to keep public land access open to the public. It is NOT, as some people might assume, just for people wanting to ride dirt bikes or 4 wheelers. It is an organization for ALL sportspeople, outdoorsmen and women who just enjoy being or actively recreating in our public land. Whether you are a hiker, snowmobiler, horseback rider, cross county skier, rock collector, geo-cacher, wood cutter, hunter, nature photographer, or a sight-seer enjoying the beauty of the outdoors, we all need and want unrestricted **access** to the public lands WE pay taxes on. The SAC gives input to the land management agencies, as they organize the future Travel Management Plans. They provide a powerful voice of the forest users.

As for Jedidiah's funeral service on Sunday, everyone is invited to attend or not attend, as you so choose. We, the family, will in no way hold it against you as to how YOU wish to remember Jedidiah.

There will be an open casket viewing at the LDS Church from 3:00 to 4:00 PM on Sunday Jan. 9th. I want to emphasis that this is strictly optional. We think it is important to provide friends and relatives an opportunity to say good-by to Jedidiah's body. It is ok to touch his body, kiss him, hold his hand and talk to him. We know that his body was just a temporary shell for him to use while he was here on earth. His Spirit IS still alive and well, with his Heavenly Father. If you do not wish to participate in this, that is ok too.

Regular Funeral Service for Jedidiah will be held at 4:00 PM, Sunday Jan. 9th at the LDS Church, on the Bucks Lake Road (next to the hospital)

We really appreciate all your kindness, and offers of assistance. We are doing okay now, as we manage to plan and organize Jedidiah's funeral and services. We don't need much physical help right now, thank you. We do appreciate the kind hugs, nice words, and thoughtful smiles. Thanks!

We promise to keep you posted as we have needs that we would like assistance with.

"I can do all things through Christ which strengthened me."
Philippians 4:13

Jan 4, 2011

Jedidiah's memorial service will be held this Sunday, January 9, 2011 at the L.D.S Church On Bucks Lake Road in Quincy, CA.

There will be an optional open casket visitation from 3:00 to 4:00. The Service starts at 4:00, with a pot luck reception following. Quincy First Baptist Church's Pastor George Tarleton will be conducting the Service.

In lieu of flowers, please send tax deductable donations to these non-profit organizations in honor of Jedidiah:

    Johnsville Jr Ski Team
    Central Plumas Recreation & Parks District
    PO Box 1551
    Quincy, CA, 95971

    Sierra Access Coalition
    PO Box 944
    Quincy, CA 95971

"For God so loved the world, that He gave his only begotten Son, that whosoever believeth in Him should not perish, but have everlasting life. For God sent not his son into the world to condemn the world: but that the world through Him might be saved." John 3:16-17 KJV

"Then shall the dust return to the earth as it was: and the spirit return unto God who gave it." Song of Solomon 12:7

"Wait on the Lord: be of good courage, and He shall strengthen thine heart: wait, I say, on the Lord." Psalm 27: 14 KJV

Cynthia Lusk

"Rejoice in the Lord always: and again I say Rejoice!" Philippians 4:4 KJV

Jan 10, 2011

Here is what Jessica wrote for Christy to read at Jedidiah's Funeral:

Ten months ago I started missing seeing Jedidiah running around all over the place, almost a month ago I started missing hearing his voice, a few days ago I started missing him completely. I'm thankful that this loss was gradual: we managed to have a ton of fun and create some amazing memories since Jedidiah's diagnosis. But by gradual, in no way do I mean easy. Jedidiah was such an amazing, fun loving, goofy kid that it's hard to understand why we only got him for such a short time. I don't feel the need to go into detail about what a great person Jedidiah was or how much he inspired us all, you all are a testament of that. Instead, I want to share some things with you that are helping me cope with his untimely death.

If you're sad, Cry!

The saddest and yet most healing thing I've ever experienced was the night Jedidiah died. Our whole family holding him as he left us is a privilege I would not give up for anything. After he took his last breath our pain flowed freely from our eyes as we hugged each other and cried. It felt like our hearts were simultaneously ripped open by our grief, yet held together through our shared pain and love. Crying bleeds out the pain we feel, that if withheld would drown us.

Nicholas Wolterstorff wrote, "If sympathy for the world's wounds is not enlarged by our anguish, if love for those around us is not expanded, if gratitude for what is good does not flame up, if insight is not deepened, if commitment to what is important is not strengthened ... if hope is weakened and faith diminished, if from the experience of death comes nothing good, then death has won."

The bible says, "and these three remain: faith hope and love, and the greatest is love" 1 Corinthians 13:13

Love with all your heart, All the time!

John Bratner wrote, "only people who avoid love can avoid grief."

The immense pain of losing Jedidiah is no doubt worth the incredible privilege of loving and being loved by him!!

I know nothing can take away the pain from Jedidiah's death, but I hope these words help ease the sting some for you as they have for me.

I'd like to finish by saying: Jedidiah, I love you SO much. I still say I love my two little brothers. And you still are the world's best-est ever, littlest brother! WE WILL ALWAYS REMEMBER YOU!

Jan 11, 2011

Thank you all who attended Jedidiah's funeral service on Sunday afternoon. We appreciated your presence, the sharing of our grief, the sharing of your wonderful stories and memories of Jedidiah.

We especially appreciate those courageous souls who stepped up to share their words at the front microphone. THANK YOU!!

I know the beautiful music by Johny McDonald, The String Beings and the Kepple girls, was greatly appreciated by everybody. Their music was very special and healing for us too. THANKS!

We are grateful for the thoughtful cards and letters people have written to us and Jedidiah, the mailbox has been full of well wishes from our long-distance friends.

Thank you to the LDS Church for letting us use their facilities, thanks to the folks who organized and brought all the great food, and those who did the clean-up.

"The spirit of the Lord God is upon me; because the Lord hath anointed me to preach good tidings unto the meek; he hath sent me to bind up the brokenhearted, to proclaim liberty to the captives, and the opening of the prison to them that are bound; to proclaim the acceptable year of the Lord, and the day of vengeance of our God; to comfort all that mourn; to appoint unto them that mourn in Zion, to give unto them beauty for ashes, the oil of joy for mourning, the garment of praise for the spirit of heaviness; that they might be called trees of righteousness, the planting of the Lord, that He might be glorified." Isaiah 62: 1-3

Cynthia Lusk

Feb 3, 2011

February 3, 2011

Dear Jedidiah,

It was a month ago today that you departed this earth and went to join Jesus. We miss you very much!! We think of you many times each day and always think of things we want to tell you. So what is Mom's solution? To write you a letter!

Pep is still as peppy as ever, though I worry that I may be feeding her too much, as she is getting a little chubby around the middle! She did the silliest thing yesterday morning, that reminded me SO MUCH of you. As I was reaching to make the bed Pep scrambled up the pile of clothes at the end of the bed, and she ran under the sheet as I was lifting it up. You would ALWAYS dive under the covers like that, giggling and laughing, when I wanted to change the bedding.

Pep crawled out all wriggling and happy- I know that was a grin on her face! Then I reached for the cover to pull it over, and she ran under that one too! She was bouncing around and scurrying all over the bed. Thinking of how it reminded me of you- I laughed and I cried!

The three black cats are all doing well. Your kitten, Black Lightning, looks like a full grown female cat. She is lithe and slender, and very self-possessed. She shares Blue Nanny's room with her cat Emerald. The two boys, Midnight and Baby Cakes, grew large and hairy. They are big cats and spend most of their time playing outside. They hang out near the hay stack and have become great mousers. Sometimes they come inside to play with Pep and she enjoys that a lot. But if they stay inside too long, they start causing trouble. If they are inside at night they try to sleep on Blue Nanny's head! Justin has reported being smothered by too much cat fur a couple of times too.

Speaking of Justin- he has been playing lots of Basketball lately. His picture was on the front page of the Sports Section this week- in color! I am cutting it out to send to all your cousins. Justin has three Home Games this week. The last couple weeks I have been driving the boys to away games all the way down to Esparto, by Woodland, and over to South Lake Tahoe, but it has been fun. Justin got his Report Card last week and he earned four A's and two B's, (the B's were in his AP classes, he tells me they are like A's).

Jessica took a neat trip down to Maui, and had a really fun time for a week. Now she is back to school at FRC for the Spring Semester. She says she has filed her petition to Graduate in May, so that is something to look forward to! Jessica is taking a Speech Class this semester, along with her CNA program. She had to give her first speech on Monday night. The topic she was assigned to speech about was, "My Favorite Thing", and she picked her family to talk about! So I asked for a copy of her speech but she said she did not write it down. I was thrilled that she spoke about our family and asked what she said. Jessica said she used the analogy of dominoes in a circle, and said our family surrounds each other like that, and how we hold each other up in love. If one domino is knocked over, the next one catches it. So, even if all are pushed over by adversity, they are still leaning on each other, so the circle is still connected and strong. That's pretty cool, isn't it?

Nanny is taking a Drawing class at FRC this semester that is two days a week and she is taking a painting class downtown too. She is still playing the harp and is taking lessons from Johny McDonald. Nanny is doing great with that instrument and Johny says she is a natural for it. With all the art and music she is doing, ("Artsy Smartsy" as Dad would say) she is still finding time to volunteer with Horses Unlimited. And guess what? Nanny's photo was in the paper this week too! She is on the front page of the Regional Section- in full color!!

Dad had to go down to Sacramento last week for a Forest Service INFRA computer class, so he is happy to be back at home this week. He is looking forward to coaching a JJST Ski Race this Saturday, with Jessica as his Assistant Coach. Hope there is still some snow for them to ski on.

Can you tell the weather patterns, by looking down from heaven? Northern California has been stuck under a high pressure bubble for a couple of months now. I call it, "The High & Dry". I went snowmobiling at Bucks Lake last week. You would not have enjoyed it very much because there was NO deep powder to blast through. The snowpack was more like a cover of concrete. Guess that's why it's called, "Sierra Cement"!

Yesterday was Ground Hog Day, and the Official Word is that the groundhog saw NO shadow. Yay! That means we are in for an early spring! That is great news for those folks back east, in the Midwest, and in New

England. They have all been hit with record snowfall, terrible blizzards, and the worst winter conditions they've had in a long time.

With all this nice weather I have been able to hike on the Pacific Crest Trail, ride horses, and work the young horses in the round pen. Your horse Adam is doing well. I put him in the round pen a couple weeks ago and put the saddle on him for the first time. Like you, he seems to take everything in stride. He did NOT care about that saddle one bit. I think he was just happy to get out of his winter corral and PLAY! I hope to get him out riding on the trails some this summer. He is a nice horse and I will take good care of him for you.

When the sun is out and the blue sky is so bright, it is hard for me to stay inside the house. But last week I forced myself to stay in one day, and began the process to clean the upstairs. I sorted through some of your things, since you don't need them anymore, and made a bag of stuff to take to the thrift store.

I remembered how much you enjoyed going to thrift stores and looking thru all the treasures. Now some other little boys can enjoy your clothes and toys too. I am glad you like to share.

I found some neat things in your stuff. One plastic bag had four small items, wrapped in Christmas paper. Hmmmm, I thought, what could these be? Apparently they were Christmas presents you forgot to hand out, that got lost in your room somewhere. There was a name on each one- for Mom & Dad, Justin, Jessica, and Nanny. I removed the wrapping paper on the one to Mom & Dad, to reveal a cute little soccer photo of you from fall 2009. Wow! You would be happy to know I handed them out to the appropriate people. Guess you must have been saving them to surprise us now? I put that soccer photo of you, up on the bathroom mirror upstairs see I can see it every day. Thank you!

I discovered a pair of your little boy sized Wrangler jeans in the corner. They were a faded blue, and one knee had a hole, ripped across the front. It looked as if you had just taken them off and threw them in the corner last week, but I know it must have been last year- the last of January of first week of February- before we discovered your brain tumor. There were still things in the front pockets! I removed what you had put in the pockets, they were all little boy treasures and it made me cry! I found some wood chips from the elementary school playground, a collection of small, pretty rocks, a pencil eraser, a little, round bouncy ball, and a piece of an orange peel.

You would be glad to know that I have been back volunteering in Mrs. Hochrein's Fourth Grade class at Quincy Elementary School. I go on Wednesdays and have been twice so far. It is good to see all your classmates again! They are doing well, and are working on fractions in math now. I don't imagine you would enjoy the math too much, but Mrs. Hochrein has some really fun games for the students to learn from. There are cardboard pizzas, sliced up with fractions written on them, and a dot-to-dot picture to make when you plot the answer to the fraction questions.

QES is hosting the Family Science Night next week, and I am going to bring my animal skull collection again. I remembered how much you loved going to that Science Night. Once you got there, you would be immersed in the event, captivated by all the projects! You would run back and forth between the tables, all excited to see everything. It was always hard to leave, and we would be one of the last still in the cafeteria, as the floors were being swept.

Well, Jedidiah, I got to go for now. I will write to you again later, as there is so much to tell you. Always know that we love you very much! And, we will ALWAYS REMEMBER YOU!!!!!

Love, Mom

<u>Feb 4, 2011</u>

Hi Jedidiah,
    Wait! There is more.
    More stuff to tell you!

The new deck around the front of our house is DONE! Coach Richard Daun and his son Robin finished that last week. It turned out great! I will have to take a new photo. They built benches around the edge for us to sit on, complete with a back railing, that are super nice. Your Dad is so thrilled! Our only regret with the deck is that you did not get to see it finished and enjoy the final product. I have a feeling we will sit out there on that deck for days to come and think of you, many, many, times in the future.

Your Dad and I returned the four wheeler to Dee Vajart last weekend. It was sure nice that you were able to borrow and ride it for a while. We still look at pictures of you riding it all by yourself on Dad's Birthday Camp-Out. It made us all so happy to see you smile! That sure was a fun time for the whole family.

Dad gave back the gray van to Quincy Auto the week before last. I remember the first time I saw you in that van. You were camping out at the Taylorsville Rodeo Grounds on July 3rd. I drove down from Oregon to join you, Dad and Justin. You were looking forward to watching the Silver Buckle Rodeo on the Fourth of July. Dad had set a tent up to camp in but you and Justin wanted to sleep in the back of the van. As I was sliding open the side door of the van to check it out, I could hear your voice loud and clear, telling Justin, "The Rules of the Van". You were very authoritative as you stated the rules you made. You were just finishing up your speech when I heard you yell, "AND JUSTIN, GET YOUR STINKY FEET OFF THE CEILING OF MY VAN!!!!!!"

I chuckled when I heard that. You made me laugh a lot, Jedidiah. That is one of the things I really miss about you. Your humor, intentional or not, had me laughing whenever you were with me. You saw the funny side of life and shared it with others.

Your brain tumor was diagnosed last year on February 14.

The one year anniversary of your diagnosis is coming up in ten days. Knowing it is going to be a sad day for all of us, I decided to make it happier. Guess what, Jedidiah? I ordered some new baby chicks to arrive on that day!! They will arrive in the mail on Valentine's Day, Twenty five fluffy, little, peeping, baby chicks. If you were here I know you would name them all, take good care of them and watch over all of them like a mother hen. Justin will have to help me get everything set up before they arrive.

I took a cool photo on my hike yesterday. It is of a meduim sized douglas fir tree, maybe 50 feet tall, growing out of a rock! I thought you would enjoy it. How does that tree do that? Where do the roots go? How long has it been growing there? It looks healthy too. It is not just growing, but thriving there. I thought of the many lessons that tree could teach us all. So, I wrote them down to share:

1. Start with a solid foundation.
2. Grow where you are planted
3. Thrive despite your circumstances.
4. My best friend is the rock I cling to.

And Jedidiah, you could probably come up with a dozen more. I learned so much from you!

I love you and miss you!!

Feb 9, 2011

Hi Jedidiah,

I've got a photo of the new deck for you! Dad and Justin were enjoying it last Sunday morning, and the big, hairy, black cat, Baby Cakes jumped up on Dad's lap for the picture. Guess he wanted to say hello to you too!

There was a photo of your Cub Scout Pack in the paper last week! They held their Pinewood Derby on Jan. 22 this year, and there was a short article about it announcing the winners. There is a paragraph in the paper that reads, "The race was held in remembrance of Bill Hopman and Jedidiah Lusk". I remember just how much you enjoyed that Cub Scout Pinewood Derby Race last year. I am so glad your brother filmed you racing the truck you made in January 2010. Your Dad still keeps your Pinewood Derby truck in a special place in Aunt Myrtle's hutch, right next to the Pinewood Derby car he made as a child!

I was wondering if you knew that Bill Hopman had died too? Maybe you welcomed him to Heaven, or ran into him somewhere up there? Your Dad said he was skiing with him on Saturday, January 8th. He came to your funeral service on Sunday, January 9th, and then he died on Monday Jan. 10th. If you see him, please say hi and tell him we miss him too!

Speaking of Heaven, I read a great book called, "Heaven is for Real", by Todd Burpo with Lynn Vincent. Mrs. Beer at Quincy Elementary School loaned it to me. I was so impressed with that book, I ordered 15 more copies of it to share with other people. The book is a true story about a little four year old boy who temporarily visits Heaven, while he is being operated on in the hospital for a burst appendix. It's very interesting, to say the least!

Jedidiah, that book, and the parents who wrote it, have inspired me to commit to writing a book about you. Of course, you told me many times during this past year, to write a book about you. Other people have mentioned it to me also. But it is such a huge step to decide to take on such a large challenge! It is SO easy to sit around and talk about doing things, but it is quite another matter to REALLY do those things! I am sharing the responsibility, and have made assignments to others to help. I have already asked your Blue Nanny, Justin, Dad and Jessica to each commit to writing a story about you. You will get a kick out of this one Jedidiah: I also asked two of your teachers if they were willing to take on the assignment of writing about you! Mrs. Lemnah and Mrs. Hochrein, being the great teachers and wonderful people they are, both said, "Of course, we would LOVE to write about Jedidiah!" The assignment is due from everyone on April 3rd. (To anyone else out there who likes to write and wants to contribute- you are welcome to mail your Jedidiah story to me.)

Your book is going to be called, 'Always Remember Me- The Story of Jedidiah Lusk.' I will be putting together stories this spring and summer, but really won't have time to sit down and focus on the whole project until next winter. So, it is going to be a big job to complete. But you know, Jedidiah, it's like I've told you and your brother and sister about taking on large projects. It is a lot like eating an elephant- you do it one bite at a time! The other day Jessica mentioned that she likes to work on things a little at a time- "I am doing it in INSTALLMENTS" she said. That's kind of how I am picking away at cleaning the upstairs, too! I've got another day scheduled next week to work on it again.

Jedidiah, we found a new home for your Go-Cart. I hope you and Robbi both approve! Last Saturday I loaded it up in the horse trailer- after first loading my two horses and closing the center divider, and hauled it to Quincy. I unloaded your Go-Cart at Quinn and JD's house. It's mostly for Quinn, but the family can share. We thought of Quinn because he is the little brother, just like you were the little brother in our family. I am sure they will enjoy it. Quinn's Mom, Devon, said she would keep me posted on their go-carting adventures.

Dad said to tell you at the first Johnsville Junior Ski Team Race of the year, the Director was handing out a new sticker. Dad got a couple to bring home. The sticker reads, "Racing In Memory of Jedidiah". The words are written in bold, black letters around the edges. The background is white, like the snow, and there is a ski racing figure in red, leaning around a racing gate in the middle of the sticker. There is a pretty red heart in the middle of the "O" in Memory. That is a super neat sticker! THANKS JJST!

Last night Justin played Basketball in Portola. I really hate to say it, but the Portola Tigers whipped the Quincy Trojans in that game. You know how it is, you win some, you lose some! Next we go to Los Molinos on Friday for an away basketball game. The last Home Game is going to be next Tuesday against Biggs. Then we travel to Hamilton City for the very LAST basketball game of the year on the following Friday.

Did you know that today, February 9th, is your Grandma Betty Lusk's Birthday? We called Wawee this morning and sang "Happy Birthday" to her on her cell phone. That was fun! And, indeed, she did sound happy! Jessica also got a card for her, that we all signed, that she put in the mail today.

Since today is Wednesday, I will be heading to QES this afternoon to help in Mrs. Hochrein's class. Two weeks ago she told me that she had an idea, of planting a fruit tree on your birthday next month. She asked if we thought it would be ok to plant the tree in the QES garden, and they will put a plaque next to the tree that reads, "In loving memory of Jedidiah Lusk. Always Be Positive". Everybody in your family thought that would be great, but we all thought of a different kind of fruit tree. Dad liked apple, I liked peach, Justin said pear, and Jessica thought plum. So I ended up telling Mrs. Hochrein to pick one that would grow best. I think you would be honored to have any one of those fruit trees planted at the school in your memory.

Speaking of next month, it will be March soon! My boss, Eric Graff, called and said it will soon be time to return to work at the Air Tanker Base- in March! Wow, how quickly the time has passed. Jedidiah, I will sure miss having you come up to Oregon and visit me at the Tanker Base this spring and summer. I know there are some Tanker Pilots that remember you, and they will miss your inquisitive questions, natural curiosity, and interesting conversations. I invited Jessica, Justin and Dad to come up for Spring Break, when school is out for the kids. Justin said he might, and Jessica said she may be in Santa Barbara visiting your cousin Christy. So, we will have to see what happens then. Dad is always interested in visiting Central Oregon, especially when it time for the Small Farmer's Auction. Lynn Miller hosts that at the Madras Fairgrounds and this year it will be April 15-17th.

Well, I better go for now, Jedidiah. Have more to say, but will save it for next time. We love you and Always Remember You!

Love, Mom

"*We also rejoice in our sufferings because we know that suffering produces perseverance; perseverance, character; and character, hope.*" Romans 5:2-4

Friday, February 11, 2011

Hi Jedidiah,

I went riding yesterday near Taylorsville. I rode Rose and lead Adam with a saddle on him. You would be glad to know he is doing great in his training. We made a large loop that consisted of going up the mountain above Foreman Ravine, across the side hill on a narrow trail, down a steep trail through the forest, across a creek, on a road through the snow for half a mile, up another hill, then down the Beardsley Grade road, which was dusty the last three miles. We saw wild turkeys, quail, and a couple of deer herds.

It was a super, wonderful day for riding! The sky was that beautiful, deep blue, which was your favorite color (the color Jessica christened, "Daytime Blue" quite a few years ago). The air was crisp and clean, and the snow on Grizzly Peak and Arlington was all a sparkle! It was not too cold, and I think the bright sunshine made it feel warmer. I rode Rose on that same loop last year, and there was more snow then, (but winter is not over as I hear it is going to snow more next Tuesday night). I just looked at my calendar to see when it was last year, and it was March 14th.

Jedidiah, I thought about you most of the day yesterday, especially since I was reflecting on how I felt on that ride last year, and how I was SO worried about you!

So here is my story about last year's ride: What I remember most was that my mind was surrounded in a painful fog. You were lying in a hospital bed at U.C. Davis Medical Center, still there one month after being diagnosed with a brain tumor. Your stay in that hospital lasted 33 days! Whew! And it was the first time I had been out and about, that far away from you, in a whole month! I was so steeped in worry and concern for you that it was very hard for me to think of anything else on that day. I remember thinking that it would do me good to get out and have some "Riding Therapy." I focused so hard just to get the horse trailer hooked up and all my tack together. I called my riding buddy and I bragged on myself that I had hooked up the trailer and gotten everything ready. That took a lot of concentration for me! My friend said, "Well, put the horse in the trailer and let's go!" I did not bother to try to explain how much energy it took to just accomplish the first step, and now it was time to move on to the next. Whew! But I finally made it to the riding area, and it was a good thing that I went out to spend the day on my horse. It was very therapeutic! While we rode the first couple of hours, my mind was still in a whirl of frenzied activity remembering the first few days with you in the hospital.

You were in so much pain that first night at U.C. Davis. You were having intense, painful headaches. I held you in my arms and rocked you while you lay crying, "Help me! Help me! It hurts Mommy! Make it stop!" I put my lips to his forehead and kissed you, and told you I would suck out all the pain in your head. The nurses gave you Tylenol and Ibuprofen, but to no avail. Your pain just kept getting worse. "We are going to have to do something else to take away his pain," I told the nurses. "What other, stronger painkillers can you give him?" You lay limply, whimpering quietly, "owh, owh, owh…" as I tried to comfort you.

One nurse replied, "Well, the next step would be to give him a shot of morphine."

"So, what are you waiting on?" I asked hotly, "He is in so much pain now!"

"Well, the doctor should ok it," the nurse hesitated. Another nurse walked up, "Let's just give him some now so he can rest tonight." The nurse looked at me with sympathy, "I am so sorry he has to be going through this. He is such a beautiful child!"

I looked down at you, Jedidiah, my youngest baby. You were only 8 years old, and a very wonderful little boy. Quite special to your family. Your face was all scrunched up in pain. I said a prayer for you, "Dear Lord, Please help my Jedidiah! Please ease his pain. Thank you. Amen."

I shook my head hard, back and forth, to clear those painful memories, telling myself I needed to get back to the present. I was on my horse, trying to enjoy the day. Rose flicked her ear and tilted her head back to see what I was doing. I rubbed her chestnut neck, "Thanks, Rose! I am glad we can get out today. I am just worried about my little Jedidiah!"

After two hours of riding, my friend proclaimed, "Its Lunch time!" We were near a little clearing in the woods, so we pulled over to tie the horses up to the trees. We each pulled out our lunches and settled on the dead grass, in the sunshine. There was a comforting warmth radiating from the sun into that clearing. After eating my snack, I laid down and stretched out in that sunshine. I put my sweatshirt under my back and my riding helmet under my head. I put my arms over my head and used my hands to block the sun from my eyes. I took a deep breath, and let it out. Another deep breath in. "Relax", I told myself. "It's ok to let go of the stress. You NEED to let go of the stress. Ok, breathe again...." I cleared my mind. It was the first time I could do that in the past month. Lack of sleep, intense stress, concern over you, thinking about the cancer, worrying about Jessica and Justin at home- them trying to press on while their little brother was in the hospital fighting for his life.... All of those matters, constantly swirling in my head while I stayed in the hospital with you for the past 30 days. "Wow", I thought. "That sure takes a toll on the body! It's been a rough go for all of us!" While living through those kind of conditions, it's just surviving day-to-day. Trying to hang on, one moment to the next moment. You don't really realize how much stress builds up in times like this.

I don't know how long I laid there. It must have been at least 30 minutes. The peace and quiet in the woods was wonderful! The sunshine was warm and healing! I was able to let the awful stress out of my body, and finally have room for peace, and I prayed, thanking God!

"And the peace of God, which passeth all understanding, shall keep your hearts and minds through Christ Jesus." Philippians 4:7 KJV.

Sunday night, February 13, 2011

Whew, Jedidiah, this has been a VERY busy last three days! We had an action packed weekend, so I thought I'd better tell you about it:

On Friday at 11:00, Jessica, Nanny and I all went riding together down at Sloat. Jessica rode Joy bareback, I rode Stormy, Nanny rode Treasure, and Nanny's friend Claire, rode Britches. It was another beautiful, spring-like day in February, so we thought we'd better get out and enjoy it while we could. So, enjoy it we did!! The horses all behaved themselves and acted happy to be out enjoying the day as well. We rode a loop, one that goes above the Middle Fork of the Feather River and has some wonderful views. So, guess we'll call that one "The Riverview Loop". It was a relaxing ride, and we made it back to the barn around 2:00 PM. Just in time to unsaddle and brush the horses, and get back home by 2:30. Then I had to change clothes and drive off to be at Quincy High School to pick Justin up, and drive him and three other boys to the Basketball Game in Los Molinos.

We stopped at In-N-Out Burger in Chico to let the boys have a snack before the game. We arrived in Los Molinos in time to see the last half of the QHS Girls Varsity game. I think the girls won that game, but the Boys Varsity lost. Justin played pretty well, I think he made 12 points, got some rebounds, and played pretty good defense. It is fun to watch him play basketball, just because he has fun playing. He doesn't get too upset. He just plays the game. Justin said the other team was kind of rude. But, you just got to smile and do your best anyway.

It was a late night. We did not get back home to Cromberg until 1:00 AM. Then we hurried off to bed. Made for a short night because the alarm clock went off at 0500 AM! I got up to make breakfast for the Ski Coaches, Scott and Jessica- who were headed off to Alpine Meadows. Then Justin woke up and went skiing too! He didn't want to miss out on all the FUN! I fed the horses then left the house at 0630, to head up to Bucks Lake. It was time for the Bucks Lake Poker Run, sponsored by the Bucks Lake Snowdrifters! So, I spent the day up there helping out with serving the tasty lunch! The snow was not too great- it is still frozen solid in the mornings, and finally warms in the afternoon, to thaw out to be a little mushy. We need some new snow to refresh the trails.

On my way home I stopped in Meadow Valley to say hi to Shawn Webb. It was so great to see him and his family, and give him a big hug! I am so grateful to Shawn, and all the things he did for you, Jedidiah. He is the one who got the Plumas County SWAT Team to come down to visit you while you were still in the hospital at U.C. Davis. They "Deputized" you and made you an Honorary Plumas County Sheriff's Deputy, AND a SWAT Team member. They gave you a Special SWAT jacket that we still have hanging in my closet. I still have the little badge they gave you too, and the Plumas County Sheriff's coin, also! Shawn has the same kind of brain tumor you had, those dreaded Glioblastoma multiformes. Darn! I hate those brain tumors!!

I got home about 5:30 PM, fed the horses and changed clothes. Dad, Jessica, and Justin got home at 6:00 PM, they changed out of their ski clothes, and we all headed into Quincy together. We had dinner at the First Baptist Church of Quincy- the Youth Group hosted a Valentine's Spaghetti Feed. It was GREAT! We had a really fun family time, being served and eating at a small table for four. We laughed a lot that night. (Maybe for Justin and i - it was sleep deprivation from the night before?) The room was decorated superbly, with hearts on the table cloths, pretty candles, and red heart decorations hanging from the ceiling. The Youth Group did a fantastic job! Your Dad loved the spaghetti and meatballs! We all did! Justin cleaned up his portion with no trouble at all. I couldn't quite eat all of mine. So, I helped fill Justin up. Then the CAKE arrived. A yummy desert too! We all left quite satisfied, with full tummies and a happy spirit!

On Sunday I hooked up the horse trailer and Dad, Nanny and I took our horses to Greenville to ride with Kassandra. Dad rode Red Horse, I rode Rose and Nanny took Joy. We rode on part of the trail that makes up the Patriot's Day Endurance Ride, and we went up "The Zipper" trail that is the hill climb up Keddie Ridge. We climbed and we climbed!. You should have seen the beautiful view, Jedidiah, it was breath taking! Jessica stayed home to sleep in, and Justin said he had homework to do, so your brother and sister missed out. I don't know that Justin ever did all his homework or not, Jessica said he was on the computer, reading Facebook all day!

When we got home from riding, Dad and I took out your brother and sister and treated them to the movies! We watched, "True Grit" at the Town Hall Theater. It was an adventure movie.

But the neat thing was, on our way driving to town with Jessica and Justin- we tuned in the new Radio Station, where at 6:30 PM we listened to a pre-recorded Family Radio Show, where Jessica and Justin read, "The Cremation of Sam McGee" by Robert Service, in your honor! They did such a fantastic job, you would be SO proud of your brother and sister!! Justin has a really good "Radio Voice", and Jessica was really quick thinking to come up with great answers in the interview after the poem. I don't know how they managed to sound so calm and organized. I am going to try to get a CD of that show so we can send it to your Cousins in Idaho.

Well, Jedidiah, I've got to go for now. Justin is having his LAST home Basketball game for the season tonight! I've got more to write, but I will tell you tomorrow. And tomorrow I will tell you all about our Valentine's Day! We LOVE you and we Miss You! But we will Always Remember You!!!

Love, Mom

"As soon as Jesus heard the word that was spoken, he saith unto the ruler of the synagogue, 'Be not afraid, only believe'." Mark 5:36, KJV

<u>Monday, February 14, 2011</u>

HAPPY VALENTINE'S DAY!

At 0700 Dad had us all gathered around the kitchen table opening Valentine presents! It was lots of fun! Jessica was a little bit of a sleepy head, but Nanny, Dad, Justin and I were all wide awake. Of course, there were gifts of chocolate- and a lot of it! Everybody in the family had picked a different kind of chocolate to give the rest of the family.

Jedidiah, it was one year ago today that you got diagnosed with the brain tumor. That Valentine's Day morning last year, you felt so sick, you did not want to open the presents that Dad got for you. You were so weak and tired, you did not even want to LOOK at the presents on the table that morning. So, I scooped you up and carried you to the car. It was a Sunday, and the doctor's clinics were not open, so i drove you straight to the Emergency Room at the hospital in Quincy.

THE CHICKS HAVE ARRIVED!!

I picked them up at the Post Office this morning at 0830. All 25 of them are alive and well. I hurried them back to the house, where I had their new home already in a small, rubber, horse water trough. I had put clean, dry hay in the bottom for bedding, plugged in a warming lamp, had a chick water container set up and chick food awaiting. The day old chicks are so cute and fluffy, and their "peep, peep" chirping sounds so happy!.

After I got the chicks all settled in their new home, I drove to Quincy Elementary School, to deliver Valentine's Day cards to Mrs. Hochrein's classroom. They had their party after lunch. It was neat to see at the kids enjoying cupcakes and opening their Valentine's cards. Jedidiah, all your classmates are such neat children. They are very polite!, They all said thank you, when I gave them each a glass of water and a napkin. Mrs. Hochrein is a good teacher, and the students reflect that.

Jedidiah, today is also your cousin, Carlin's, Birthday! She turns 16 years old. Jessica got a card for her that we all signed, and sent our Best Wishes to her.

Tuesday, February 15, 2011

All the chicks are still alive and doing great today! I am so happy for them. I think this is the healthiest bunch we have ever received in the mail from Murray McMurtury Hatchery.

Justin played his last basketball home game tonight. Quincy BEAT Biggs!! GO TROJANS! We head to last regular game of the season in Hamilton City on Friday night.

Wednesday, February 16, 2011

And Winter is back!! There is FRESH SNOW this morning! If you were still here with us Jedidiah, I know you would have jumped on your snowmobile FIRST thing this morning and went for a ride!! We all thought of you, and how much you enjoyed the new snow. I took a photo of the house for you, with snow on the deck!

This morning I told Justin he would have to leave early to drive his car slower than normal to get to school safely and on time. But as he was clearing the snow off his car, I received a message on my cell phone saying the Quincy Schools were on a 2 hour delay. So, Justin did not really have to leave early. Instead, he went for a drive around the neighborhood, to get the feel of how his car handles in the snow.

Jedidiah, we did have a Family Memorial Service for you at the Chicken Tree several weeks ago. We kept it private, with just our immediate family. We decided that whomever was there when you were born, and the same people who were with you when you died, could come to our family service for you. I have just avoided talking about it because it is SO HARD and HURTS so much to realize that you are REALLY gone from us- (Until we get to Heaven to meet up with you again). But, we talked about you, laughed and cried, and read the Will you had written back on September 13, 2010. As you requested: Nanny got your Cotton Candy Machine, I got your "Weindeer", Justin got your Snowmobile (and the urinal you said he could have!), You gave Dad your blue Nano I-Pod, and to Jessica you gave your large, stuffed Easter Bunny (and you wrote that she could have your bedroom!). We all got a chuckle when we read the part you wrote that your cat, Black Lightning, had to share her toys with Nanny's cat, Emerald!

At your service, Justin read a story called, "The Fork", that Dr. Segura gave him at school one day. I am going to ask Justin if he still has that, so I can make a copy to keep. It was pretty interesting. Maybe I can write it down in one of my letters to you also.

Then we each grabbed a handful of your ashes and let the breeze blow them around the woods at the Chicken Tree. We thought of the love we all shared together, and how you made our lives so much richer, with your humor, your jokes, your tenacity, and your courage. Thank you Jedidiah!!

Thursday February 24, 2011

Hey Jedidiah,
    We still miss you a ton!
    We are sad a whole lot without you!
    Last night was Justin's last basketball game of the season. It was the first playoff game, but Quincy lost to Durham. It was an away game in Durham. Funny thing was that Quincy AND Durham both shared the "Trojan" mascot. So, I had to yell, "Go Quincy", instead of "Go Trojans!"

Justin played well! He made three 3 point shots and one regular basket, (but he missed both of his free throws) for a total of 11 points in the game. He grabbed plenty of rebounds and made some assists too.

Durham started off the game by stealing Quincy's pass. Then they went down and made a basket! They were good players who made a high percentage of their attempted shots. Quincy did NOT. So, we lost. Basketball season is over.

Justin started Baseball practice today. Though I think it will be another month or two before QHS can play baseball on their baseball field. It is BURIED in snow. So the baseball team has to practice inside the gym. More snow is on the way tonight and tomorrow. We already have THREE FEET of snow on the ground at our house, Jedidiah.

Dad and I have been riding snowmobiles from the house. There is plenty of snow to go blasting through. In fact, we found there is SO MUCH snow- that it is TOO easy to get stuck in! So we have gotten good at digging the machines out and turning them around. Dad says we need bigger snowmobiles, with longer paddles! But I think then we would just get stuck worse.

Saturday February 26, 2011

Jedidiah, we received a couple more feet of snow Thursday night and Friday morning. Too much snow! We have been busy digging the vehicles out and running the snowmobiles down the driveway and back to pack the snow down. The snowmobile you earned has been running great, and has been very helpful to have this winter.

Justin has had no school this week, due to "Winter Break". His baseball practice was cancelled on Friday. He has been catching up on his homework, shoveling snow off his car, feeding the chickens, and riding the snowmobiles with Dad. We think of you often, and know you would be just LOVING this week of SNOW and Winter Break!!

We received word on Friday, Jedidiah, that your friend, Shawn Webb passed away early morning yesterday. Shawn died from a Glioblastoma multiformes brain tumor too. Hope you two are sharing some good jokes and conversation in heaven, now that you are both free from brain cancer!

Justin made a copy of the story he read at your family memorial service. This is what Dr. Segura, the Principal at Quincy High School, gave to Justin. I have no idea who wrote it. There is no author's name on the page. That's too bad, because someone had the bright idea to write it down to share it. Now, I can't give them the credit. But, anyway, here it is:

"A WOMAN AND A FORK"
Author Unknown

There was a young woman who had been diagnosed with a terminal illness and had been given three months to live. So as she was getting her things "in order," she contacted her Pastor and had him come to her house to discuss certain aspects of her final wishes.

She told him which songs she wanted sung at the service, what scriptures she would like read, and what outfit she wanted to be buried in...

Everything was in order and the Pastor was preparing to leave when the young woman suddenly remembered something very important to her.

"There's one more thing," she said excitedly.

"What's that?" came the Pastor's reply.

"This is very important," the young woman continued. "I want to be buried with a fork in my right hand."

The Pastor stood looking at the young woman, not knowing quite what to say.

"That surprises you, doesn't it?" the young woman asked.

"Well, to be honest, I'm puzzled by the request," said the Pastor.

The young woman explained. "My grandmother once told me this story, and from that time on I have always tried to pass along its message to those I love and those in need of encouragement. In all my years of attending socials and dinners, I always remember that when the dishes of the main course were being cleared, someone would inevitably lean over and say, "Keep your fork". It was my favorite part because I knew that something better was coming... like velvety chocolate cake or deep dish apple pie... something wonderful and with substance."

Then I want you to tell them: "Keep your fork, the best is yet to come..."

The Pastor's eyes welled up with tears of Joy as he hugged the young woman good-bye. He knew this would be one of the last times he would see her before her death... but he also knew that the young woman had a better grasp of what Heaven would be like than many people twice her age, with twice as much experience and knowledge... She KNEW that something better was coming.

At the funeral people were walking by the young woman's casket and they saw the cloak she was wearing and the fork placed in her right hand. Over and over, the Pastor heard the question, "What's with the fork?" And over and over he smiled.

During his message, the Pastor told the people of the conversation he had with the young woman shortly before she died. He also told them about the fork and about what it symbolized to her. He told the people how he could not stop thinking about the fork and told them that they probably would not be able to stop thinking about it either.

He was right... So the next time you reach down for your fork, let it remind you, ever so gently, that the best is yet to come. Friends are a very rare jewel, indeed. They make you smile and encourage you to succeed. They lend an ear, they share a word of praise, and they always want to open their hearts to us.

Show your friends how much you care. Remember to always be there for them, even when you need them more. For you never know when it may be their time to, "Keep your fork!"

Cherish the time you have, and the memories you share.

Hope you enjoyed that story, Jedidiah. After Justin made a copy of the story for me to keep, Dad engraved on one of his favorite forks, "Jedidiah Lusk- 3/30/01- 1/3/11." Then we took the fork up to the Chicken Tree on the snowmobiles, and screwed the fork to the tree, in your honor. So, every time we go past the Chicken Tree and see that fork there, we will think of YOU! We will always remember you, Jedidiah!

"And to know the love of Christ, which passeth knowledge, that ye might be filled with all the fullness of God." Ephesians 3:19 KJV.

Thursday March 3, 2011

Hi Jedidiah,

This past week has been a regular whirlwind of activity! Busy, busy, busy as usual...

The biggest thing we have been dealing with is: TOO MUCH SNOW!!

I finally hollered, "Uncle!" and called a backhoe in to remove some snow. Mr. Caley drove his backhoe down from the top of Gill Ranch Road, and started plowing from the corner of Gill Ranch and Cat Tail Roads. I asked him to push the snow out of the way to make room to park a car or two right there at the road junction. Jessica's little car can't make it in the driveway in four inches of snow, much less four FEET of snow. So, now we have a place for her to park.

Mr. Caley pushed snow out of the quarter mile dirt driveway to our house, then he moved snow from the loop around our house. When you remove snow from one place, you need to find another place to put it. So Mr. Caley piled a bunch of snow from the loop around the house, in a corner between the horse trailer and the basketball court. It made a HUGE mountain of snow! Mr. Caley worked nearly three hours, moving snow for us. When Dad came home at lunch time, he saw that large mound of snow and remarked, "Wow, wouldn't Jedidiah have loved playing on that pile of snow?!"

"Yes, he would." I said.

When Nanny came home later that afternoon, and she saw that pile of snow, the first thing she said was, "My, wouldn't Jedidiah have loved to play 'King of The Mountain' on top of that snow?"

"Yes, he would," I replied for the second time that day. Of course, Jedidiah, these days, practically EVERYTHING reminds us of you.

Here is a photo of Dad riding his snowmobile. An activity we did almost daily during this past week. The snow was so deep, Dad was pushing snow up over the hood of the snowmobile. We had to stand up while riding, to see past the snow flying over the windshield!

Yesterday I went to Mrs. Hochrein's class. Her students are working on a really cool musical play. I got to watch them practice the play on the QES stage. It looks like a whole lot of fun! There is lots of singing and dancing, plus the speaking parts. Plenty of activity for everyone in the class. I don't know the title of the play, but it's about the Westward Movement. The kids are learning some good history lessons too.

After the play practice, we performed a science experiment involving dirt, water and rocks. With the combination of those three items, you know the students had fun! I did the experiment three times, for three groups of kids, so each small group could have some hands on learning. We talked about the role of water and gravity in soil erosion.

I know you would have enjoyed that Jedidiah! As the eight year old boy you were a year ago, I think you had become somewhat of an expert in what happens when you mix soil and water, plus a few rocks. On the Friday before you got sick, when there was no school that day, you and Justin spent practically the whole day 'working' in the small stream of water near the house. You boys were making rock and soil dams, directing water into several different rivulets, floating things down the rivers, racing bark boats, mixing up the mud, stomping your feet in it, jumping across the streams, and who knows what else. Basically, you were learning science, hydrology, physics, and geology, plus doing P.E., all rolled into one fun day!

Justin played his first Quincy High Baseball Game on Tuesday, March 1. They played down in East Nicolas, and Dad drove some boys down so he could watch the game. QHS lost. Justin said the game was called because of darkness, but really, he said, "They called the game before Quincy had time to make a comeback!" Justin was just getting ready to go up to bat.

Monday March 7, 2011

Hi Jedidiah, Its Monday, after a busy weekend.

We all went to Shawn Webb's Memorial Service on Saturday. There were a lot of Police Officers there, and I saw many of your fellow SWAT Team Members. Sheriff Greg Hagwood gave a very nice speech, about what a gift Shawn's life was. I think the same thing about your life, Jedidiah. Your life was really a gift to your family and to our community.

We are all missing Shawn very much too. He was a great man, friend, and police officer.

Pastor George Tarleton was there also, at Shawn's service, in the role of Sheriff Chaplain. At the reception following the service, George said something that made us laugh. He asked, "and how is the Purple

Grandma?" I didn't get it for a few minutes, then it popped into my mind he was referring to Blue Nanny. She was there with us, chuckled, and said she was fine.

The 25 baby chicks are all doing fine too. They have grown SO much this past two weeks. They have feathers now, and are trying to flap their little wings and fly. I am going to put them in a larger trough and move them to the tack room, so they have more room to exercise and grow out there.

The chicks are very curious about their world around them. When Nanny plays the harp up in the loft, the chicks want to see out, to see what is making that noise. One little chick learned to jump up and sit on top of the water container. He did that while Nanny was playing, and he got to watch her play the harp. I think he rather enjoyed the concert!

Justin brought a couple chicks down to the kitchen the other night, put them on the floor, and brought Pep over to see what she thought of the baby chicks. Pep did NOT know what to think ! She ran away barking and growling. Then she came back to sniff and investigate the two chicks. One was a white chick, and the other was brown. Pep did not like the white chick. It was bolder and tried to peck Pep on the nose. She ran off growling again, but came back to see if the brown chick was nicer. Brown chick just looked at Pep, and cocked his head like he did not know what to make of a tiny Chihuahua, either. Guess it was a stare-down between the two different species.

We didn't let the two large male cats in the house much, while the chicks were little. One time they got in, and I caught Babycakes laying on top of the chicken wire covering the chick's container. He was sticking his paw through the round openings in the wire and he was trying to reach they chicks- with his claws! Of course they were all chirping for help, running and flapping all over. That's what got my attention, and I kicked the cat OUT!

We miss you Jedidiah! We all LOVE YOU SO MUCH!!

With a Lotta Love, Mom

"Then said Jesus unto his disciples, 'If any man will come after me, let him deny himself, and take up his cross, and follow me. For whosoever will save his life shall lose it: and whosoever will lose his life for my sake shall find it. For what is a man profited,

if he shall gain the whole world, and lose his soul?'" Matthew 16: 24-26, KJV.

Mar 9, 2011

WHAT IN THE WORLD IS A "CHICKEN TREE"?

A few people have asked me this question, so I thought I might as well tell everybody.

The Chicken Tree is where we scattered some of Jedidiah's ashes, and also put a fork with his name on the tree.

It is a large tree, of the Black Oak variety, (Quercus kellogii), that lives up in the woods about 250 yards north of our house.

For the past five years, since we purchased this property and built our home, the Chicken Tree is the place we take our dead critters; such as chickens, rabbits, ducks, turkeys, etc. Since we have a small farm and raise lots of animals, the children have seen the whole cycle of life, from reproduction, to new life, to old age, and death.

Our Chicken Tree is hollow in the middle, and we deposit the dead animal inside the hollow space. The kids would always go trudging up to the tree with their beloved, dead pet, say a prayer for the animal, and a few days later they would come back and see that the animal's body was gone! It must have seemed quite mysterious to them.

I always explained that even though their pet was dead, it would be providing life, in the form of a meal, to the next animal that came along. We have many wildlife neighbors, and have seen, in person, or signs of: gray fox, coyote, bobcat, black bear, mountain lion, raccoon, and skunk.

Now, I do not like to make a practice of feeding the wildlife, so don't get me wrong. But, in a way, this kills two birds with one stone, so to speak.

As Jedidiah was growing up, I guess it made a pretty big impression on him, as he did ask us to spread his ashes there.

We miss you very much Jedidiah! We WUV YOU!

"Peace I leave with you, my peace I give unto you: not as the world giveth, give I unto you. Let not your heart be troubled, neither let it be afraid." St. John 14:27 KJV

Saturday March 19, 2011

Hey Jedidiah,

The good news is:

We awoke to two feet of fresh snow here in Cromberg this morning! Yippee, we hopped on the snowmobiles and went for a ride! Snow was light and fluffy, just like you would have enjoyed. Dad and I thought of you as we poured gas in the snowmobiles and took off this morning. It snowed all day yesterday, and most of the night last night. Dad took this photo of me, almost to the Mud Road. We rode down towards the highway and then headed up Rattlesnake Road. We only got partway up, and got stuck! It's all uphill, you know, and we were pushing snow over the front of the snowmobiles. So we got the machines unstuck, turned around, headed back down to the packed road, turned around again and made another run at it. Got another 100 yards past our previous stuck area and that was it. Oh well! Dug out again... So, we just enjoyed riding back over our packed trail. As you know, Dad's back can only take so much of digging, lifting, and getting his snowmobile unstuck! But, we sure did have fun. Tomorrow it will be Justin's and Dad's day to go play on the snowmobiles, as I have to drive to Oregon to be at my Aviation COR Training in Redmond on Monday.

The bad news is:

Yesterday we learned that our young friend, Dozer Garret, has developed a new, "Inoperable" brain tumor, in a new area of his brain. **Darn! Darn! Darn!**

Dozer is ten years old and lives in Oklahoma. We have been hoping and praying with his family since we learned about him last May. He was diagnosed with a GBM, and has been traveling to Pittsburg to take an experimental vaccine to help fight the brain cancer. We are STILL praying for him!!

On a lighter note, Jedidiah, your Dad and I went to QES on Wednesday and watched Mrs. Hochrein's class perform their play about the Westward Movement. It was great!! Your classmates did an excellent job of remembering their lines and singing their songs. We sure did enjoy that.

Well, more things later. Love you! We Always Remember You!

Love, Mom

"Blessed be God, even the Father of our Lord Jesus Christ, the Father of mercies, and the God of all comfort; who comforted us in all our tribulations, that we may be able to comfort them which are in any trouble, by the comfort wherewith we ourselves are comforted of God." 2 Corinthians 1: 3-4 JKV.

Apr 6, 2011

Okay, one last update in CaringBridge to tie everything together for you folks out there, then I am going to focus on writing the book about Jedidiah.

It's been over three months since Jedidiah died on January 3, 2011. It has been a tough go for ALL of us- family, friends, and classmates of Jedidiah. That pretty much encompasses everybody who ever met Jedidiah. Once Jedidiah met someone, he wanted to be their friend. Not just their friend, but their Good Friend!

I am still running into acquaintances, who heard bits and pieces about Jedidiah last year, and they ask, "….and your little boy, the one with the brain tumor. … Oh, yes, and how is he doing?"

And I have to look them in the face and tell them, "Well, Jedidiah died in January."

Their eyes widen in disbelief, and they say, "I am so sorry! I am SO, SO, very sorry!"

"Yeah, so am i."

So, life goes on… But it is only with the grace and courage from our Lord above, that we can find the strength to go on too. God is good, and don't let anyone tell you anything different!

March 30, 2011 would have been Jedidiah's 10th Birthday. We celebrated.

I guess we actually started the celebrations the weekend before, when Scott, Jessica, Justin and I met at the Peppermill on Saturday night. I drove down from my job in Oregon, and Scott and the kids drove over after skiing with Johnsville Junior Ski Team at Homewood. We met at the Peppermill because it was always one of Jedidiah's favorite places to go, and because we were combining the celebrations of Scott & Cynthia's 25th Wedding Anniversary, Justin's 17th Birthday, and what would have been Jedidiah's

10th Birthday. AND- because Jedidiah paid our way with the money he left in his Piggy Bank!

Jedidiah would NEVER let anyone touch his Piggy Bank while he was alive. He must have started saving about five years ago. He was saving ALL his money for a Snowmobile! That started even before his Dad told him he could learn to play a certain fiddle song to EARN his snowmobile.

As Justin was growing up, he liked to take out his money to count it. He would sort thru it, put it in piles, re-sort it, add it up, take it away, put it back, re-count it, etc. Justin kept asking Jedidiah, "Don't you want to count your money?" Jedidiah would simply say, "No." Justin kept at him, "Well, if you don't want to count your money, then can I count your money?" Jedidiah would answer with a resounding, "NO!" As time continued, his answer never changed. He would not ever count his money, let anyone else count his money- or even touch his piggy bank, for that matter.

It was hard for us to do, but we all finally agreed last month that Justin could open Jedidiah's piggy bank and count the money. To our surprise, Jedidiah had left almost two hundred dollars! So, then the discussion was: What shall we do with the money, in Jedidiah's memory? The general consent was to do something fun, to use the money for something Jedidiah would have enjoyed. Then we thought of the All-You-Could-Eat-Buffet- that was a big highlight for Jedidiah when he got out of the hospital and was finished with his radiation. He enjoyed inviting all his cousins to join him there. That was a happy memory for all of us. So, we took Jedidiah's money to Reno! (And, no, we did NOT try to double it first!!). We slept and ate, talked, laughed and cried- All in Memory of Jedidiah!

Then, on Jedidiah's Birthday, we were invited to Quincy Elementary School to plant a young, bare-root, Peach Tree at the school garden. Teacher Mrs. Hochrein and Jedidiah's class of fourth graders came outside to assist, on what was a beautiful, sunny, Spring day. It is always fun to watch the children when they are excited, and being outside in that garden, planting a tree for Jedidiah was no exception! Principal Mr. Williams and Secretary Mrs. Beer even came outside for the occasion. It was a great time!

Jedidiah's Mom and Dad, brother Justin and sister Jessica, Grandma Blue Nanny and Uncle John were all there. A plaque was made (and after some upgrades) will be installed at the base of the newly planted peach tree. It reads: "In Loving Memory of our Friend, Jedidiah Lusk, March 30, 2001- January 3, 2011, 'Always Be Positive'".

THANKS SO MUCH TO ALL!!

"We are confident, I say, and willing rather to be absent from the body, and to be present with the Lord." 2 Corinthians 5: 8 KJV

Cynthia's Stories
Deputy Shawn Webb

I pulled my Subaru into the multi-storied parking garage at UC Davis Medical Center, found a parking spot and turned off the engine. I just sat in the car for a few minutes, steeling myself for yet another week long stay inside the hospital. I had just driven the three hour trip from home, while Scott had stayed at the hospital with Jedidiah over the weekend. Two quick days at my house, and back here again. I removed my hands from the steering wheel, took some long, deep breaths, and settled into the driver's seat of my car. Leaving my small, beloved mountain home and driving down to the city of Sacramento always stressed me out. But I had made it here safely, with a couple nights of good sleep under my belt, and a recharged spirit from visiting my home and horses.

I glanced over at my open notebook and the words I had written earlier that day. There was a name: "Shawn Webb, with the words: "Plumas County Sheriff Deputy" and "GBM brain tumor"", and some other assorted, scribbled notes. There were some phone numbers and other names, the blue ink scrawl barely recognizable. I had been calling around, talking to friends of friends, trying to track down this person. I recalled reading an article in the local newspaper a while back, about a man who had been recently diagnosed with a brain tumor. I had not paid much attention at the time. It was not anybody I knew. In fact, the article said he and his family were new to the community. There was a recent fundraiser that had been planned and held to benefit this man, to cover some of the costs of his treatment for brain cancer.

My cell phone rang, cutting into my thoughts. "Hello, this is Cynthia," I answered.

"You don't know me," said a man's voice. "My name is Shawn Webb."

"No kidding?" I interrupted him. "I was just sitting here staring at your name in my notebook!! I was trying to find out your phone number..."

"Well, I have been thinking about calling you for the last few days. I just thought I'd better do it now."

"I am so glad you called!" I was incredulous. What timing!

"I have the same tumor as your son."

"Whoa, that is weird. I heard that GBM's are very rare."

"I'd like to meet your son sometime", he went on. "Maybe we can get together?"

"Well, he will be here at UC Davis in the hospital for awhile. I just drove back from Quincy today. Next time I am in town I will give you a call. I would like to meet you."

"That sounds good!" Shawn said. "Maybe I can bring the SWAT Team down to visit your son in the hospital. Would he like that?"

"Oh, Jedidiah would love that!" I answered, wondering if he was serious, and if really would follow through. If so, that could be a really special day for Jedidiah to look forward to.

"Listen, I've got to go now," he said. "But let's stay in touch. Here is my phone number. Call anytime, and come see me next time you are in town."

"All right, thank you. I will do that!"

"Good bye now."

"Bye-Bye."

Suddenly, I was smiling to myself. For some reason, the call from this man cheered me up. I was so glad he called. I was looking forward to meeting him. Just that little bit of human contact, a positive sounding voice, and it made my whole day seem brighter.

I got out of the car and strode into the hospital with purposeful steps.

Scott glanced up as I entered the room. He looked tired. He was sitting in the chair, bent over close to Jedidiah's bed.

"You would never guess who just called me" I said excitedly.

"Who?" asked Scott. "Was it Ed McMahan with a million dollars?"

"No! It was Shawn Webb."

"Who is that?"

"It's the guy from Quincy who has the same brain tumor that Jedidiah has. He is a deputy sheriff"

"Another GBM?"

"Yep. And he said he might bring the SWAT Team down to visit Jedidiah here in the hospital."

"That would be great."

"Yeah, I bet Jedidiah would love that"

"How could be get all those guys to come all the way down here, just to visit Jedidiah?" Scott wondered.

"Don't know," I answered. "But it would be super cool for him." I looked over, where Jedidiah laid sprawled sideways across the bed, asleep.

And Shawn did come to the hospital a couple weeks later! And the next day, he did bring the Plumas County SWAT Team with him!! They came fully dressed in camo gear, all looking like strong, confident men. There were four of them, plus Shawn. They made quite an appearance, striding through the Pediatric Ward of UC Davis Medical Center! I will always remember that day with great appreciation to each and every one of them.

CaringBridge Journal

When Jedidiah was admitted to the UC Davis Medical Center in Sacramento, I received a handful of paperwork; brochures, notes, admission slips and a bunch of informational pages...Okay, so it was more than a handful- it was more like an armload full of STUFF! It was too much for me to deal with at the time. So, what does a good leader do, before they get overwhelmed by too many things? They DELEGATE!! So, I started doing just that....

I went thru my piles of paperwork. I handed some to Scott, some to Justin, some to Jessica, and some to my mother, followed by the verbal instructions: "Please take care of this for me!"

I had not known that Jessica received the CaringBridge brochure when I was making the rounds handing out "Stuff" to each one of them. She took my advice to heart and set out to create a website, through an organization called "CaringBridge". This website allowed many people to get regular updates on Jedidiah's condition without calling and possibly bothering us at inconvenient times.

According to the website at: www.CaringBridge.org, "CaringBridge is the world's first and most widely used free online service for keeping families and loved ones connected when facing a serious medical condition, receiving treatment and while recovering. Its mission is to bring together a global community of care powered by the love of family and friends in an easy, accessible and private way."

We are extremely grateful to this organization. It was an amazing idea! We utilized their free services and were very happy with how easy it was to post updates and notes into the Journal.

Jessica was the one who initiated this for Jedidiah. She took the time each and every day to update the website, while he was in the Intensive Care Unit. She poured her heart and soul into this project. While worrying about her little brother whose life was in grave danger, she was also a freshman at Feather River College, attending her classes, completing assignments, doing homework and studying for finals.

It was a very stressful time in Jessica's life, yet she unflinchingly took on this additional project, and succeeded with flying colors. THANK YOU JESSICA!

When the time came that I decided to get serious about writing this book, I wanted to get stories and input from lots of people who had contact with Jedidiah. I especially wanted to get the very best stories from those closest to Jedidiah- his brother and sister. When I approached Jessica to ask for her story, she just looked at me with that exasperated, "How come you don't understand, Mom?" look on her face.

I did not understand, so she had to spell it out for me. "I already wrote my heart out! I put everything I had into that CaringBridge Journal, Mom. Okay? I don't have any more desire to write anything else about Jedidiah. It's just way too hard!"

I did NOT realize how hard it was for her to update Jedidiah's journal, until I took it over, after Jessica got burned out on it. After each entry, I would be emotionally drained. Yes, Jessica, I understand now. Thank you for what you did.

With Justin also, he did not directly give me any written stories about Jedidiah. Though, he did tell me he had written one- while sitting high upon the mountain behind our house, at a special place we call "The Overlook." Justin was trying hard to focus on getting through school, one day at a time. His outlet was sports. I got his stories indirectly, by bits and pieces- about Jedidiah, in the speeches he wrote and spoke.

I found out the hard way, it was most difficult for the ones closest to Jedidiah, to write about him. It was like pulling teeth to get the family to write. I made a few half-hearted attempts myself, to get it together enough to start to write a book. I invited many other people to submit their letters and stories to me. But I did not receive a whole lot of submissions or help. Apparently, the process of putting all your emotions, thoughts, and feelings in writing is just too painful for most people. It was just too soon, I decided. Maybe I can ask them later… But I was afraid if I waited too long, then the memories would fade, along with the pain that was felt, of trying to conjure up all those memories of Jedidiah….

Scott, bless his heart, tried really hard to write his story down too. After repeated requests and pleading, Scott proudly handed me his 18 page story. The content was there, with much love, and some history. But the story was all jumbled up; there was no logical order to it. It was kind of how my brain felt also, the memories of Jedidiah, so many, many of them…. and where to start? His story bounced from recent times, to Jedidiah as a baby, then to a story in the past, then jumped forward to him being in the hospital, and how mad Scott was at the doctors at U.C. Davis, for not doing more for Jedidiah. How could I unravel this story, to make some sense of it, to interpret it for someone else to read?

How am I ever going to be able to follow through on writing a book about Jedidiah? The thought caused utter panic. Repeatedly I would ask myself HOW will I do this, WHEN will I do this?….Aaaahhh!

So, I just started compiling my stories together….some from here, some from there. Little by little… I tried, just for Jedidiah's sake! I am NOT good with computers. I do enjoy writing, but I hate sitting still for any length of time. I am also easily distracted….I have WAY too many things to get gone around the house, the yard, with all the animals…and I still have to work some of the time….There is just NEVER enough time.

Secrets of a Cancer Caregiver

(I wrote this when asked to give the "Caregiver Perspective" speech at the 2010 Relay-for-Life, in Quincy, CA)

CANCER!! Just the very word can strike fear into the heart of most people. But, honestly, it wasn't something that I spent much time worrying about. I just did not think about it. I had never participated in this Relay-For–Life. I have never been involved in any other cancer fundraiser, either. Cancer was <u>always</u> someone else's problem.

Hello, my name is Cynthia Lusk. I am the mother and caregiver of a nine-year-old boy with a Glioblastoma Multiformes brain tumor. My son, Jedidiah, has brain cancer.

Now, suddenly, cancer IS MY Problem!

So, what is it like to be the Primary Caregiver of someone with Cancer?

Well, for me, it has been mentally terrifying, financially draining, and emotionally devastating.

And, oh, did I mention, it's been totally and completely EXHAUSTING?! It's only been 4 months since my son was diagnosed with brain cancer. Feels more like 10 years!

So, what is a mere mortal to do when faced with this sort of situation? How does a caregiver approach this humungous job?

Being a caregiver requires lots of strength and a ton of courage.

Many of us caregivers did not get a choice in this matter. We were thrust, unwillingly, into this role solely by the fact that our loved ones got cancer.

The grief begins the moment of diagnosis, the minute you hear that CANCER word.

You need to acknowledge the grief. Yes, it hurts! Yes, it's sad! Yes, it's bad! And, yes, you will get mad!

If you have been around horses much, you may have heard of the "Fight or Flight Response". It is that first instinctive response to a sudden surprise or scare, the initial surge of adrenalin that can be used to run away really fast to save yourself or to pump up the muscles to get ready to fight. YEAH, it would have been nice to just run away and <u>not</u> deal with it. The Flight option sounded pretty good at the time of diagnosis! But, as a parent, you really do not have that option. So you stay there and Fight.

In order to fight, you need to gather your strength. You need to know just where your source of strength comes from. Gather up all the strength you can, and utilize it. You will need ALL of it you can find, because being a caregiver is such an overwhelming job.

It is also a very humbling job. At times you feel completely powerless. You need to turn to your source of power to fight the cancer. Turning to God, reading the Bible, praying, talking to your friends and family... you need to do all of these. You need to gather up your support group for yourself. You can't cope alone.

For me, it was such a blessing knowing I had 2 or 3 good friends I could call any time day or night. Not that I really needed them every second, but just knowing they were there, provided me with a great feeling of comfort and relief. I am still thanking God for putting those people into my life.

The next important thing you will need is your sense of humor. Laughter TRULY is the Best Medicine. Jedidiah's favorite gift he received in the hospital, was a huge Joke Book. He begged us to read it to him for hours at a time. One of the best things I learned from Jedidiah is: "When in doubt, LAUGH!"

It REALLY does work! Laughter dissolves stress! It is impossible to feel hopeless when you are holding your side that aches from too much laughter. So, laugh anywhere, anytime, all the time!

Recently, someone asked me, "How can you even THINK about laughing at a time like this?"

In turn I asked them, "How can you even SURVIVE without laughing at a time like this?"

Make a point of having fun! Enjoy every day!

But how does one bridge that huge gap between emotional devastation and being able to enjoy the time you have with your loved one?

I learned from another cancer survivor, who told me, "Start by finding one positive thing a day and build on that."

Surely you can find just one good thing within a 24-hour period?! You may have to look hard, adjust your attitude, squint your eyes, and look again....

But, wait! There it is! That one POSITIVE thing! After seemingly hours and days of dreary dread and anguish. And then.... You find another one-... something positive in the place you least expect it!

Sooner or later, you are seeking, and finding, MORE positive items! Wow.

And that is how it is. We live hour-by-hour, day-to-day. We are here to celebrate LIFE!

That is NOT to say there won't be any more challenges, any more intense sadness, or sudden onset of fear.

Those will continue also, but don't let them overpower you.

From my standpoint, the Secrets of a Cancer Caregiver are:

1. Acknowledge Grief
2. Gather your Strength
3. Embrace Humor
4. Celebrate Life

SOME STORIES ABOUT JEDIDIAH
By Cynthia

The Biggest Booger

Jedidiah sat in his brown chair at home. He had his finger in his nostril, digging around, like little boys often do. I looked away for a few moments. When I looked back, he was still at it, a look of intense concentration on his face.

"Jedidiah! Just what ARE you trying to do?"

"Well, I've got this big booger way up inside my nose, and it just won't come out! I keep trying and I keep trying, but it's just out of reach..." and he was digging some more.

"So, what's the matter? Is your finger too short?" I joked with him.

Jedidiah frowned at me. "No, Mom, I just want to get it out. It's blocking my breathing! See?" He breathed heavily in and out a few times, just to show me.

"I think you are still breathing."

"MOM! Here, you look. Maybe you can get it out?"

I looked up the appointed nostril, and only saw pink mucous membranes. "Looks all clear to me." I quickly said.

"No, it's up further. Get a flashlight!"

So, I humored him and got a flashlight. I shined it all around to show him how bright it was. Then I went for the nostril. "Say AHHH! No wait, that's for the throat. Where is that booger? Oh, it is in the NOSE!"

Jedidiah tilted his head back and I focused the light. This time I saw bright pink, shiny mucous membranes. I wiggled his nose around, shined the light around this way and that. Nothing new that I could see.

"No boogers in sight," I announced. "The coast is all clear!" I turned off the light.

"But I know one is in there!" Jedidiah insisted. "And I have to get it out!"

"Well, let's try this then. Blue Nanny says to spray saline water up there." I grabbed the bottle off the table and presented it to him. "Here, just a dab will do you." I took the lid off, inserted the tip in Jedidiah's nostril and squeezed the bottle. "You want some in the other side, just for good measure too? And here is a tissue so you can blow." I wanted to make sure Jedidiah felt comfortable. He let me squish the saline mist up each of his nostrils, and accepted the tissue to wipe his nose. He looked up at me. "I sure hope it comes out soon!"

Four days later, I am in the kitchen washing the dishes, when Jedidiah calls out for me, "Mom, come quick!"

"Do you need the potty?" I ask.

"No, just come here!" I dash over to his side, wondering just what could he want this time?

"I got it!!" he beams at me, a triumphant look on his face.

"Got what?" I ask, puzzled.

"The giant booger," Jedidiah explains. "I have been trying to get it for this past hour. Then, all of a sudden, it just slides out. See?" He proudly proffers his pointer finger, with a gooey mess at the end of it, as large around as my thumb.

"Uhh, Yucky.... Now, what are you going to do with it?"

"Hey Mom, can you put this booger in a sandwich bag? I can't wait to show this to Justin and Dad!"

Getting Pep or "**Mom, I want a Chihuahua!**"

"Mom, I really do want to get a little Chihuahua puppy. Remember when Dad gave me that gift certificate for a kitten last Christmas? What I **really** wanted was a puppy. Did you know that?" Jedidiah asked, in all seriousness.

"I know you'd like to get a dog. But we already got you three new kittens and..."

"Black Lightning is my kitten," Jedidiah explained. "But Midnight and Baby Cakes are Justin's and Jessica's kittens, not mine."

"Besides, the cats won't stay in my lap when I want to pet them. They jump up and walk off when they want to. I can't teach them tricks, and take them to town with me. A puppy would be a whole lot more fun. And I want a special kind. It has to be a Chihuahua!"

"You are sure of that? Only a Chihuahua?

"Yes," Jedidiah answered earnestly. "My very own Chihuahua!"

"You think this Chihuahua will make you happy?" I questioned.

Jedidiah looked me straight in the eye, making sure he had my attention, and he paused. "Yes, Mom, I know it will," he said. "My Chihuahua will make me very, very happy." Then he paused, and finally asked: "Mom, you don't want me to die unhappy, do you?"

Just then, I felt a knife-like pain in my heart. I could hardly speak. But I knew this was something important I had to address. "No,... of course not, Jedidiah. I don't want you to die unhappy! I don't want you to die happy..... I just don't want you to die at all!" I engulfed Jedidiah in a tight bear hug, blinking away my tears.

Jedidiah hugged me back briefly, and continued on about his puppy, undeterred.

"I will love my Chihuahua, and she will love me." Jedidiah said brightly. "And I will take REALLY good care of her!"

"Oh, I don't doubt that."

Jedidiah immediately started on his checklist of his dream puppy. Number one, it had to be a Chihuahua. Number two, it had to be female. Number three, it had to be cute. Number four, he wanted a tan color. Number five, it had to have 4 white feet. And number six, it had to be smart.

So, we started on our search for a Chihuahua that afternoon. I called around to the County pound, then to the local animal rescue. The rescue group said they had a one year old, neutered male, that was half Chihuahua. I asked Jedidiah if that would work, but he wasn't too excited about it. I thought it would make a good back up plan, in case a full blooded Chihuahua did not materialize. I asked the rescue group what I would have to do to adopt from them. They told me I would have to fill out the five page, on-line application, provide two character references, and then pay a $260.00 Adoption Fee. Sounded like a lot to do just to get a little half-blooded Chihuahua...so my excitement waned about that prospect too.

Next I turned to the weekly local newspaper. BINGO!! An ad for Chihuahua puppies was listed in the "Pets For Sale" column!

"Jedidiah!" I excitedly called to him, "There is an advertisement for Chihuahuas in the Feather River Bulletin!"

"Where are they? Let's go!" Jedidiah was already struggling to sit up in his bed.

"Well, just wait a sec. Let me call the number to see if they still have them." I took out my cell phone and dialed the Greenville phone number that was listed in the ad.

"Hello?" I held my breath. "Do you still have Chihuahua puppies for sale?"

"Yes, we do." A kindly women's voice said.

"How much are they?" I asked, keeping my fingers crossed that they were not outlandishly expensive.

"Two hundred and fifty dollars," she stated. "And they are purebreds!"

"Great!" I said with enthusiasm, thinking to myself, wow- that's even cheaper than the rescue place. "Where are you located and when can we come to take a look at them?"

"We are in Greenville and tonight would be fine if you would like to come see them."

I proceeded to write down the directions and promised the lady we would be there that evening. I glanced over at the bed in the living room, and saw Jedidiah literally wriggling with excitement. "When can we go Mom? Do they have puppies? What color are they? Can we go now?" He was overflowing with bubbling happiness, much like a puppy himself.

"Well, let's wait for Dad to get home from work, and Justin to get home from school. It would be a lot more fun for them to come with us, wouldn't it?"

"Yeah, they could come with us to get a Chihuahua puppy! As long as they HURRY!!!" Jedidiah was already bouncing himself on the bed. "Come on, come on! Let's go get me a Chihuahua puppy!! You will never regret this, Mom. I will be SO happy! And I will always take such good care of my puppy!"

"Okay, Okay, it will be fun! We just have to wait a few hours. Then we get to go see if they have the right puppy you want."

"Yes, you will see Mom, they WILL have the puppy I want, I just know it. And I will teach her all kinds of tricks, and she will really love me...." Jedidiah's excitement was uncontainable. He continued on, "I will love this puppy and she will be my most favorite pet ever. We will go everywhere together, I can take her to town, she can go to school with me, and even sleep in bed with me. I am going to buy her the favorite food she likes, and LOTS of good toys to play with..." He went on for the rest of the afternoon, talking about his dream puppy. He was so excited, I could barely get him to eat any lunch.

As soon as Justin walked in the door at home, back from school, Jedidiah was bombarding him with information and stories about his soon-to-be new Chihuahua.

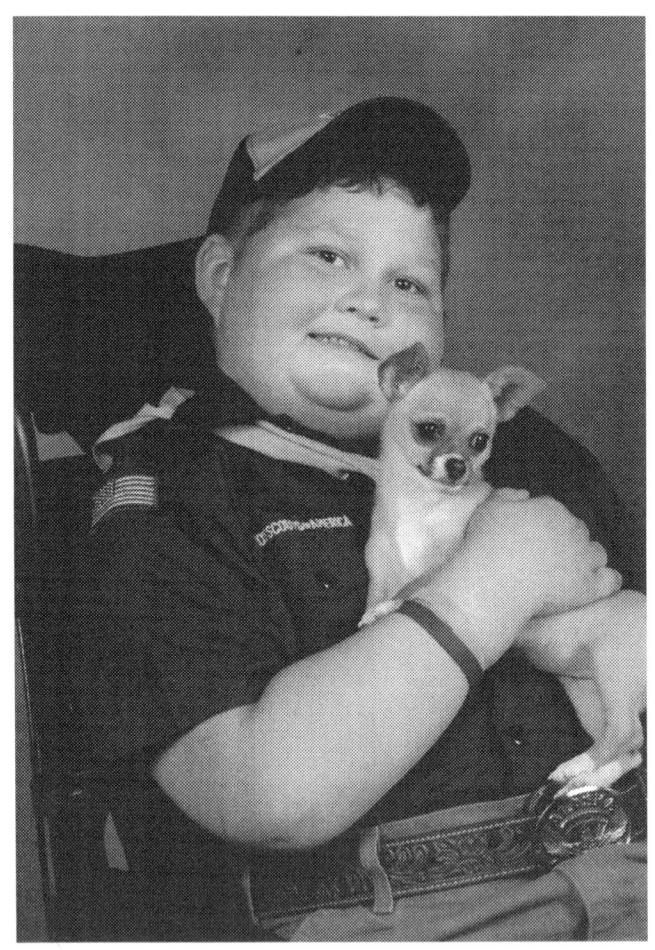

Jedidiah with his Cub Scout Uniform, and his puppy, Pep, 2010. Photo by Leslie Froggatt.

STORIES FROM JEDIDIAH'S FAMILY & FRIENDS

Won't Never Forget 'Ya Jedidiah Lusk
By Uncle Rick Lusk

Jedidiah, I never had the opportunity to
Get to know you well. You always lived over
There, and, me way over here.

You and your family would stop by our
home on your way from one place to
another. Usually it was late at night. Ya'll
could take a ten hour drive and make it last
all week.

So, sometime around midnight the door
would crash in, the dog would start
howling, and in you'd come. Most of the
time you were being carried, asleep- or
halfway there, with crumbs on your face
and sleepy dust in your eyes.

In the morning, out you all would creep.
The dog would start barking- the door
would crash wide. I'd see you, usually being
carried, asleep- or half way's at least, with
no crumbs on your face and sleepy dust in
your eyes.

Cynthia Lusk

I got to admire a guy who likes to eat and sleep!

Robert and Sarah and I had the pleasure of
Meeting with you and all the "Cousins"
For some mountain biking one year. At
Moab. Of course.

Sarah and Robert and I were going along
fine, till Bob's brakes started dragging the
rim. Sarah kept going, Bob and I turned
around and started heading on in. Way up
ahead was it, just a mirage?

We got closer and surely did see, your Mom
hunched over pushing a little bike type
thing. You were sitting high and proud, not
riding side saddle, pedaling right along,
headed to home.

We asked if Yun's needed a hand.
Cynthia smiled that smile that mom's only
Can and said, "Nah, we've just about got the
bike trip licked." You licked your lips and
said, "I need a juice drink!"

The only time I have gotten to do the
Hiawatha Ride, Robert and you were riding
by my side. Before I knew it, Bob was two
furlongs ahead. I said, "you fall back with
your dad, Jed. I'm going to ride hard and
fast to catch up with Bike Rocket Bobster."

I took off pedaling as hard and fast as I
could. The wind was whistling through my

hair, blood pounding through my eyes.

What did I hear? The soft whisk, whisk,
whisk of your pedals and cranks. I looked
down and you looked up at me and said, "Ya
going to start pedaling yet?"

Thanks to you, we caught up with the rest!

All of us "Cousins" met up one year at
Farewell Bend State Park, in the Oregon
Territory. For camping and
Family's sure like to bike an

Farewell Bend is a great place to bike and
Camp and play with a ball. It's flat. Well
Paved. Lots of green pretty grass.

Until our tubes started swooshing and our
Tires started flattening. Goat head thorns of
Course. You were the only one not to suffer
A flat- How's that?

Kind of like the time your Dad on one of our
Bike rides, "Here, Rick, let me show you how
To 'pop' the bike pump off the stem."
Didn't work- Twice...

Or,

The time Scott and Cynthia, on their Bike
Across America, in Kansas or someplace like
That, eleven flats in less than a mile...
And,

Cynthia Lusk

Scott was quoted in a local paper one time
On that trip, "Well, if Cynthia makes it
Across the country with me, I might just
Have to marry her, ya see..."

I am glad they made it. The years went by
And bye, along came our Jedidiah.

JEDIDIAH- Written by Connor, Carli and Cole Williams

There is a special bond that "Cousins" share.

And no matter how far apart we live, it is always there.

Our youngest cousin left this world and is no longer here,

But in our thoughts, memories, and hearts he is always near.

His fun, adventurous spirit made our world more bright,

He taught our families how to be more thankful and to unite.

We have a little sky blue light to hang on our Christmas Tree,

To show he still shines on in our lives, for you and me.

Even as we go our separate ways, we all will remember him forever,

For he touched our lives and tied us cousins together.

The youngest cousin of all, taught us how to live,

And no matter what we encounter in our lives, to...

ALWAYS BE POSITIVE

Cynthia Lusk

To Jedidiah from Carli

Dear Jed,

Hey Jed it's Carli. I think about you all the time and wish we were watching "Hotel for Dogs", or "Beverly Hills Chihuahua". It was so much fun playing in the pool with you as you would dunk me under, over and over again as I guessed the wrong color or fruit, or whatever the topic was. I want to thank you for teaching me how to be brave and strong like you. You are such a tough little guy. You have also taught me to think of other's feelings more. You always made sure everyone got a chance to participate and have fun with whatever activity we were up to, like having us all sing together a song you made up about your little "Mini Cheese Grater". You made sure we all got to use it!! And WOW, how we all love your cotton candy. You make the best warhead cotton candy ever, and again, your kind and caring heart made sure we all got some before we got to have seconds. You know how to share better than most adults! We all thought your new van was awesome and again you made sure we all got to open the doors and put the ramp out with a button on your key chain, as long as we did not push the Emergency Button!!! Your new i-pod was so cool and as long as we put it away correctly in your i-home, we could listen to it as much as we wanted. Jedidiah, I will never forget when you came up to visit a month after my ACL surgery, you offered me your wheelchair because you said that I was the hurt one. You said you could stand or sit in another chair. You even ended up pushing me for a while. Lastly, Jedidiah, you have taught me to always smile and enjoy the life I have. You taught me not to feel sorry for myself if things don't go the way I want them to, but enjoy what is happening and appreciate all I have. You showed me to never give up, but to work hard and make it happen. I have leaned on you so many times during my second ACL surgery and rehab. Thank you. You also taught me to give hugs to everyone. Your smile was contagious! I love your huge hugs to everyone and how you said you would never let go. You would just keep squeezing me so tight. I look up to you so much. I am only a kid myself but I know you have changed my life, my attitude, and my outlook. Because of you, I will be a better person and adult. I try hard every day to live like you taught me and always be positive. To live life each day, to enjoy the day I have, and to be kind to everyone. I know I will carry these traits with me forever. Thanks for making me a better person! You always have been and always be truly the favorite, littlest cousin. I always do and always will think about you. I promise I will never forget you and will always remember you. You are always in my heart. I miss and love you so much.

Love,
Your Idaho cousin,
Carli

Jedi Strong
By Anna Chavis

When my aunt Cynthia told the family she was writing a book about Jedidiah, I was very excited. I had actually, secretly, been thinking the same thing…that *someone* has to get the word out about Jedidiah. People have to know about him, his story, his humor, his grace, and his positivity throughout those 10 ½ months with a tumor in his brain. Cynthia has given me ample time to turn in my Jedidiah chapter. Here it is, months later, and I'm just now getting around to writing it.

I don't know why it has taken me so long to begin my chapter. I've always been a procrastinator, but that's no excuse. It kind of feels like I'm writing a term paper, but this will not be graded. I guess there is part of me that knows that when I finish typing that last sentence, that will be it, the end. My memories and stories about Jedidiah will all be on paper, so there will be nothing more to tell, nothing to write or hold on to. There is finality about this chapter that I have been avoiding.

I guess the main reason is that in order to write this, I will have to remember, and feel every emotion that arises in my attempt to let his story be heard. And that is what scares me, to make those feelings real again. I have grieved, I have cried, and now I will have to feel those same emotions again. It sounds silly as I write all this down. Of course writing my chapter will be tough emotionally.... but it's worth it; for Jedi, for me, for my family and for all his friends and people he touched and inspired. It will be therapeutic. It's not healthy to hold certain feelings inside for too long. You've got to let them out and be heard. It is part of the healing process......so let it begin!

I would like to tell the story of Jedidiah through my point of view, not as a family member who had the privilege of interacting with him daily, but as a cousin, hundreds of miles away. I am very pleased when I get to spend time with any long distance relative. I am the second oldest cousin in the family, so I have had the honor of watching the rest of the cousins grow up, and have changed a few diapers along the way.

When Jedidiah was born, I'm sure I wasn't the only person who was alarmed. His parents named him *Jedidiah? Really?* It made a little more sense once Scott explained that Jed was named after Jedidiah Smith, an 1800's explorer of the West, trapper, fur trader, and hunter and not after Jed, the Beverly Hillbilly. Jed was a very cute baby and toddler, a spitting' image of his older brother Justin, and just as big of a character as Justin at that age too. Whether it was a young Justin or a young Jedidiah in the room, you could always tell because somebody would be laughing. As soon as they realized they were doing something that was getting some laughs, they knew it and they played it up.

Some of my first memories of Jedidiah are when he was maybe two, and the family was camping at Farewell Bend State Park in Oregon. There is a picture that I took that pops up in my head from this trip of the cousins in Bobby and Wawee's (grandparents) RV, making silly faces and just being total goofs. It makes me laugh every time. Jedidiah was not in that photo because he was probably off with his mom somewhere (being a toddler and all) eating or sleeping. But there are a few pictures of him that I took that trip that are classics. In one, he is putting his mouth on a spigot, trying to suck out water, and dirt is just caked on all over his mouth and face. Another picture taken shortly afterwards is of him in his pajamas, with a spatula in hand and a smile on his face.

Since Jedidiah was only nine years old and lived so far away when he passed, I only got to see him a couple of times, mainly in the summer or during Christmas. As he got older his personality began to peek through. He was kind, caring, and such a sweetheart. He definitely did not let being the youngest cousin get in his way of having fun with the others. Jedidiah was included in just about every activity the cousins were doing, but he was also very good at entertaining himself. If he were the first person to awake at Camp Grandma, which he often was, he would sit on the floor and begin to build things with Lego's, or send parachute men down from the loft.

If you add the number of times I got to see and spend time with Jedidiah, and subtract the number of times he spent with the younger cousins, who are *way* more fun, that only leaves so few encounters between him and I that I could actually get to know him, an 8 year old boy. But Christmas 2009 is when I really got to know him as much as I could, and when his personality began to shine. I remember when he saw me for the first time that Christmas, he came up to me and gave me a great, big bear hug. He was abnormally strong for an eight year old!! Jedidiah literally lifted me on my tiptoes as he embraced me. That's when I knew that he had a whole lot of love to give.

Part of the reason I enjoyed that Christmas so much was that Jedidiah and his family stayed at Bob and Betty's house, which is where I stayed as well. Justin, Jedidiah and I had a lot of fun playing with these Nerf guns that shot darts with Velcro tips. Okay, I might have been the target. But Jedidiah soon discovered that he could shoot the darts at my pants, mainly at my butt, and they would stick. I did not mind because he was having so much fun doing it, and I enjoyed seeing that smile on his face.

That was the last time I got to see him before he was diagnosed with a brain tumor only a few months later. During that Christmas visit Jedidiah said something to me that I will never forget. I thought it a bit odd and funny at the time. But now, it is completely appropriate. He was about to go to sleep for the night, so I headed down the stairs to my room. After a few steps he said quickly, "Hey, Anna. Remember me!" I did a quarter turn, looked at him, and said something like, "Um, ok." I didn't know where that came from, or why it was important. But of course I would remember him. It's not like I'm going to forget who my littlest cousin is!

Today I think I know why he told me to remember him. Jedidiah didn't want to miss out on *anything*. Since he was the youngest cousin, he felt it was his duty to jump in head first, and shout out for all to hear, 'Hey, I'm here! Don't forget about me! I'm part of the family too!" None of us would forget this in the first place, but I guess he felt he should stand up and be heard. It must be hard being the youngest. Everyone's older, smarter, stronger, faster, and more independent. I soon found out that Jedidiah was all of those things, and much, much more.

It was Valentine's Day weekend, 2010. My parents were about to go skiing with friends in Utah later in the week, which meant I got to pet sit for them while they were gone. While at my parent's house that weekend I had heard from them that Jedidiah was rushed to the local hospital because he might have the swine flu. But he was soon rushed to the UC Davis hospital because something wasn't quite right.

Before my parents left, Scott was on the phone with my dad, asking him questions about what could possibly be wrong with Jedidiah. My dad is a surgeon, and that comes in handy whenever a friend or family member has a medical question or concern…or if someone needs stitches after almost slicing the tip of my, I mean *their* finger off with a wood carving tool. My dad comforted Scott, told him not to worry yet and informed him of how rare brain tumors are in children, and that it might just be an infection of some kind. We wouldn't know for sure what was going on until all the tests were done.

My mom informed me that Blue Nanny used to be a nurse and she thought Jedidiah might have a brain tumor. That's why he was having blurred vision, nausea, vomiting, and horrible headaches. I really hoped that Blue Nanny was just completely wrong. I was still hoping for swine flu.

It was later that week when my parents were gone that we received the news that it was, in fact, a brain tumor. And not just any brain tumor, the most aggressive, persistent kind of tumor there is. My mom broke the news to me over the phone, and we started to cry. I never realized until that moment just how wonderful, and necessary it is to have a family member or a friend's shoulder to cry on in times of need. I looked around the house and only saw two big slobbering dog faces staring back at me, and an unpredictable cat that could start to attack at any moment.

I had no idea how to handle this information. I've never had a close family member pass away or have a terminal illness, not until Jedidiah. After an hour or so of uncontrollable sobbing I became angry, *really* angry. I felt that someone, somehow, was to blame. That was the easiest solution; find someone to pin it on. But I quickly realized that this was obviously irrational. How could I possibly think that? Of course no one was to blame here. For some unfortunate reason, that damned tumor found its way into Jedidiah's brain, and all we could do was figure out what to do next, and hope it was treatable.

It's funny how bad things seem to happen to good people. Well, it's not the slightest bit funny, it's simply unfair. I tried to put myself in the Lusk's shoes, and I started to think about how I would feel if it were my little brother who had been diagnosed with brain cancer. But that is something I can't even begin to comprehend. I like to think that I could handle something like that, and try to remain positive throughout it all, like Jedidiah did. I like to think that I could have stayed in school and finished the semester with good grades like Jessica and Justin did. I like to think that I could have gone back to work like Scott or Cynthia did. I like to think that I could have remained strong and positive for my brother or son or grandson. But I don't know if I would have had the same amount of strength, courage, and bravery as the Lusk's did. Because how do you say goodbye to someone you just got the pleasure of getting to know?

Slowly, one little step at a time, and with a whole lot of support is the answer to that question. I can't even imagine how hard that is to accomplish, because I'm just a cousin. I wasn't there day to day to hear his voice, to spend time with him at school, to watch him ride his dirt bike, to be on the receiving end of one of his wonderful hugs, or to see him smile. All I have is precious memories, pictures, jokes, and stories that I will hold on to forever. I guess in the end that is what we all have.

The motto that arose from Jedi's hardships was "Always Be Positive." When you think about that, it's not *always* an easy task. There are so many things that happen in life, large or small, that make you want to give up, to stop trying or scream at the top of your lungs. But no matter what happens in my life nowadays, I try my absolute hardest to remain Jedidiah Strong. It's not an easy task for me, and sometimes I do fail. But I try to stay positive and to think of other ways to overcome an obstacle, because that's what Jedi would do.

It's utterly amazing that Jedi never once asked why he was dealt the hand he was given. That would have been one of the first questions I would have asked. Jedidiah had more guts and grit than anyone I've ever known. Even when he started to gain weight from the steroids he had to take, it was as if he was unfazed. He stood out from the rest of the kids his age, with his wheelchair, his new hairdo, weight gain and his partial paralysis. But he was still the same Jedidiah. That never changed. That is how I will always remember him.

In the summer of 2010 Jedidiah got to come visit his cousins here in northern Idaho, with pictures from his Make-A-Wish trip to Alaska and of course his cotton candy machine!! Another amazing thing about Jedi is that a few weeks before he got sick, he recited Robert Service's poem *The Cremation of Sam McGee* from memory at his school's talent show. My mom pointed out to me that she recited that same poem from memory...in the fifth grade!! That is one long poem for an eight year old to memorize. But what almost brought me to tears that summer was when he recited *The Cremation of Sam McGee* for us. Even after the biopsy, chemo and radiation he still remembered the majority of the poem, and he did a darn good job reciting it.

But it is another poem by Robert Service that I believe best describes Jedidiah, much better than I can. It's called "*The Quitter*"

Whenever I read this poem, or look down at my Always Be Positive Jedidiah bracelet, I think of Jedidiah's attitude throughout it all, and I am reminded of his unsinkable spirit. It was his spark, his wit, his smile and his zest for life that made him so admirable and inspirational.

Last summer (2010) was the best summer of my life. I was lucky enough to be able to spend it with Jedidiah and family, and cousins! What else can you do for someone who has a terminal illness except pack as much fun, family, and friends into each day as humanly possible? That's what last summer was all about. Jedidiah shared his cotton candy maker and remote control wave runner with *everyone*, so we all got to have a turn. I got to share Jedi's much beloved fascination with Cobalt boats and yachts and took a tour through one with him and Scott. We all went camping at Bungalow in Pierce, Idaho where my grandfather used to work as a ranger, and Jedi even got to take part in the local parade. We made s'mores and ate Bob's famous Bungalow breakfast. We got to bike the Hiawatha Trail, and the trail of the Coeur d' Alene's where we saw a moose! Jedi didn't seem too impressed because he saw plenty of moose in Alaska. Talk about living life to the fullest! That kid did more living, from the day he was diagnosed till the day he died, than most people do in an entire lifetime.

But like all good things, it had to come to an end. That day, after the parade, Jedidiah was in his van and Scott was ready to get on the road. I don't know if he heard this somewhere or if he made it up, but Jedidiah had a new saying, "I don't like you. I don't love you. I WUV you!" He had been saying that all summer, and it caught on quick. Wuv is the highest one can go on the Love scale. So before they drove off, I leaned in for one last Jedidiah hug and I told him, "Jedidiah, I like you, I love you, AND I wuv you!"

Those were the last words I spoke to him. And I am so grateful I did. Some people don't get the chance to have last words with a loved one. Others might love someone, yet say something they regret before a person dies. When Jedi passed away, I took myself back to that summer and tried to remember what it was that I last said to him. I remembered that it was "I wuv you", and I smiled. How wonderful to end on that note, to use his phrase but twist it around and still have it stay meaningful and true.

I believe Jedidiah was wise beyond his years, like a little Buddha, or a Jedi warrior. That's why I like calling him Jedi. He was faced with the ultimate test, and he passed with flying colors. At his funeral I had finally gotten enough courage to stand up and say a few words about him. I hadn't turned around to look at how many people showed up. But when I got on that stage I was struck with awe. *Hundreds* of people crowded into the room, all of them there to honor a nine year old boy. It was an incredibly humbling experience. Cynthia would like me to include a copy of my speech from Jedi's funeral. It is not word for word, but it's close enough:

In our family we draw Name Persons every Christmas. This year I feel I was the lucky one...because Jedi had my name. I'm wearing the SpongeBob Wrappie he gave me. Not a Snuggie, but a Wrappie! Big difference. Jedidiah knew I'm a big fan of Sponge Bob, like himself. I guess he saw the Wrappie somewhere and knew it would be perfect for me. On the plane ride over here, I got it out of my bag & was going to take a nappie in my Wrappie when my mom sees it and says, "It's like you're wrapped in love." That's exactly how I feel wearing the Wrappie. That's exactly how I felt around Jedi, and that's exactly how I feel as a member of this family.

Jedi was the youngest of the cousins, and the youngest of 11 grandchildren. Being the youngest meant he missed out on a lot of family adventures in earlier years simply because he wasn't born yet. He was just getting to the age where he could have fun with the cousins on his own and not have to have his parents around.

Last Christmas the whole family gathered at Camp Grandma in Coeur d' Alene, Idaho. Jedi and his family were leaving to go home later in the day, but that morning Jedidiah and I were playing with a Nerf gun that shot darts with Velcro tips. He soon found out that if he shot at my pants, the darts would stick. He then purposefully started to shoot the darts at my butt. After our Nerf battle I was headed downstairs when all of a sudden he says, "Remember me!" I thought this was a funny thing for an 8 year old to say. But as I thought about it, I guess it made sense. He was so happy to play with and get to know his older cousins; he didn't want the fun to stop! He didn't want to wait another year to see his cousins again. And he didn't want me to forget what a kind-hearted, fun loving person he was.

But after I learned the news last February 14th, that it was indeed a brain tumor, I thought back to last Christmas and those two little words, "Remember me!" Maybe it was a premonition. Maybe on some deep, subconscious level his brain knew it had a cancer, and his brain told his heart to say those two words. I don't know the answer, but I do know this is true: Of course I will ALWAYS remember you, Jedi. How could I possibly forget your cute little face, and that contagious smile? To quote from his favorite poem, The Cremation of Sam McGee: "He wore a smile you could see a mile." ...which brings me back to this Christmas...

This year Jedidiah gave my mom what I thought was a goody bag, but I just learned today it was actually a goody bag from the dentist. It has his name on it, and on the bag is a smiley face and the words "A smile is Forever"

So yes, Jedidiah. I will always remember you, and your smile is forever in my heart.

This past summer Jedidiah had a new saying. "I don't like you. I don't love you. I WUV you!!" Wuv being the highest level, and like being the lowest. I don't know where he saw that, or how he came up with it, but my last words I said to him in person were as he and Scott were about to drive back home. I reached in the van, gave him one last hug and said, "Jedidiah, I like you, I love you, AND I wuv you!"

I would now like to share my favorite Jedidiah joke. I don't know if he came up with this one himself. But I like to think he did, because it comes with a disclaimer. Jedidiah warns you NOT to try this at home:

Q: What do you call your cat after you put it in the dryer and it is never seen again?
A: Socks!!

Jedidiah's story touched so many hearts and inspired so many people. The amount of help, support, and love Jedidiah and the Lusk family received from the little town of Quincy, California, from Alaska to Virginia, all across the nation, was unbelievable. Thank you to all who participated in Jedidiah's life and his fight. The effect Jedidiah had on family, friends, friends of friends, even on complete strangers was absolutely beyond belief. There will always be a special place in my heart for my special little cousin. I will **always** remember you, Jedidiah. You can count on that!

OUR MEMORIES OF JEDIDIAH

by Bobby and Wawee Lusk
Summarized and written by Anna Chavis

We are Bob and Betty Lusk, (known by our grandchildren as Bobby and Wawee) Jedidiah's paternal grandparents. Including Jedidiah, we have 11 grandchildren. We live in northern Idaho, so whenever any of our children or grandchildren can make it all the way out from California, Oregon, just across the border in Washington, or anywhere else they come from, we consider that a real treat.

Since Jedidiah was so young, he only got to visit us a handful of times for summertime fun or a large family Christmas before that lousy tumor was found. And even then, Jedidiah got to spend one last wonderful summer with his cousins here at "Camp Grandma," playing in the water, camping, making cotton candy, and reciting Robert Service's *The Cremation of Sam McGee* from memory. Jedidiah was a special little guy who we loved so, so much, and he will always be in our hearts. We would like to share some of our favorite memories of Jedidiah with you, so that he might *always* be remembered.

Summertime at Camp Grandma on the lake, means boat rides, tubing, playing on the big raft, jumping off the dock into the water, skipping rocks, and much, much more! Each time we got to see Jedidiah we could see just how much he'd grown, physically and mentally. The last summer before he developed the brain tumor, he was so happy because he was finally old enough and strong enough to not need a life jacket anymore! Jedidiah was right in there with all the cousins, playing their version of King of the Mountain, goofing around on the raft in the water. But one of the fondest, and cutest memories we have of Jedidiah on the dock is when he caught his first fish. Jed was two years old, in a diaper, fishing pole in hand, and binky (pacifier) in his mouth when that tiny fish grabbed hold! That snapshot became an instant family classic.

Another fond summertime memory of Jed involves him steering the boat while sitting on Grandpa Bobby's lap, looking all around with a smile on his face. It was known from a very young age that Jedidiah was mesmerized by anything with moving parts and was very technically inclined, whether it was cars, trucks, cranes, snowmobiles, tractors, bikes, or boats. Out of all the grandchildren, and even at two years old Jedidiah had the best touch on the boat's controls.

Jedidiah was an independent and courageous kid. He was never scared to take a different route, a road less traveled. There are lots of stairs, both outside and in, that one must climb in order to get upstairs in our house. Jedidiah would always climb the short, steep trail that takes you around to the front door instead of taking the stairs. The last summer he spent at Camp Grandma, even with his wheelchair and with one side of his body partially paralyzed, Jedidiah still chose to sleep downstairs when he was already upstairs, and vice versa.

One of the features of our house that Jedidiah loved was the loft. Like any young boy, as you can imagine, he would spend a lot of time playing with toys, games, hide & seek, Lego's, etc. Jedidiah would play school or draw pictures up on the chalkboard in the loft. But Jedidiah loved sending parachuting army men down to the floor below, and any other random toy down on a string just for fun. He had such a vivid and wonderful imagination.

We reflect on these, and other memories of our youngest grandchild Jedidiah, and hope that he has touched your heart and inspired you in some way, like he has to us and so many others. We miss you Jedidiah, and we will always love and remember you!

THE DAY MY SON DIED

By Scott Lusk

**Jedidiah Lusk Spotting for Alaska Smokejumpers.
Photo by Mike McMillian.**

I dedicate my chapter to all "The Cousins" who were Jedidiah's Best Friends: Cole, Connor, Carli, Robert, Sarah, Christy, Anna, Reid, Linda, Rich, Richard, Julie, Tim, Bobby and Wawee; to all Jedidiah's classmates who did not make fun of Jedidiah when he was paralyzed, confined to a wheelchair and doubled in weight from the Decadron, and to Bill Cramer and the Alaska Smokejumpers-who made my little boy's Dream come true.

The title of my chapter comes from my oldest son, Justin. He read a story he wrote for Pioneer School's, "Young Author's Night," titled, 'The Day My Brother Was Born'. Justin was seven years old and in the second grade. He stood in front of the entire school and read his story out loud. He was so proud to have a little brother. I paraphrased Justin's title, 'The Day my Brother was Born," and changed it for the title of my chapter, "The Day my Son Died."

Justin had finished a ski race with the Johnsville Junior Ski Team the day before his brother was born. His Grandparents had come down from Coeur d' Alene, Idaho to watch Justin race, and to be there when Justin's brother was born. Justin's grandparents, Bobby and Wawee (Bob and Betty Lusk) took Justin and Jessica to Taco Bell, the Dollar Store, then to our Plumas District Hospital, where their little brother was born. We have pictures of all of them holding the new, little baby, Jedidiah in the delivery room!

The two brothers were inseparable. They always played together. Justin was very nice and patient with his little brother. Two days before Jedidiah was diagnosed with an inoperable brain tumor, the two of them were outside building bark waterfalls in the creek by our house. I yelled at Jedidiah, "Don't get your good school shoes dirty." Jedidiah was unresponsive to my request. Then he looked at me, grinned, and stomped his feet to send mud flying all over his brother! I was not ready for the 'unresponsive' Jedidiah that Cynthia warned me about, while Jessica, Justin and I were gone visiting the cousins in Coeur d'Alene after Christmas that December in 2010.

The day my son died, I was oblivious to the fact. I did not know he was going to die, that day, then, right now! I did not read the booklets Hospice had left us that Cynthia asked us all to read. The girls were lying next to Jedidiah's side, on his fold-out couch-bed we had used the past 11 days short of 11 months. Blue Nanny was a Registered Nurse, Cynthia and Jessica were current EMTs. They knew the signs of impending death; shallow, rapid breathing, weak pulse, blue color. Justin and I were watching Monday Night Football. I was bidding on a pair of cowboy boots for Cynthia on e-Bay.

Cynthia walked over and told me quietly, so not to scare Jedidiah, 'Your son is dying'.

I knew that. Dr. Z had told us on July 13th that he'd be dead by the end of July, that's how fast the tumor was re-growing. I did not know Cynthia meant he was dying and taking his last breaths, right then. Cynthia had us hold hands, touch Jedidiah, and led us in a prayer. He breathed in, and he never breathed out again. He just stopped breathing! Jessica said I was brave and held myself together. Not true! If I'd known Jedidiah was literally dying, right then, I would have been screaming, 'No, No, Don't Die! Don't go!' Cynthia said it was best I wasn't screaming.

Jedidiah weighed 67 pounds when we first brought him into the Plumas District Hospital on Valentine's Day 2010. The ER doctor said it might be the flu. There were six children that had come on that day, with the same flu-like symptoms; throwing up and a headache. Cynthia said no, look closer, his eyes are dilated. Cynthia insisted they do a CAT scan. The CAT scan was sent to Reno. The doctor was just getting ready for her 12:00 lunch break. She said she'd get back to us in 3 hours. Five minutes after the CAT scan was emailed she received a call right back from the technician who said, "Life Flight that little boy to UC Davis. There is 'something' walnut-sized on his midbrain splattered to his brain stem'. Jedidiah was life flighted to UC Davis. His mama flew with him.

I went home to feed the horses and finish moving some corral panels. Justin came to help. I fell down twice moving the panels. My body just wasn't working right. I could not focus.

Glioblastoma multiformes are brain tumors that involve the cells that make the fluid that cushion the brain. For some unknown reason, Jedidiah's brain cells thought they were supposed to start dividing and growing again. No one knows why they did. Researchers are working to find the cause and cure, but very little new information has been has learned since the 1960's. Because these kinds of tumors are so rare, more research is spent on other types of cancers.

When Jedidiah was at UC Davis they gave him Decadron to reduce the swelling in his brain. The biopsy paralyzed his left side. We were at UC Davis for 33 days. We had to wait 10 days for the results of the biopsy. There were 161 different kinds of brain tumors. They needed to see what kind of tumor it was, to know what kind of treatment he'd need. The neurosurgeon asked Cynthia to sign a release form saying he could paralyze Jedidiah or kill him while performing the biopsy and Cynthia resolved him of all responsibility. The choice was to go ahead and do the biopsy, or not do the biopsy and Jedidiah would die from the swelling.

Two weeks into the hospital stay we were getting ready to go home. That night Jedidiah started talking incoherently. Cynthia recognized that as a bad sign. The nurses said it's no big deal go on home. Finally Cynthia convinced them to let her see the doctor. Only two nurses that I met, Nichole and Angela, actually looked at Jedidiah and took the time to care for him instead of just walking into his room and heading straight to the monitors he was hooked to. His brain wasn't swelling, the tumor itself had grown! It started as the size of a walnut when he was first Life Flighted to UC Davis, growing to 2 inches by 2 inches within the first two weeks we were there.

Jedidiah had to come back and be fitted for a radiation mask and they would 3D image the tumor for radiation treatment. In hind sight I would've only allowed the Decadron for two weeks, not 10 mg for 8 months. The tumor was growing, it wasn't his brain swelling from the treatment. Decadron made Jedidiah think he was hungry all the time, so he ate, and ate, and ate. It also made his whole body and face swell. It's a steroid. The radiologist would argue with the doctor to stop the Decadron. He said it was making his face swell too much for the mask they used to hold Jedidiah down for his radiation treatments. The radiologist had to cut holes in the mask for Jedidiah's huge cheeks. Later, they had to make a whole new mask- when Jedidiah's face swelled to twice his normal size from the Decadron. Jedidiah swelled from a skinny little 67 pound boy- clear up to 167 pounds from the steroid, Decadron. Finally in July, Cynthia and I reduced his Decadron from 10 mg/day to 6mg, to 4mg, to 2mg, to 1mg to 0.5. I wish we would have done that earlier.

We went to Deputy Shawn's funeral on March 3rd, 2011. Deputy Shawn Webb lived in Plumas County and developed a GBM at 38 years of age. He did a fund raiser for Jedidiah with the Plumas County Sheriff's Department and made Jedidiah an honorary member of the Plumas County SWAT. Deputy Shawn went to UC San Francisco for his brain tumor treatment and tried an experimental chemo. It still did not cure him. Cynthia told me that she had done her own research on GBMs and had read that they are 100% terminal - there is no cure. GBMs are the most aggressive, most lethal, and the rarest form brain tumor. I heard her, but it did not register with me, even on Thanksgiving Day when Jedidiah only wanted to eat a little Top Raman, and that was the last food he ate. He drank juice and milk up until Christmas. From then on Jedidiah would only accept a tiny bit of water when his mama would squeeze it from a bulb syringe to wash his mouth out.

    I would like to share some stories that shows Jedidiah's positive spirit. We drove Jedidiah back to UC Davis for a PIC change in May. We took off Jedidiah's shirt to show Dr. Z how fat and swollen Jedidiah was getting. Dr Z said that's not the usual response to Decadron something else must be wrong. He ordered an emergency CAT scan and told Jedidiah he'd have to stay in the hospital. Jedidiah broke into tears. He did not want to stay in the hospital again. He just wanted to go home! Within two minutes, Jedidiah pulled himself together and said, "it's Okay. Do whatever you need too". I went outside and cried. Jedidiah was my "tuff guy". As it turned out, nothing new was revealed by that emergency CAT scan, and Jedidiah did not have to stay overnight in the hospital after all. That's the spirit my little guy had.

    Jedidiah was my play buddy. He wore the #21 ski bib. He dove head first down the high school GS ski course at Diamond Peak when my young team gripped up on the icy course. I got a snowmobile and a dirt bike because Jedidiah had one, and his mama said he couldn't ride alone. I miss my little guy!

    Here are several more short stories that capture Jedidiah's Spirit for me. The first three I wrote on his August 29, 2010 Web Page. Jessica began this CaringBridge website back in February 2010, when Jedidiah first went to UC Davis Hospital. Jessica kept up the web page while a freshman at Feather River College in Quincy, and still made A's and B's, then graduated in May 2011 with Highest Honors:

1) Jedidiah skied with the Johnsville Junior Ski team when he was four years old. He was a dues paying member at five. Director Elliott made a special name for Jedidiah and called him, 'Biscuits and Gravy' (That was the 'Breakfast of Champions' he would feed his son, Elliott, before they raced). Ski Team members were supposed to be seven years old to be on the team or be in the second grade. The director made an exception for Jedidiah…and

he was on the Team and racing...just a tad bit younger! On a real icy day in 2008, when Jedidiah was 7 years old and wearing the #21 bib, he made an impressive statement. It happened during the first practice run down the High School GS ski course at Diamond Peak. Jedidiah skied down to Dayne, who was wearing the #20 bib and helping a new racer who had just fallen, slid, and gripped up. I overheard Jedidiah say, "The Coach says, 'self-check, if you fall and land with your head uphill, you're doing it wrong, but if you fall and land with your head downhill, you're doing it right', like this," as he dove head first downhill sliding on his belly with a loud, 'Aaughhh!' The community, in lieu of flowers at Jedidiah's funeral, sent $1,850 to JJST in honor of Jedidiah!

2) Jedidiah had to have an emergency MRI on March 1, 2010. It was late at night after most of the staff had gone home. The nurse on duty forgot to bring the anesthesia, and then she brought the wrong kind. I was asked to help, by holding Jedidiah down, because he kept moving around too much. Finally, the nurse brought the correct anesthesia, and gave him some. Three times they kept giving him more anesthesia so he'd lay still, on the third time, Jedidiah motioned for me to lean in close, uncrossed his eyes, looked me straight in the eye, and said, 'I'm just trying to scratch my left butt cheek Dad."

3) Jedidiah kicked the PICU nurse when she tried to pull some sticky tape off his IV arm. It hurt him and Jedidiah asked her nicely not too, that he would do it. She laughed at Jedidiah, 'How you going to change it on your right arm when you can't even move your left arm? Jedidiah said, 'leave it alone, I'll do it!" When she tried again, he kicked her in the chin with a right round house kick from under the covers. The Nurse looked at me and winked, and said, "I like Jedidiah's spirit!"

4) After Jedidiah was confined to a wheelchair from the immobility of the biopsy and all swollen from the Decadron, he didn't whine or complain. He remained polite, patient, cheerful, and positive! He had such a positive attitude, he would say, "I don't mind being in a wheelchair, people get to push me around and it feels like I'm flying in a chariot". Jedidiah looked forward to pushing

the blue wheelchair button to open automatic doors. He'd point at the button and say, "That's me! I get to push that button!" Jedidiah made "Cotton Cloud" cotton candy for his friends. He'd sell it for a dollar a bag. If you didn't have a dollar, he'd make you cotton candy if you gave him two pieces of hard candy. If you didn't have any hard candy you could use his! Coach Elliott ordered 20 bags of cotton candy! Jedidiah gladly made and delivered them to Coach Elliott's office. A Win/Win Situation for two nice people!

5) Jedidiah delighted in life, as only little 9 year old boys do! He enjoyed remote control 4x4s, helicopters, and snowmobiles. He was always collecting things and putting them in his pockets. His Mama emptied a pair of his pants pockets a year after he died and found: four colorful rocks, a bouncy ball, three little wooden sticks with bark, and a yellow piece of twine. Jedidiah appreciated things as the way they were. He delighted in living the moment. He saw Zenda's brother drive up to the Fairgrounds in a limo. Jedidiah asked, right then, if he could have a ride. Zenda's brother said, "Sure, hop in!" I got to go with him too. Jedidiah waved at everybody as we drove all through Main Street and East Quincy! Jedidiah asked him for his autograph. Jedidiah asked the pilots and crew that flew him to Alaska for their autographs. Jedidiah asked the Smokejumpers for their autographs! Jedidiah asked the Make-a-Wish limo drivers for their autographs. Jedidiah got all the American Valley Speedway Stock Car Driver's autographs on a T-shirt. Everybody was surprised and delighted to give Jedidiah their autograph. Jedidiah enjoyed the real things in his everyday life. Jedidiah had an invitation to hear a Tim McGraw concert and go back stage after the concert. Instead he focused his energies on getting the Kepple Family to come play at his "Jedidiah Celebration Day", -and they did! Make-a-Wish wanted to send Jedidiah to Disneyland. Jedidiah said he'd much rather to go to Alaska and see real Alaska smokejumpers instead!

6) Jedidiah loved riding snowmobiles. He kept pestering me that he wanted to get one of his very own. He started that when he was four years old. He would always look at them on the ski hill and

just drool when the ski patrol would drive by, pulling a toboggan. I let him ride one of the mini snowmobiles at Soda Springs when he was five. He was hooked. Finally I told him when he memorized "O'Keeffe Slide" on his fiddle, he could get one. He worked and worked until he got it memorized. On November 18, 2008 standing on the runners of the green Arctic Cat 370 snowmobile at DuPont's Power Tool in Quincy, in a snowstorm, he played 'O'Keeffe Slide'. In attendance was Mrs. Ducoe, from Bucks Lake. Her daughter, Alexis, had outgrown the small snowmobile. She gave Jedidiah "thumbs up" and said he had earned it by playing 'O'Keeffe Slide'! And now it was his! I am so glad I cashed $850 from my retirement to pay for it!

7) Cynthia and I would take turns sleeping downstairs with Jedidiah all night, on his fold-out couch bed. We would be there beside him, to spend time hugging, reading 'Hank the Cowdog' and other stories, and talking with him. Sometimes he needed to go potty at night. Rarely, very rarely, were Cynthia and I ever able to share our upstairs bed at night. One evening, both of us just happened to be headed upstairs together, at the same time, to the bedroom we shared. Jedidiah yelled up to us, "Hey...and just what are you guys doing? I'm piecing it together... I'm piecing it together," and he cupped his hands in building block motions.

Here's the update I wrote to John Gould on Jedidiah's web page on July 13th, 2010 when we had just come home from our Alaska Make-A-Wish Adventure on July 11, 2010, and Cynthia had taken Jedidiah into UC Davis for just a regularly scheduled MRI visit on July 12, 2010.

July 13, 2010

John, I got your phone message today. I'd planned to call you to say, 'Thank You'. Yes, we made it home safe and sound! We picked up the envelope at the front desk at Pikes from Lindsay Wyatt. Mike met us at Hot Licks Ice Cream the night before we left Fairbanks. He gave us the photo album and DVDs he made, and a card signed by 13 workers from the Alaska Fire Service Mess Hall. You guys are the greatest!

I've learned these GBM tumors are rare in children. They are the most aggressive of all brain tumors, with the shortest life expectancies.

Your timing was perfect! Jedidiah had a blast! He kept the streamers Jessica and Justin retrieved stumbling across the tussocks and has been demonstrating spotting stories to all who will listen!

He's gained strength back from his biopsy and radiation/chemo treatments and was there physically and mentally for his Alaska Smokejumper trip!!! What you guys did for him was amazing:

Putting him in Rookie Training under the Head Rookie Trainer, Loft Foreman, Lead Spotter and PC, letting him eat meals with the Bros, making him a jump suit with his own PG bag, taking an air tanker/lead plane tour, parachute manipulation and Spotting 101 classes, putting him right at the door with the headphones and letting him talk to the pilots and kick the jumpers, then presenting him his Alaska Smokejumper wings, plague, print, T-shirts and hats in front of all of Alaska Fire Service at the Awards Ceremony, letting me give him his Alaska Smokejumper belt buckle, followed with the Chena River jet boat ride, grayling fishing, eating moose-on-a-stick and drinking root beer at Rookie Camp! Jedidiah is one of the Best of the Best, the 650th Alaska Smokejumper in 51 years! This is HUGE!!!

Jedidiah went in for his follow-up MRI on Monday. Dr Z said he's awful sorry to say, news he knows were not ready to hear, but the MRI shows the tumor has re-grown tentacles and there's nothing else Dr Z can do. He told us to enjoy every day we get with Jedidiah -and to keep making those memories!

I never imagined you and Bill would make Jedidiah's Make-a-Wish this BIG, with me and Cynthia in the jump ship, and Jedidiah's brother, sister, and grandma there to participate! From the bottom of my heart, 'Thank You', for making my little boys dream come true!!!!

We held a family funeral for Jedidiah at the Chicken Tree in February 2011. We read Jedidiah's will that he wrote September 13, 2010. Jedidiah asked me in September that when he died to have him cremated, to give half his ashes to Justin and Jessica, scatter half at the Chicken Tree, (where we put all the pets that died), to give the other half to his kids, and to never forget him. Jedidiah told me he wrote a will but would not tell me what was in it. He said I had to wait until after he died. He did tell me what he gave

Jessica. Cynthia told me his will was just a bunch of sentimental, broken, kid's toys, and not to get too excited.

Jedidiah gave Justin his snowmobile. I thought he would give Jessica his Cotton Candy Maker. She was the first one he certified to use it and Jessica made lots of cotton candy. Instead, he gave Jessica the big, six foot tall, blue, Easter bunny he won from the hardware store when he was five. Jessica helped him fill out the form for the drawing. They drew Jedidiah's name. He was so excited! He thought it was a real bunny. He gave Blue Nanny the Cotton Candy Maker. He gave his Mama "Weindeer"-a small, stuffed toy, reindeer Santa gave him at the North Pole. He gave me his Blue Nano i-Pod. I gave away some of Jedidiah's stuff that he gave me. I was going to keep it... but...

I gave Jessica: Uncle Bob's bear claw that Wawee mailed to Jedidiah for Christmas- to give him strength and courage, his yellow Sponge Bob blanket that he laid on at Ronald McDonald house with Aunt Linda, reading jokes before he got his 'Extremely Comfortable Chair', His Alaska Smokejumper Wings, the Mini Cheese grater he made a song up about, and the stainless steel teapot we used to melt the lead for his Pinewood Derby Truck.

I gave Justin his Alaska Smokejumper knife and his Alaska Smokejumper belt buckle and his red "Yes We Can" blanket Chloe made him. I kept his Pinewood Derby Truck and his blue Jedidiah blanket. I scooped Jedidiah's ashes out and put them into two Daytime Blue aluminum water bottles for Justin and Jessica. We each grabbed a handful of Jedidiah's ashes and scattered them around the Chicken Tree. His Mama kept some we'll put into the blue Darby vase from Marty Almquist, we'll keep to give to Justin and Jessica's kids...

For two months, while Jedidiah was in the hospital and at the Ronald McDonald House getting radiation and chemo treatments, he went from bad to worse before he got better. Dr. Z said he would get worse before he got better. Dr. Z just didn't know how worse he'd get before he got better. Jedidiah had to wear diapers because he pooped in his pants, he couldn't feed himself, he sucked on a pacifier, he didn't even know who his own Mama was! For a while, he couldn't even talk. Jedidiah doesn't remember his stay at the hospital or Ronald McDonald House.

He got better. I smuggled him out of Ronald McDonald House to bring him home for his birthday on March 30, 2010, when he turned nine years old. The first sign he was starting to come back was, out of the blue- after he waved goodbye to his best friend, Nano, at his birthday party- he giggled when his Mama kissed him goodbye! She was headed up to work at the Redmond Air Tanker Base and I took him back to Ronald McDonald House!

Here's a couple of additional stories I like telling about Jedidiah- that capture his humor, his care free abandon, and his zeal for living that made Jedidiah special. He had a SPARK!

'People Hugs,'- Whenever he stood up, Jedidiah decided that he had to hug everybody that was present at the time. We were usually in a hurry, but we did it anyway, just for Jedidiah. He would say, "I'm standing...what does that mean?? It means: it's time for a People Hug!!" And he would envelope us in a big bear hug. It wouldn't matter who was there. Jedidiah liked to hug everybody!

The Cousins came down to the "Eat, Swim, Eat, Swim, Eat, Swim, Sleep, at the Peppermill- All- You- Can- Eat -Sea Food –Buffet," with Jedidiah in August of 2010. Jedidiah could swim at the Peppermill outdoor pool with complete mobility! Everybody had a blast!!

We went back to the Peppermill in March of 2011 to celebrate Jedidiah's 10th birthday party, but sadly, without Jedidiah. We went in honor of him. We used the money Jedidiah left in his piggy bank. He would never tell us how much money was in it. He would never let anyone count it, especially not Justin. The day we scattered his ashes at the Chicken Tree we came back and let Justin open Jedidiah's Piggy Bank and count his money. Jedidiah had saved $197 in his little bank. We thought swimming at the Peppermill and eating the "All You Can eat Seafood Buffet" would be a good use of his money. Just family went. We missed the Buddy Werner Championships that was held that Sunday, but we got to ski with the team on Saturday for Race #6 make-up at Homewood.

Jedidiah would also have loved us to go to the Buddy Werner Championships and BBQ with the A and B teams at the Franciscan, which we have done with Jessica, Justin, and Jedidiah for the past 10 years. Jedidiah made the B Team, in 2009. Jedidiah attended his first Buddy Werner when he was 4 years. He was tagging along with the B

Team, which I had the honor to coach. It was spring skiing in the Sierra's at its worst. Three feet of wet, heavy "Sierra Cement" snow fell the night before the race. It rained the day of the race. The snow was too deep and heavy for us to practice running gates on the course. The gates weren't even set. I was coaching the B Team. I decided we should go in. I looked over at Jedidiah. He was crying and had snot hanging down from his nose to his belly. I said, "Hey, Jedidiah, what's wrong, are you cold?" Jedidiah said, 'No, I'm crying because you said we have to go in'. Hanging with the Buddy Werner Team would have been a good tribute to Jedidiah, too, on his 10th Birthday!

When Jedidiah returned home from the Ronald McDonald House and had time to recover and rest up, we signed him up for Physical Therapy in Quincy, with Cory Felker. We thought it would be good for Jedidiah to swim in the warm, indoor pool they had. But after a short time of going Jedidiah got too tired out. He decided that Physical Therapy wasn't any fun because they worked him too hard. Jedidiah said the PT for Physical Therapy really stood for 'Pain and Torture'. So, we let him stop going when it stopped being fun for him.

Jedidiah got his go-cart when he was eight years old. Cynthia was staying at Robbi Pruitt's place in Central Oregon while she worked at the Air Tanker Base in the summer. The boys went to Oregon and stayed with Cynthia for the last two weeks of August in 2009. Jedidiah got the go-cart by asking Robbi Pruitt. He said to her, 'Your kids have left home, and don't use this Go-Cart anymore. Hey, can I have it?" Robbi said yes, and we brought the go cart home in the back of the horse trailer. Jedidiah was so excited!

Jedidiah was an aggressive driver. He did power slides around the driveway. Jedidiah loved riding his go-cart! Thank you Robbi!!

Jedidiah got his first dirt when he was four years old. He started riding his little dirt bike with a 'stability' system. Cynthia said he couldn't ride all by himself. So I had to get a dirt bike too! Thanks to my brother, Rick, I could accompany Jedidiah. We rode up the roads and trails behind our house. Jedidiah loved to go! He was a tough, little rider. One time he got his stability system high centered on some rocks, and he was frustrated because he couldn't go anywhere. Another time, he fell over backward when his back tire got stuck in a mud hole in the creek… then his bike fell on him. I was afraid he was hurt. Jedidiah was wet and muddy, but he bounced up laughing!

A story I like telling is about the time Jedidiah and I we rode our dirt bikes to Happy Valley in October 2009. It was a few months before his brain tumor started growing. There are nine miles of dirt roads from our house up to Happy Valley, on the Beckwourth Ranger District of the Plumas National Forest. That Saturday we rode to Happy Valley, Jedidiah stood up on his dirt bike the whole way! That's how our neighbor, Sean, taught Jedidiah to ride. He told Jedidiah that REAL dirt bike riders ride by standing up over their foot pegs.

It was cold outside when we departed for Happy Valley. Jedidiah did not complain, he just wanted to get going. We left in such a hurry he did not make time to grab his coat. When we arrived at the aspen stand he was shivering cold. I let him wear my red Quincy Soccer sweatshirt during lunch in the aspen patch because he was so cold. We ate lunch with Jedidiah sitting on my lap. Then we looked for Basque carvings in the aspen tree. Who ever found the oldest date carved on the tree would win. Jedidiah found the oldest tree with the year of 1913. The Basque sheep herders were often lonely. Jedidiah also found a carving of a topless lady!

Before Jedidiah learned how to swim, we made him wear a life vest when he went swimming with the Cousins in Coeur d'Alene Lake. One day after swimming, Jedidiah wore his life vest all day at Camp Grandma. He also had his bicycle helmet on, and a fish stringer tied around his waist. Jedidiah caught his first fish of the dock by the 'Leaning Tree' when he was two years old. He caught it on his second cast. His cousin, Reid, took a picture of him wearing his diaper, with a binky in his mouth, and the fish in the air on his line.

Jedidiah did not like doing homework. He ran down the driveway screaming on the first day of 3rd grade when I tried to make him do his homework that night. Jedidiah's 3rd Grade teacher, Mrs. Lemnah, called us and said she thought Jedidiah had a learning disorder. I didn't know if he just didn't like doing homework or if it was beginning of brain tumor. Jedidiah did not like doing homework in the second grade, either. Dr. Z said their observations on how fast tumor grew in the lab petri dish made them think tumor only started growing in December 2009. The tumor was approximately the size of a walnut on Valentine's Day 2010, then 2" x 2"x

2" two weeks later when we were supposed to go home, but ended up going to emergency radiation instead.

Jedidiah was always suspicious of Santa. Santa never brought him what he asked for, so Jedidiah wondered why should he bother telling Santa what he wanted each year. Jedidiah asked for a blue puppy when he was four years old in 2005. He did not want a fake dog, but a real puppy- that's blue. All he got was a Blue Elk Wagon I could use to move hay bales.

He sat in Santa's lap at the lighting of the Christmas tree in Quincy in 2006. (I remembered that year, because on the walk from the Courthouse back to our car at the Post Office, Jedidiah "froze solid". It was so funny, because he locked up and wouldn't walk anymore. He told me he was so cold that he froze solid and we would have to carry him home. So, his Mom and I had to carry him, stretched out, flat as a board, while he was frozen stiff!) I heard him ask Santa that night for a Red Rocket that really goes to the moon. All he got was a rocket that you could launch, the kind you can get from Wal-Mart. First we launched it at home to try it out. The jet blast scream noise scared the horses so bad that Scrub ran through the back of the shed. Then we launched the Red Rocket from the QHS soccer field. It was a dry winter with no snow on the field and we caught the grass on fire. But we stomped the fire out, and the principal couldn't even tell where the fire was by spring time.

In 2007 Jedidiah asked Santa for a Blue Nano i-Pod. I thought it was too expensive for a little kid. So in 2007 Santa gave Jedidiah a remote controlled helicopter. Jedidiah flew it up one time inside the house and hit the ceiling and it crashed. We have that on video and you can hear someone saying, 'Oh look, here's the instructions!'

I gave Jedidiah a KHS bicycle from Paul's Bike Shop in Quincy, with a front shock and 5 gears! In 2008 Jedidiah asked Santa again for a Blue Nano i-Pod. Santa left another "helicopter what flies", this time a bigger one. That one lasted one month.

In 2009 I had Jedidiah's name and got him the biggest present under the tree. Jedidiah asked for a Chihuahua. I got him a coupon for a kitten and wrapped it up in a great big box. I didn't like Chihuahuas. I thought a kitten would be better. We couldn't find kittens in the winter. We looked at PAWs, and everywhere else we could. Just before Jedidiah's Celebration Day in May, Mike and Linda Hoover, from Bucks Lake, brought Jedidiah a black kitten from Reno. Jedidiah named her, 'Black Lightning', because she ran really fast all over the house. At Jedidiah's Celebration Day, on May 27th, 2010, another lady brought Jessica and Justin each a black kitten. Jessica named hers, 'Baby Cakes' and Justin named his, 'Midnight'. We went from having no cats to having three black cats, inside the house.

Cynthia bought Jedidiah a Chihuahua the week before my Birthday in September 2010. Jedidiah named the dog, 'Pep'. Jedidiah wanted a Chihuahua, because he liked to watch the movie, 'Beverly Hills Chihuahua'. Jedidiah used to watch that movie over and over even before he had his brain tumor. We took Pep on the BD camping trip. It was freezing at night so she got to sleep in the tent, in the sleeping bag with us. Jedidiah asked his mom in September, "Do you want me to die unhappy?" If she did not want him to die unhappy, then she needed to get him a Chihuahua!! Jedidiah told me that if I let Mom buy him Pep, I was off the hook for buying him a 6x6 and we'd call it even. I weighed the difference in price between DuPont's Polaris 6x6 with reverse, a snow plow and a trailer, and a two pound puppy. I said, "OK, let's get a Chihuahua!"

I bought Jedidiah a Blue Nano i-Pod as an 'I Love You Present' in June 2010. He took up to AK when he became the 650th Alaska Smokejumper. Jedidiah wiggled and wiggled when he got his Blue Nano i-Pod. There was only one blue one in the store. It was the display model. I pleaded with the store's manager to let me buy it. Jedidiah was so excited! He had Justin load it up with songs. Jedidiah would share his headphones with me or Justin so we could listen. Jedidiah used his Nano i-Pod everyday and took real good care of it. He had a case for it, and he kept it in its case all the time unless he was listening to it. Justin let Jedidiah use his bags he won at the Fair; "Plumas County Fair Best of Show Duck and Geese" and "Best of Show Chicken", sponsored by Dave and Jane Roberti and Kingdom Backhoe. Justin won them as 4-H Poultry Awards. Justin was so proud of them.

Jedidiah loved to answer any question you could think of about how to run, store, play, set, and save songs on his Blue Nano i-Pod. Jedidiah would sit for hours listening to his Blue Nano i-Pod. Jedidiah gave me his Blue Nano i-Pod in his will.

John Gould called me while Jedidiah was in the Pediatric Intensive Care Unit. Jedidiah's stay in the PICU was the worst 7 days of my life. The whole 6th floor had PICUs in each of the four corners of the wing,

There were 20 beds in each room, all attached to monitors. Whenever a monitor would flat line, all monitors would show the child's name so all emergency nurses would rush in to that bed. The monitors would flat line about once a night… and the whole family would stand around and cry. One crying mama held her dead daughter for 2 hours. Yet, every night, still the helicopters would land on the roof bringing more kids to the UC Davis Regional Children's Hospital … It was in that setting John Gould called me. He asked if there was anything he could do and to let me know that whenever Jedidiah wanted to go to Alaska- the trip was his. When Jedidiah could talk again we wrote down a list of things we were going to do when he got out of the hospital, a list of positive things to keep our spirits up. A trip to AK with John Gould was number one on the list!

The Social Worker at UC Davis never told us about Make-A-Wish. Cathy Rahmeyer in Quincy did. I applied. Make-A-Wish is an organization that grants wishes to terminally ill kids, a trip to Disneyland, a room make-over, a cruise. I remember the day they called back, I text the Cousins, 'the good news is Jedidiah is eligible for Make-A-Wish, the bad news is Jedidiah is eligible for Make-A-Wish'. They told me Jedidiah could wish for anything. Jedidiah only wanted one thing, a Polaris 6x6 so he can help do the chores, feed the horses, move hay, drive it by himself sitting up. We looked at brochures from DuPont's for hours and compared all features to get everything he wanted, reverse, headlights, winch, snowplow, trailer, etc. They showed up to ask Jedidiah what he wanted. Jedidiah said a Polaris 6x6. They said no that has a motor, that's against company policy, wish for something else. Jedidiah said a Polaris 6x6 without a motor. Duffy at DuPont's can put a motor in later. They said no, that's still considered a motorized vehicle. Jedidiah said then how about a Dragon 1,000 snowmobile, that doesn't have wheels! They said no, that's still not within our guidelines it still has a motor. Jedidiah got discouraged. They said how about a trip to Disneyland? Jedidiah said I do not want to go to Disneyland. They said how about a cruise? Jedidiah said how about a cruise to Alaska then to Hawaii with a cotton candy maker in my room when I get to Hawaii. They said no, that's 3 wishes, we can only grant one. Then to change tactics, they said, what do you want to be when you grow up? Jedidiah said, 'I want to be an Alaska Smokejumper, just like my dad!'

Make-A-Wish said okay, we'll fly you, your mom, dad, and Justin to Alaska for an Alaska Adventure. But since your grandma and sister are over 18 we can't pay any of their expenses.

June 1, 2010 to Make a Wish:

As requested Friday afternoon on the phone to reply on Tuesday, Jedidiah thought about his wish more over the weekend while swimming with his cousins, who flew down to spend Memorial Day weekend in the 4' heated pool in Reno with him for his, 'All You Can Eat Seafood Buffet, to Eat, Swim, Eat, Sleep, Eat!' Jedidiah said Plan B is to tour the Alaska Smokejumper base in Ft Wainwright AK, with his family, to watch a practice jump. We're available July 7th to July 12th!

John Gould is the Director of the Alaska Fire Service for a contact name. He's my, 'Rookie Bro'. His phone number is: (907) 356-5600. http://fire.ak.blm.gov/

Please be careful with how you ask my 9 year old downhill ski racer, who's raced on the Johnsville Ski Team since he was 4 and wore the #21 bib when he was 6 years old, you have to be 7 to be a member. Jedidiah was a dues paying racer at age 5!; he earned his own snowmobile; rides his own dirt bike; go-cart, and horse; plays a mean fiddle; who recited, 'The Cremation of Sam McGee' for his school talent show on February 12th, 2 days before he was life-Flighted to UC Davis Children's Hospital fighting a Glioblastoma multiformes brain tumor (http://en.wikipedia.org/wiki/Glioblastoma_multiforme), son what he really, really wants. To tell him its ok to be selfish and to think of himself. What does Jedidiah really want; a thing, a place to go, a person to meet, electronic equipment. Then to say no to a Razor, no to a Razor without a motor, no to a snowmobile, no to a trip to the AK SMJ base and RV to Mt McKinley with a cruise to Hawaii with a cotton candy maker in his room, and no to his big sister and grandma to accompany him, -but to use his imagination and think of something he really wants...

Jedidiah restated Plan A, is he really, really, really wants a Razor, with a winch, lights, reverse, radio, utility trailer and a snowplow. I don't have the money to buy him one. Jedidiah is so kind hearted and good natured he's happy with Plan B. So please be careful how you ask him what he really wants.

Please visit his web page his big sister has been keeping up to date to learn more about Jedidiah, to see how special he is and well loved by his family and our small Quincy community: http://www.caringbridge.org/visit/jedidiahLusk

I was friends with Terry Strle when I went to school at UAF. I called Terry to let her know we were coming. She said she was the Mayor of Fairbanks and we could hang with her at her cabin at Harding Lake for a BBQ and jet boat ride. North Pole, AK is 16 miles south of Fairbanks. I planned to stop there so Jedidiah could have a word with Santa.

In 1987, when Cynthia was a Rookie Smokejumper out of Redmond, OR, she got to go on a Fire Assignment to Fairbanks. That was back when girls couldn't do it. Her picture was on the inside door of my locker and her last name was on the front. She showed up wearing a blue tank top t-shirt that said, 'Alaska, where men are men, and women win the Iditarod'. I jumped out of Fairbanks at the tail end, when Para Cargo was Good and the Loft was Evil; when we did more before 0800 than most people did all day; when Clarkson was the King and Nemore was the Queen; when Dow for 7 was written on the Chinese Wall; when the first man in the door was handed the radio and was the fire boss; when C's still came in cans; when Mike Dirtshe skied on the US Ski Team, started #57 paying his own way racing in the World Cup and finished #17; when Don Bell was still telling stories around the jumper's camp fire; when Brown was on Black and Black was on Brown; when whenever Troy flew we, 'were off in a cloud of horse poop'; when it was, 'Oh what a feeling to be dancing on the ceiling!'; when there were no bad deals, -just deals; when the Big Flip was $25; when Tony Pastro stopped long enough to kick the last 500 gallon Rollagon out the back of the flaming C-119; when we carried our 44's in our left leg pocket and a fifth of Jack Daniels in our right leg pocket; when beer was sold for a dollar a can out of the pop machine in the Standby Shack, when first load rode in a van with the door open to the midnight meal; when you could log 24 hours a day with no days off while on fire; before there were 'Limited and No Attack'; back when I could do 10 pull ups, 35 pushups, 65 sit ups, and run 1.5 miles in under 8:12 minutes; when Fairbanks Area Research and Technology (FART) developed the Ram Air square parachute and we brought it down to Grand Junction where Sean Cross waived the Jolly Rodger on the ramp at BIFC, and said, 'We will jump any base, anywhere, at any time'. I'd often start telling stories to Jedidiah with, "There I was, no escape, flames all around me…"

I still wear my Alaska Smoke Jumper belt buckle every day. I didn't know I had told Jedidiah so many stories. It meant so much to me to hear Jedidiah say he, 'wants to be an Alaska Smokejumper, just like his Dad, when he grows up!'

I was hoping that maybe, with our connections with John Gould, my Rookie Bro, and Cynthia having jumped fires with the Base Manager, Bill Cramer, we might get to tour the Alaska Smokejumper base on one day and maybe even get to eat lunch with the Jumpers. Boy was I surprised how the Bros treated Jedidiah! Bill Cramer is a man among men!

We left the kids at Pikes Landing. We were supposed to meet at 1000 then bring the family in at 1300. Cynthia and I got to the base alone at 0800. We drove past the Married Housing barracks where Big Mac would ask to see your marriage license before he'd give you keys to your room. We drove past the spot where the Jump Shack used to be. We stopped and walked to the Chena Bridge at the Trainer Gate on the PT course with beavers still slapping the river that led to the Chena Pump House, where I asked Jedidiah's mama to marry me 24 years ago. I took all the kids back for supper after Jedidiah's Rookie ceremony where we all wore our best Carharts and Jedidiah made me get on my knee at the same table and propose to his mama again.

The Alaska Smokejumpers had it all planned out. We spent 3 days with the Jumpers. They put Jedidiah through Rookie Training, gave him an orange Rookie arm band, put him through parachute manipulation, spotter training, mock ups, and a tour of the whole AFS. We got to eat lunch, supper, and breakfast with the Bros. There was a bust going on so I got to see some of the old guys I jumped with:, Bozo, Colonel Major, Ron Lund, Ken Coe.

They let Jedidiah sit in the door and literally kick jumpers out the door. His pigtail was too tight he couldn't slap them on the back so he kicked them. He talked to the pilot and told him, 'left, left, more left, your other left, oh shoot, Get Ready, Go!' They let me and his mom go up in the Casa with him. Jedidiah kicked out Derek Patton- Lead Rookie Trainer and

Togie Wiehl- Loft Foreman. Gary Baumgartner was the Lead Spotter, Base Manager Bill Cramer was the Assistant Spotter. Mike Macmillan was the official photographer. They drove Jessica, Justin and Blue Nanny to the jump spot to watch. Jedidiah got to kick cargo at 200'. They drove us out to watch the second load.

Then the whole Alaska Fire Service gave Jedidiah an awards ceremony where they took off his Rookie armband. They gave him the 'Checking the Wind Drift' print, t-shirts, ball caps and cash from each base that was there. Bill Cramer presented Jedidiah his 'Rookie Wings' and Mr. Cramer let me give Jedidiah his Alaska Smokejumper belt buckle. Jedidiah stood and walked to me to get his belt buckle. I cried. The next day was a 'Mandatory Day Off' where, nowadays, if you work more than 14 days you have to have 1 day off or 2 in 21, (it's a bad deal to be off because you can't make any money). They set up 'Jumper Camp' with cargo chute hooches, 14 miles up the Chena, took us up by Jet Boat, saw moose on the ride in, cooked moose on a stick over an open campfire, fished for Grayling in the Chena River, drank root beer, and told stories around the campfire in the light of the Midnight Sun.

Then the very next day, big burly Alaska Smokejumper Jedidiah, got to go to the North Pole to sit on Santa's lap. Instead of asking something for himself, Jedidiah put in a good word for JD, Nano, and Quinn, who received letters from Santa in December 2010. Santa had a line of kids already waiting to see him, but he looked up and said, 'Come here Jedidiah, I've been expecting you!'

Jedidiah got out of his wheelchair and stood next to Santa. Santa gave Jedidiah "Weindeer" and an autographed 'Twas the Night before Christmas" book and took Jedidiah outside to help him feed his reindeer. Jedidiah forgot his doubt in Santa, he is real!

Each Christmas Eve I always tell the kids the story of when we were poor and had just moved to Terrebonne, Oregon. We didn't have enough money to buy more than just one present per kid, for Jessica and Justin. That year, on Christmas Eve, as Mom went to get a log from the woodpile on the porch, she reached for the handle on the sliding glass door at the very same time Santa's hand was reaching for the handle from the outside. Mom screamed! Santa dropped the 3 bags of presents outside and ran off! But that was back before Jedidiah was born…

In the afternoon we got to hang with the Mayor of Fairbanks, my college friend, Terry Strle, and her family. The kids went waterskiing and rode a wave runner. I rowed. Jessica and Justin took Jedidiah out in a paddle wheeler. There weren't any bugs to bother us and it was beautiful weather, with temperatures in the 90's.

On the drive up to ID to see the Cousins after our Alaska Adventure, we camped at Skull Hollow on the Crooked River National Grassland in Central Oregon. A Sherpa from Redmond Smokejumper base flew over and threw streamers then dropped a load of Jumpers. Our tent was 200 yards from the jump spot. We wheeled Jedidiah over to watch them land. Jedidiah told Tony Johnson, "I don't know how you do it down here, but in AK when I was Spotting, my Jumpers all hit the jump spot."

John Helmer, with the National Smokejumper Association drove to our house and gave Jedidiah a check for $3,350 for his trip to Alaska. The Alaska Smokejumpers started 'Jumping for Jedidiah' where each jumper at each base gave $5.00 to Jedidiah for each Fire Jump as the summer progressed. We used that money to help pay Blue Nanny's and Jessica's expenses to AK, buy Jedidiah a Wii he always wanted, bought Pep, and to help pay Jedidiah's funeral expense, -which came way too early.

I love you Jedidiah!
I will always remember you!
I will never forget you!

Here's a note I wrote to Lynn Roby on April 15^{th,} 2011 when our friend from Terrebonne, Oregon, Laurel Skelton, was told she had a GBM in April 2011.

Our 9 year old son, Jedidiah, was diagnosed with a GMB on Valentine's Day 2010. We never gave up hope for a cure. We played hard, prayed, talked, and laughed lots!

Early on the morning of Valentine's Day last year, we had Life Flighted Jedidiah to UC Davis because the cat scan at our small local community hospital had showed 'something' on his brain stem. UC Davis took 10 days to grow and diagnosis Jedidiah's biopsy culture to make sure of their diagnosis. The day of the biopsy, the neuro surgeon told us it was a GBM. Pathology confirmed our fears 10 days later.

We learned there are 161 different kind of brain tumors. That's why UC Davis wanted to make sure of their diagnosis. Jedidiah had a Glioblastoma multiformes brain tumor, "GBM". Glioblastoma are the cells that produce the fluid that cushion the brain. Multiformes means they come in many different forms. Not much is known on them and little research has been done since they are so rare. They said GBMs are the most aggressive.

Our UC Davis PICU nurse dismissed herself from our case. She had a 9 year old son with a GBM 10 years earlier. She said she'd answer any questions I had. I did not know what to ask her. Deputy Shawn, one of our Plumas County Deputies, was diagnosed a year before Jedidiah with a GBM and would often stop by. He brought the SWAT Team in full regalia and made Jedidiah an Honorary SWAT Team member, took him to shoot his SWAT guns, and held a golf fund raiser for Jedidiah! Cynthia leaned on Deputy Shawn a lot to ask questions. The three of them would often meet for lunch. Deputy Shawn went to UC San Francisco for surgery and had radiation and tried an experimental new chemo.

Dozer is a 10 year old boy in Oklahoma, we heard about through some friends of friends. He was diagnosed two months before Jedidiah. He had 3 small tumors that were removed. He had surgery and radiation in OK then went to Pittsburg for an experimental new vaccine. He flies to Pittsburg once every 3 weeks for the 1 minute vaccine. We talked with his folks a lot. Jedidiah's tumor was too deep for surgery. The Neuro-surgeon paralyzed his left side doing the biopsy. He left the hospital strapped in a high-back wheel chair. But he did grow nerves in his brain from his left side to connect to his right side to enable him to move his left side and take steps again. He had 33 days of isometric radiation at UC Davis, which shrank the tumor 20%.

With Make-a-Wish and the Alaska Smoke Jumpers, Jedidiah became an Alaska Smokejumper Spotter and kicked Smokejumpers out of the jumpship last summer in Alaska! Dozer's Oncologist told Dozer last month his tumors have regrown and spread. We plan to meet Dozer at Bishop Mule Days in Bishop, CA on Memorial Day Weekend and buy a jack donkey from his grandparents. We went to Deputy Shawn's funeral last month. Dr Z. told us every case is different and everybody reacts differently. Dr. Z told us GBM's are extremely rare, and are 100% terminal.

On July 13th, last summer, on a routine MRI visit, Dr Z shocked us with the news that Jedidiah's tumor had quadrupled in size, grown tentacles, and there was nothing else he could do. He said, "Call Hospice, and enjoy every day you have left with him". Dr Z gave Jedidiah two weeks more to live, until the end of July. Dr Z said Jedidiah would get sleepier and sleepier, then one day, just not wake up. We did not call Hospice, but we played hard, prayed, talked, and laughed lots all through the summer and fall!

Jedidiah went to school to be with his friends this fall. He would raise his left hand, just because he could, and tell the class, 'I'm still alive, today!' Jedidiah outlived the Doctor's prediction -and We Lived Each Day! Jedidiah stopped eating on Thanksgiving.

On December 8th he just wanted to rest in bed. He slept most of the day after that but would wake up and talk with me from 0100 to 0400. He sang Happy Birthday to his Mama on December 14th! He smiled when we unwrapped his presents and told him what he got for Christmas! He stopped drinking on New Year's Eve. He remained conscious and would ring a bell, or raise an eyebrow to communicate with us. Then on January 3rd, at 8:58 at night, with all of us gathered around, he just breathed in, and never breathed out again. Cynthia accepted the diagnosis last year, back in February. I'm still in shock, anger, disbelief and denial. My unopened 2010 Valentine's Day present to Jedidiah is a water bottle and a Sierra cup filled with Hershey Kisses for our PCT hike that I'm going to give to Dozer when I meet him at Bishop Mule Days in hopes that Dozer gets to use it on a hiking trip!

There are a lot of tuff choices involved when a loved one has a brain tumor. I would do radiation again. I think that is what extended Jedidiah's life. They said 33 days was the maximum dose, any more would kill good brain tissue. I would not do chemo again. We stopped chemo after the first round. We were scheduled for 6 one week treatments with 6 weeks rest in between. The chemo UC Davis prescribed was used to make Mustard Gas. Jedidiah's blood cell counts plummeted the 5th week, as they said it would. We decided to have quality of life vs. length of life. I would not do Decadron again. It made his face swell beyond recognition and he doubled in weight.

Jedidiah was never in pain.

Jessica kept a web page on Jedidiah at www.caringbridge.org/visit/ jedidiahlusk. It's free! You might want to have someone set one up and post updates for you. Jessica posted updates to keep everyone in the loop and we didn't have to answer every one who asked how's he doing? People asked, 'What can we do to help?' It took us awhile to make a list, we're not used to asking for help; but people really wanted to and liked to help!

Our List: Look me straight in the eye, touch my shoulder, and say, I'm here; freeze meals since no one feels like cooking right now; bring over a complete hot meal on Wednesdays; fix the Scout so Justin can get his driver's license; split and stack the firewood rounds; rake pine needles to reduce fire hazard; finish nailing the boards on the tack room. FS held two work Saturdays, with BBQ's! The Rodeo Team held a Rodeo benefit! The Plumas County Deputy's held a golf fund raiser! The elementary school and coworkers organized a Jedidiah Celebration Day for us that we wanted to use to say Thank You back to the community for all their help, but instead it turned out to be another fund raiser with items donated that raised over $12,000! His classmates sang songs, played the recorder, and had his favorite musicians. Jedidiah joined in! Jessica had a PowerPoint slide show loop with 650 photos of Jedidiah with his family and friends playing in the back ground. Another lady took all our bills, I would hand them to her unopened. She would organize them, fight with the insurance companies, write and receive grants to pay the bills.

Play hard, pray, talk, and laugh lots!

I'm here! I'm a phone call away. Cynthia is at RAC for the summer if you want someone to talk with!

Sunday, January 2, 2011 12:49 PM, PST

January 2, 2011

We're back! Justin, Jessica and I spent the week after Christmas in CDA with the Cousins! We were all here for Christmas. Jedidiah actively participated on Christmas Day! Jedidiah would feel presents with his fingers when we gave them to him and ring his bells, smile with his eyebrows and wiggle his legs to show he liked the presents! When we left, we all kissed Jedidiah and said we'll see you in a week! I sat on his foot and he said, 'Ouch'! Jedidiah kissed Jessica back on her cheek, -and he aimed a right round house at Justin!

Our plan was for all of us to go to CDA, but as it turned out, Jedidiah was too sleepy to travel that far, so Cynthia said she would stay home with Jedidiah. We had a blast shooting skeet off the deck at Tim's Cabin; skiing powder at Silver Mountain; spending the night in the Condo; surfing at the water park; playing several games of pick-up basketball at the Kroc; bouncing off the walls at the trampoline park; watching Carli step in to play after her ACL surgery as her team won the Championship tournament game; and spending quality family together time driving 18 hours up and back!

I read Cynthia's updates. She wrote Jedidiah was unresponsive. To me, an unresponsive Jedidiah means when you tell him not to get his good school shoes wet in the creek the day before Valentine's Day in 2010, then he jumps in past his ankles and he sends mud splattering all over his brother, grinning ear to ear! I was not ready for this kind of 'unresponsive' when I got back and saw Jedidiah last night. I knew it was coming and have had a while to prepare. But I'm not ready for it. Cynthia has been doing the daily physical hands on part the past few days of rolling Jedidiah to change his hospital pants, holding his head to brush his teeth, and lifting him to change his clothes. But that's not what I wanted to write about. I want to tell people about Jedidiah's unconquerable spirit! My little guy who rides snow mobiles fast, stands up on dirt bikes, floors 4-wheelers, wore the #21 bib in ski races, the second fastest on my team, plays the fiddle, and -who does not like homework!

Throughout this entire 10 month ordeal Jedidiah has remained his sweet, caring, funny guy. He never once said, "Oh why me" or "Oh pity me" or even be ashamed of how huge he had gotten, from 67 pounds to 142 pounds! When he went back to school at the end of the third grade last year some kids said you don't look like Jedidiah, he said it's because the Decadron made my face swell and gain weight. When asked why he had no hair, Jedidiah explained because he had had radiation and chemo for a brain tumor. When asked why he's in a wheel chair, Jedidiah said it's because they nicked my brain stem doing the biopsy. His friends and schoolmates have been very supportive and kind. No one made fun of Jedidiah!

Jedidiah wanted to do all the activities we wrote about in his journal. He wanted to be an Alaska Smoke Jumper, so the Bros did it! Jedidiah told jokes to the Smoke Jumpers from his book of jokes he memorized while at the Ronald McDonald House. He wanted to be baptized and understands why. He told jokes at Church on the microphone when Pastor George forgot his for the sermon. He wanted to ride the school bus home the last day of 3rd grade! He wanted to go on the Hiawatha Trail with the Cousins, so we found a bike trailer and he did, and took pictures of moose on the trail! Jedidiah loved to swim because he had unlimited mobility again and could do all the things he used to do on land in the water. At the pool this summer a little girl said, 'Oh, you're the little boy with brain cancer who's going to die.' Jedidiah replied, 'Yes, we are all going to die at some time, live life now'. He wanted to make "Cotton Cloud" Cotton Candy free for his friends and only charge $1 for the others, but if you didn't have a dollar, he said just mail him two hard candies and he'd mail you yours. He donated all the money he made at the Farmer's Market selling Cotton Clouds for the Quincy History Club's trip to Greece this year. He loved going to school this year and being in the 4th grade because he got to see all his friends and he didn't have to do any homework! He would raise his hand and answer questions at the start of the 4th grade this year.

Jedidiah made a list of things he wanted to do after he left the hospital and he has crossed most of the things off of his list. His list is amazing for a 9 year old! Travel to Alaska to meet John Gould and the Alaska Smokejumpers; Camp out at Mike Donald's Cabin at Lake Almanor; Set up a 'Cotton Cloud' Cotton Candy business with the cotton candy maker he got from the Cousins; Camp out at 'Cowboy Camp' and help in the Cook Shack at the Taylorsville Silver Buckle Rodeo; Play with the Cousins in CDA; Get a Chihuahua; Ride in a limo; Get a 4-wheeler. Thank You to all of you who have made it possible! He died before he got to: Hike the Pacific Crest Trail; Go elk hunting in AZ with Dan Key; Kiss Rxxxx!; or Live to see if the world ended on December 21, 2012.

Jedidiah told me a couple months ago that after he dies, he wants to be cremated, like Sam McGee, and to give half his ashes to Justin and Jessica and to spread the other half under the Chicken Tree.

Jedidiah asked me not to forget him! I said, "I never will"

After breakfast, we gave Jedidiah the Christmas presents his Cousins made for him. He's wearing the Whitworth Football shirt Connor gave him. We passed around the jar of hot peppers Robert and Sarah gave him. Jedidiah spread his fingers to help when Justin put on the bracelet Cole made for him out of turquoise, white, and black duct tape and he squeezed the day-time-blue water bottle with the smiley face sticker Carli made that says:

"Always be Positive for Jedidiah"

Jedidiah and Family in front of their newly built home, in Cromberg, CA, 2007.

REFLECTIONS ON JEDIDIAH

By Helene Lemnah
Jedidiah's Third Grade Teacher
Pioneer/Quincy Elementary School

When Jedidiah entered third grade in the fall of 2009, he could have been described as a classic "fly on the wall." While he was a very capable scholar, school was apparently not his thing. He never raised his hand to participate, and often had this far-away look that made me think that he was most likely reliving some exciting 4-wheeling ride rather than listening to the lesson. That being said, when I could "squeeze" a little work out of him, it was always excellent. In fact, it was outstanding. Math was a cinch for Jedidiah. He wrote and read above grade level, and always kept his desk meticulously organized. When it came to turning in homework, he would give me the funniest look of "Who, me? What homework?" I would literally have to force myself not to laugh. When I asked him any question, he would answer in a whisper. If I didn't tell him, "Jedidiah, speak to be heard!" once, I told him a thousand times. That was in class.

Outside, he came alive. Recess and P.E. suddenly revived him. He could go down the zip line and hoist himself up the whole way: a rare feat for a third grader. He dominated the soccer field and outran any of his classmates. That's when I saw his big, radiant grin. Several situations could ignite his passion: the indignation of being pursued relentlessly by a little girl who had a crush on him, the competition of his best friend wanting to take his spot in line next to another little girl they both liked, the rush of a tight kickball game. I never had to ask him to speak to be heard then.

Before school started, he would frequently tell me of his outdoor adventures, especially of his dirt bike riding exploits. He would bring me little treasures featuring the handiworks of bugs and other critters: twigs carved by larvae, pinecones chewed to the core by squirrels. He sure had a connection with animals of all kinds.

Justin and my son Alex were on the same soccer team, so I would get to see Jedidiah at the high school games, usually kicking the ball on the sideline. I can picture him in his cub-scout uniform, handing me an order form for popcorn. His only canvass was his irresistible grin. The rest was up to me to figure out. I did make him tell me about his fundraiser, just for the fun of it. He really scored with all of us sitting in the stands.

For the school talent show, which was, I believe, the Wednesday before Valentine's Day, he chose to recite "The Cremation of Sam McGee" by Robert W. Service… a most unlikely choice for a third grader. Cynthia explained to me that Justin had memorized it for an English class, and Jedidiah learned it just by listening to him recite it over and over again. For the performance, he wore a much-oversized parka with his face completely concealed by its huge fur-lined hood. The sleeves practically touched the floor. He recited the poem in a classic monotone, matter-of-fact way, which was perfect for this long narrative poem. Toward the end, Cynthia had to feed him lines from backstage. Jedidiah could not quite hear her, probably because of the thick hood over his head, and would pause until she repeated the lines loudly enough for him to hear. That was an unforgettable mother-and-son performance.

The next day, we had our class Valentine's Day Party in the afternoon. That event gave me my last snapshot of Jedidiah before he got ill: laughing with his friends, reading silly Valentine's cards and stuffing his face with candy.

The following week was our February break. I took Alex on a college tour in Southern California. On our way back, I called my husband from a phone booth off the highway to keep him updated. He told me about Jedidiah's brain tumor, and his hospitalization in Sacramento. Between the traffic noise and the shock of such bad news, I had him repeat several times what my mind could not compute: it couldn't be my little student Jedidiah, it could not be cancer, it could not be now.

But it was. At the hospital, I stared at him, sprawled over the sheets with his giant scar. I could not believe it. What was even more unbelievable, was Cynthia's strength and courage. She told me something that made a huge impression on me. In fact, I have quoted it many times since. When

Jedidiah heard of the seriousness of his illness, he likened himself to some of the animals they raised that died before being fully grown. He said something to the effect that he will probably die young, just like they did. Some die old, some die young, and that's that. Wow! Such simple, working wisdom regarding one's own death. I am still in awe.

The months that followed were heart-breaking, and yet completely inspiring to me: the rallying faith and strength of the Lusk family, the website news kept up by Jessica, the community support, Jedidiah's amazing attitude toward it all.

When he came back to class to visit in the spring, looking like his new "puff ball" self, he explained very scientifically and kindly to his classmate what had happened to him. HE was reassuring THEM! There was no more "fly on the wall" Jedidiah. He raised his hand; he wanted to contribute; he spoke as loudly as he could; he even wanted me to send work home with him. Every time he came, he had new jokes, new riddles. He was unstoppable.

That summer, I shared an extra special moment with Jedidiah, when I met him and Jessica at the pool. Jedidiah and I floated around the pool, leaning our arms over the same big noodle, side by side. He told me about his goofy dreams; I told him about mine, and we had some good laughs. With him moving in the water, away from his wheelchair, it was as if the weight of his crippling illness had vanished for a short, precious while.

The Lusks were very generous in letting me pay Jedidiah some home visits. We played the recorder together; watched his new puppy do its puppy tricks, read stories. Jedidiah let me kiss his bouncy, warm cheeks. Every time I left, I felt like I had stepped on holy grounds.

I keep the program of his memorial service on the inside cover of my planner: "Always Be Positive." Jedidiah and his family have taught me lessons about acknowledging death as an intricate part of life that I cannot quite put into words. They have certainly heightened my desire to make the best of the life I do have, and not to take for granted the health of those around me, especially the health of my students. One practical result is that I make a point of being as positive as possible when I dismiss my students at the end of a school day. I just never know if I am going to see their same smiley faces the next day. Thank you, Jedidiah.

REMEMBERING JEDIDIAH LUSK

BY Julie Hochrein, 4th grade Teacher

March 2011

Once upon a time I knew a boy named Jedidiah Lusk. I actually knew Jedidiah before he was born. His brother, Justin, was an excellent scholar in my 2nd grade class one year, and his lovely mother of many talents often came to volunteer in the classroom. Then I knew of his beautiful sister, Jessica, and his charming father Scott. I would run into all them at Forest Service functions or skiing events. When Jedidiah started showing through Cynthia's slight frame, it was amazing to see her continue all her strenuous work with animals and forest fires. Jedidiah didn't slow her down a bit, which is perhaps why he came into this world full of energy and a desire to explore every bit of his surroundings.

    I heard of Jedidiah as a young child, how he would put on his skis and want to be out there racing with the big kids. We could see this child was a force to contend with and nothing would stop him. I knew Jedidiah as a 3rd grader on the playground. People would tell me he was quiet, but I could see the sparkle and playfulness in his eyes. He was anything but quiet on the inside. I usually look over the younger children, wondering what they will be like if I have them as students, trying to get to know them a bit at recess. I hoped that Jedidiah would be in my 4th grade class, because I knew he and his family would be active participants in any class.

    It was devastating news when he was diagnosed with a brain tumor. I heard the news almost simultaneously through the ski teams, school and the Forest Service. The CaringBridge website was a daily read for me. The family's positive energy convinced me that Jed would get through this. Also, that year I had a boy who had missed my class as a 3rd grader due to cancer, and was back and thriving as a 4th grader. Of course, I was sure this would be the outcome for Jed.

As the summer progressed, it became clear that this was a different story. Jedidiah was there on the first day of school, with all his eager classmates, feeling the excitement with them and perhaps a little apprehension at the leap from the primary to the intermediate grades. This was new territory for all of us. Of course, Jedidiah was always welcome, but he really couldn't do any of the work or much physical activity. I tried to let Scott and Cynthia know when there were opportunities for him to participate. Perhaps he was relieved not to have any homework; but then again, maybe it wouldn't have been so bad to be like all the other kids. I also heard he didn't care for math; and I'm disappointed I didn't have a chance to change his mind about that. Anyone who can solve the puzzles of a motorized engine can solve the puzzles of mathematics.

One thing I noticed was that when Jedidiah was present, he always had something to say or a story to tell. (Who said this boy was quiet?) Of course, he was always polite, and yes, he had some jokes to tell, but he had much more to tell us. He told us about his experiences over the summer and fall, living an entire lifetime in a few short months, his treatments and symptoms. I remember him telling us about how in the hospital he thought his arm was not his, and wanted them to take it away. He shared his Chihuahua, Pep, and brought cotton candy to all the kids. He came for some special events and met us on a field trip.

The students were dealt with honestly, and Jedidiah was open and frank. We made 1,000 cranes as a symbol of our good thoughts and wishes, but it was explained that there was nothing magic about the cranes. Nurse Jody came in to talk about cancer, and the question came up, would Jedidiah get better? The children were thoughtful and took in all this information with a solemn sincerity.

Having taught for so many years, I can make a few generalizations about children in the 7-11 age range. One is that they are very smart and perceptive, much more so than most adults want to acknowledge. I am sure that Jedidiah knew he was touching all of us, and his classmates responded in their thoughts and hearts.

Jedidiah died on the evening of January 3, 2011. I felt so honored and grateful to be included in the first round of phone calls that evening.

I was prepared, but nervous for what would be the hardest teaching day of my career. Most of the children already knew of his death. After all, this is Quincy, where news spreads like wildfire, and many parents were reading CaringBridge daily. They were too silent and some were tearful as they arrived that morning. I just waited quietly until all were present to start talking about Jed. Then we couldn't stop. We talked and read and wrote and cried and laughed. All activities that day were devoted to Jedidiah. The children were amazing. They understood that everyone was grieving, and that they had lost a dear friend they would never forget.

Time has passed, and perhaps it seems that life just goes on. But our lives are forever entwined with Jed's. I barely knew him and I am jealous of those who knew him well, but I will never forget him. He knew he was touching our lives as he was dying, and he taught us so much. He taught us to live life to the fullest, to appreciate all that we have, and that a smile and laugh go a long ways to making someone's day special.

Jedidiah's celebration of life, his memorial service, was the most beautiful I have ever attended. That is behind us now. Cynthia occasionally comes into the classroom to help. My heart aches for her, and yet the children are so honest and healing, I know why she comes. Jed's desk remains unoccupied with his first day nametag still there. We use it for art projects. For example, I'll say, "Put your finished art in the box on Jed's desk," or "The scissors and glue sticks are on Jed's desk." We bump into hundreds of cranes on a daily basis as they continue to float in the classroom.

On what would have been Jedidiah's 10th birthday, March 30, 2011, we will plant a peach tree in the garden in his honor. This will not be a solemn event, as the kids will be excited to plant a tree and work in the garden. They will be able to tell others as the years go by, that this is Jedidiah's tree. As future classes come through and get to eat a peach from the tree, they will read the plaque and be told the story of Jedidiah, the brave and loving boy that inspired many.

Once upon a time there was a boy named Jedidiah Lusk. His life was short, but it was packed with love, energy and awe for the world around him. He taught us many lessons in his short life, and his story will never be forgotten. He is etched in my memory and of so many others forever.

"MY JEDIDIAH MEMORIES"
By Donnal Nichols *(AKA: Blue Nanny- Jedidiah's Grandmother)*

Part 1

Jedidiah was a much-loved little boy, from before he was born and throughout his life. On March 30, 2001 at Plumas District Hospital in Quincy, California, his family was anxiously awaiting his birth. We were all there to welcome him, hold him, and bond with our little Jedidiah.

I have many precious memories to remember of Jedidiah. I was so blessed to live nearby and to share in his care and experiences- bathing him, playing with him, etc. It was fun to watch his big sister and brother learns to care for their new little brother. We have lots of photographs to remind us of the special moments in Jedidiah's life. It will be hard to just sort out a few to write about.

In 2001, I lived at Philo, California, helping care for my aging father and mother. During the summers I went to live in Sloat in my travel trailer to help with Horses Unlimited, Inc. Therapeutic Horseback Riding Program. From there, I could watch over the horses used in the program and I had corrals for my horses to live in. Sometimes I would babysit Jedidiah when Cynthia was at work during the summers. When Jedidiah stayed with me in Sloat, he would happily play in the sand pile with his little cars and trucks- or when it was hot; he could splash and play with toy boats in one of the water troughs partly full of water. He was such a happy little boy and loved building roads in the sand and driving his cars and trucks along them. He would also "race" his matchbox and hot wheel cars down a "race track" created with slanted boards. He was very good at entertaining himself and playing where I could keep an eye on him.

After my father and mother both passed away, I moved back to Cromberg and rented a singlewide trailer off Gill Ranch Road, which is near Cynthia and Scott's property where they were building a home. The singlewide was on the way home for Jessica and Justin. When they got off the school bus they could stop by for a snack and do their homework while waiting for their parents to come home from work.

A seasonal creek ran by the singlewide and went through a culvert under the road. One of Jedidiah's favorite things to do was design "boats" and put them in the creek above the culvert, then run across the road, to watch them come out on the other side of the culvert. The boats would cascade out of the culvert in a waterfall, to resurface in a pool of water below. Then, Jedidiah would run down the side of the creek to a wider pool where we would retrieve his boats further down the creek. His challenge was to build a boat that would survive the trip through the culvert and over the falls and do it FAST!

Jedidiah would collect all types of containers to convert to experimental boats. He was very intelligent and mechanical, always borrowing our tools to "work" on something. Very soon he had his own tool box full of small tools that he learned to take care of. He also loved to take things apart with his tools, to see what made them work.

In 2006 I accepted a part time job as Receptionist for the U.S. Forest Service at the Mt. Hough Ranger District office just outside of Quincy. There were times when I was able to pick up Jedidiah after school and drive him home with me. It was always interesting to pick him up from Ken Nelson's Day Care. Ken provided many fun activities for the children he cared for. In the summer, the favorite was walking to the pool and park. The children loved playing on the swings and slides and wading in the pool. On these days we picked up Jedidiah at the park, it always took him a long time to leave his fun activities.

Jedidiah learned to balance on a two wheel bike after a few tries with his brother helping him. He almost immediately progressed to a mini-motorcycle dirt bike that would go FASTER.

In the winter I pastured my horses at Bob and Jamie's barn. It has a steep metal roof so the snow slides off easily. Jedidiah loved climbing up those ice and snow "mountains" to slide down the other side. He would have loved to be here this winter, with all the snow "mountains" to play on. This winter we had LOTS of snow during two large storms, instead of spaced out over the winter as usual.

Jedidiah learned to play the fiddle early in life. Since Scott, Jessica and Justin were already playing, he started too. Jedidiah memorized a fiddle tune, and played it, in order to earn a mean, green snowmobile he wanted very badly!

He was pretty good at doing his school homework- until he decided that school work was for at SCHOOL, and NOT at home. Sometimes he did his homework easily, and sometimes he would not focus on it. Then one day his teacher told Cynthia that she thought Jedidiah had a learning disability. I could not believe that at first. But, she was right- that Jedidiah COULD NOT focus, not just that he WOULD not on his homework. Jedidiah was also not doing well in the sports he was participating in- basketball and ski team. Maybe he couldn't focus there either.

One day Jedidiah decided that he was going to memorize a poem for the Talent Show at school. He was in the third grade. A favorite book of Scott and Cynthia's is the poems of Robert Service. Scott, Cynthia, Jessica and Justin had ALL memorized the poem, "The Cremation of Sam McGee", by Robert Service. Now Jedidiah decided he would also memorize this poem for the Talent Show. We have a video tape of his performance, with Jedidiah all dressed up in an Alaskan parka, reciting his chosen poem.

Jedidiah loved doing Cub Scout activities and the Pinewood Derby. Scott had made a Pinewood Derby car when he was a Cub Scout, with his father helping him. (Scott has kept his Cub Scout Pinewood Derby race car all these years!) Now, this father/son activity provided Scott and Jedidiah a chance to build a race car for Jedidiah to race, passing along the family secrets of how to make a car that goes FAST! Jedidiah worked a long time- carving, sanding, sanding some more, painting, practice runs, putting graphite on the axel and wheels, and getting psyched up to be ready for the big, official race. Cynthia and Scott were not able to attend, due to work duties. I transported Jedidiah and the precious Pinewood Derby cars (packed in bubble wrap) to the race and Cub Scout Dinner. Justin and Jessica also showed up for support. Justin video- taped the races so Scott and Cynthia could watch the action too. Jedidiah was sooo excited, as were all the Cub Scouts with their special race cars. At the end of the Scouts races, Jedidiah was allowed to race his car against the Pinewood Derby car Scott had made as a child. It was a very special evening.

One evening in February, the family went to a spaghetti feed before a wrestling match that Justin's friend Adam was competing in. Jedidiah did not feel well. Later at the wrestling match he was telling people they had two noses and four eyes. Then I realized that Jedidiah was having double vision. Why would he suddenly have double vision? Had he bumped his head or fallen off something at school? Then Cynthia mentioned that he had complained of a headache the day before.

The next day Jedidiah started throwing up. His parents thought he had the flu. The following morning he was still vomiting. He had not been able to keep any food down during that time. I was very worried. Headache, double vision, and vomiting were all three symptoms of increased intracranial pressure. If he had not suffered some sort of head trauma, then there must be something inside his skull to increase the pressure. Jedidiah was rapidly becoming weak and gravely ill. Cynthia drove him to the emergency room where the visiting ER doctor decided he had the flu that was going around. Thanks to Debbie DeSelle, RN and friend of the family's, who convinced the doctor that Jedidiah needed further testing. A CAT scan was performed and the imaging was sent to a radiologist in Reno to be read. Hospital personnel told Cynthia it may be some time before they get back with the results. The Radiologist phoned back almost immediately! He said that Jedidiah should be sent to U.C. Davis Medical Center STAT! Life Flight was called from Chico and Jedidiah was at once put on the helicopter and flown out to USDMC in Sacramento. This was the beginning of the nightmare! Glioblastoma multiformes was on his brain stem.

While Jedidiah was in the hospital having radiation and chemo treatments, someone sent him a book of jokes- Cynthia and Scott read books to him and he enjoyed jokes. Soon, he wanted us to read that book of jokes over and over to him. He was memorizing the jokes! He started telling jokes to the doctors and nurses, then everybody. Jedidiah became famous for telling jokes in times of stress, making everybody laugh. When I felt like crying in frustration, Jedidiah was telling jokes!

Jedidiah also loved watching the stock car races at the Plumas County Fairgrounds. He was given a Season Pass and probably attended most of the races that last year. He preferred to sit in the front row where he watch, feel and hear the cars coming out of the turn and accelerating for the straightway. We would position his wheelchair to the spot of his liking and wrap him in a blanket to keep him warm. Jedidiah would get mud-splattered, from all the mud flung off the race car tires…and he LOVED it! All the race car drivers knew Jedidiah by name and gave him all kinds of autographed souvenirs

When Jedidiah was diagnosed with terminal cancer, the Make-A-Wish Foundation decided to grant a final wish to Jedidiah. It was sad because everything Jedidiah wished for was denied by them. Jedidiah had absolutely no interest in the things they offered him. Finally they decided to try funding a trip to Alaska for him. The Alaska Smokejumpers got involved with an agenda of their own and made it happen- a trip to Fairbanks and the Alaska Smokejumper Base for the entire family!

It was a most memorable trip and experience! Rookie Training for Jedidiah, watching him throw out streamers from the airplane, kicking out jumpers, AND a jet boat ride up the Chena River to the Rookie Camp out! I will be forever grateful to all the Alaska Smokejumpers who participated in providing Jedidiah that precious experience, and for letting us be there to share it with him. Also, I am thankful for Mike McMillan, who created a world class photo record of Jedidiah's adventure. Even though Jedidiah is gone, we still have the photo memories of his wish.

There are many other memories, but these stand out most in my mind at this time. -Donnal Nichols, March 2011.

Part 2

NIKITA'S TUMOR
By Donnal Nichols

Nikita is Scott's Border collie that he has had for several years. Nikita is a very loving dog who helps us keep watch over the horses, mules, goats and chickens. She is happiest when she has something to herd and watch over. Nikita is very happy when I go out to check the goats or to feed the baby goats that need bottle-feeding. She runs ahead of me and checks out the little goats before I get there. When it was snowing, the baby goats slept in the back of the horse trailer at night. Nikita helped me herd them from the goat pen to the horse trailer at night and back to the goat pen in the mornings.

Sometime while Jedidiah was at UC Davis Medical Center getting his treatments, I noticed a small growth under Nikita's tail. It looked like she was sprouting a little testicle. When Cynthia and Scott got home, Cynthia took Nikita to the veterinarian to have it checked out. Nikita had an inoperable tumor- which was growing rapidly. Ironic that both Nikita and Jedidiah had a tumor at the same time. It turned out to be an interesting thing. Jedidiah had his tumor inside his skull and was unable to see what was happening with it. Nikita's tumor was on the outside so we could see it and tell how big it was growing. One day Jedidiah was looking at Nikita said, "It is a good thing Nikita's tumor is not in her head, because the tumor is as big as her head now!"

So, it is sort of like Nikita's tumor was there to help Jedidiah see and understand how the tumors grow and what his brain tumor was doing also

Part 3

A SCAB
By Donnal Nichols

When I was a teenager, I participated in a lot of activities that predisposed me to skinned arms and knees. If I crashed on my bicycle, I somehow managed to get road rash on my arms or knees. When I played softball and slid into second base, I had road rash on my leg or hip. Once the wound dried out and became crusty, they were not of much concern... until the scab started to heal at the edges and became caught on clothing and pulled on the entire scab. At this point, I usually started picking off the dry edges- thinking that a little pain off and on was not as painful as snagging the scab and getting the entire thing yanked off accidentally.

This is somewhat how I feel about my experiences with people who are dying.

As a child I loved and enjoyed my grandfather. He told us wonderful stories- some true and some fantasy. He gave us rides on his horses and taught us to help him with ranch chores and hunting. We enjoyed him. But, that changed after he had a stroke and was not able to participate in his usual activities. He became grouchy, yelled at us, and called us hurtful names. It was like he became a different person.

My father was very much like my grandfather. We enjoyed doing things and going places with him- until he was dying of cancer. It was then he became another person- cranky and mean to us.

I think these men felt frustrated that they could not do the things they used to do. They had to adapt to a new situation and were grieving for what they had lost. They had been strong men, leaders, and head of their households. Now they were becoming invalids, not having the same powers. We did not understand that at the time. It was just hurtful for us, their loved ones.

Now, I sort of feel those little hurtful times were like picking off the edges of the scab. Little hurts, so we can start letting go of that person a little at a time, so it will not be such a big hurt when they do die. That once beloved person gradually becomes a different person- that we will not grieve over so much once they are gone. It helps us to deal with their death, but we can still remember that beloved person in our memories.

Jedidiah had been such an active, cute, smart little guy that we all adored. When they did his brain biopsy, he had a bleed in his brain and became paralyzed on one side. He could no longer be the active little guy he had been. The medications they gave him caused him to gain weight and become grotesquely obese. He did not look anything like he used to. His class mates did not recognize him. It was like became a different person. It happened gradually and we became used to the "new" Jedidiah. But we still grieved for the "old" Jedidiah that we had loved for over 8 years- the skier, the dirt bike rider, and the mischievous prankster. Instead he became the kid in the wheelchair that told many, funny jokes. We still loved him, but he had adapted to his new situation and became someone new.

Part 4

<u>Jedidiah</u>
By Donnal Nichols
November 2012

I had enjoyed Jedidiah since he was born, but he was just getting to the age where he was capable of riding horses, going hiking and backpacking, and all the fun family things. He was such a daredevil riding his motorcycle and snowmobile. I was looking forward to helping him start and train his own colt and trail ride with him and my young horses. Then he was diagnosed with cancer. He lost his battle with cancer at age 9 years old. The house seemed so empty without him. His illness and death was so devastating for the entire family.

This year Jessica has moved to Chico for college and Justin has started college at Washington State University. So the house is really empty. Cynthia has been working long hours at her job in dispatch. I do not feel comfortable riding off on the trails by myself. My two young horses are not being utilized or receiving further training. What a waste.

While attending a USFS activity, I heard of a young girl who was looking so forward to 4H horse this year, but has no horse. She also has a good friend who would also love to take 4H horse. Light Bulb moment! Two girls – two horses. Maybe we could work something out. Will have to speak with parents. After discussing possibilities with parents, two girls are enrolled in 4H and we are awaiting a horse lease agreement.

Last Saturday the parents brought the girls out to Cromberg to meet my horses. We caught them up, showed the girls how to lead the horses, loaded them into the trailer and brought them to our round pen to get acquainted. The girls are learning to lunge the horses and spent time bonding and grooming their respective horse. The girls already knew which horse they wanted to work with.

Today in the new Guideposts magazine I came across a story about how a grieving grandmother mended her broken heart after the death from cancer of her beloved granddaughter. She had loved sewing pretty dresses for her granddaughter. Now, it was too painful for her to even look at the materials she had purchased for dresses. Then one day at a church meeting, the call came out requesting volunteers to sew dresses for the little girls who were left homeless by earthquakes in Haiti. After she went home and looked at the stack of material, in her mind she could see her granddaughter, as vivid as if she were there, twirling and modeling a dress with her face radiant and her eyes shining. This inspired her to sew dresses to make other little girls as happy and proud as her granddaughter had been. She had found a way to help other children while she healed her broken heart.

And that was sort of how I felt when I saw how happy those two girls were while grooming and hugging my horses. Needless to say, the two horses were quite happy with the girls loving on them and posing for photos.

LETTERS

December 11, 2010

Jedidiah-

Hello from Everett, Washington. How are you? I am an old friend of the family from way back who has watched you through cards and letters and photographs as you grew up through the years. And I am pulling for you now. I enjoy all the funny jokes you've been telling your family that I get to read in the CaringBridge web site. They really make me laugh.

What a great sense of humor you have. Where did you find that? Maybe from being the youngest child. You had to have a sense of humor.

And what a love of life you have. Where did you find that? Maybe from all the horses and mules your parents always had around.

And what courage you have in facing the things life is throwing your way. Where did you find that courage? Maybe on a dirt bike ride in the backcountry of beautiful Plumas County.

Your parents and your brother and sister are lucky folks to have you in their family. And you sure are lucky to have them in your family. It is a good thing you all got together, because it just wouldn't be quite right if you all lived in different places. Getting together for the holidays would be a challenge.

So I just wanted to wish you well, I enjoy reading about you on the web site, and I am thinking of you. Say hi to your mom, dad, Jessica and Justin for me. And of course your puppy!

With Love, CURT
Curt Spalding

Hi Jedidiah,

    I got you 2 silly things that make noise and I want one of the
Sing a mi gigs
Because then we could play them in harmony!
I got you a cow because you are a good farmer!
I tried to find a dirt bike that made noise!
Also, there are sours for Jessica and Justin because my mom
Says she knew a secret about them liking sours! I put tricky beans in for you to trick people with! I put Razzles in for you because that is one of my
    Favorites and I only get them when my card hasn't been turned for a long
Time at school!
I miss you Jedidiah. I always liked us playing together at school and
When you came to my house and played pachinko!

L O V E,
P A R K E R C A R E Y

6/13/2011

I think that Jed was a fun kid to hang around with. I remember him playing soccer with me. I thought he was better than me at soccer. I will always remember him for his parties and the Go-Cart that he gave to us. I also remember him going to Nano's party. And no matter what, I will always remember him.

-J.D. Holzer

Also, J.D. wrote a letter to Santa:

December 3, 2010

Dear Santa,
    May I have a real BMX bike for Christmas. I promise I will not take it apart. And a Wii game called Monster Jam Half Destruction.
    And can you give Jed a nice Christmas?

Love, J.D.

And from J.D.'s brother Quinn:

6-13-2011

The funniest times I had with Jedidiah was at his parties. That's where I got to see him the most. One of the parties we got to bring our go-cart.

But when I heard that he had passed away, it was devastating. But a couple days after his funeral, I got his Go-Cart. I will never forget about my best friend.

Quinn Holzer

Dear Santa, I would like to have a D.J .50 Mountain Bike and an Xbox 360. Also, I wish for Jedidiah to have a great Christmas.

Love, Quinn Holzer

Hi Cynthia,

Here is something we were hoping you could include in your book, if you'd like. Luke wrote it awhile back at School:

Jedidiah was a good friend. He was a tall, skinny boy with a mischievous smile. His favorite word was, "Hi." He was a musical person as he played the recorder and violin. He was a good friend and a talented boy. I will miss him a lot.

Jedidiah was a good friend to both of Luke and Noah, and we feel honored and are thankful that we had him in our lives. We all miss him a lot

-Susan Brandes

PASTOR GEORGE'S STORY

Dear Cynthia, Scott, Jessica and Justin, and Blue Nanny

I typed this so you would not have to struggle to read my writing. I have enclosed a copy of Jedidiah's memorial that you might want to have. I want to thank you so much for letting me be a part of your family's time of struggle and rejoicing with Jedidiah. I hope that I can continue to help you whenever you need me.

I cannot thank you enough for the picture of Scott under nylon. I told this to Scott and I will share with the rest of you about the picture. When I came into the hall where the display of Jedidiah's stuff was, I saw the picture under the airplane picture. As soon as I looked at it, I did not think of Scott coming down to earth, but I saw Jedidiah being lifted up to heaven on the breath of God.

When I told Scott about this, he told me to look on the back of the picture and that it was for me, from Jedidiah. Well, I just about lost it. I cannot tell you how much this picture means to me. It is already up on the wall by our door. And every time I look at it, I think about that fine young man. I am getting a copy of the Smoke Jumpers Prayer to put along side of it. If you want a copy of the prayer, let me know and I will get one for you.

If you want to keep "The Chicken Tree" private, I understand.

May God bless you all.

Pastor George

WELCOME

Good afternoon and welcome. Thank you for all being here to help celebrate the all too brief, but jam-packed life of Jedidiah. We are all here united in our grief of Jedidiah's tragic passing, but we are also all united in the joy that Jedidiah brought into our life. We have all found joy in knowing a very rambunctious and energetic young boy before he was sick and we have found awesome wonder how that same young boy looked his death straight in the eye. And he said to those around him, I am not gone yet, so sit down, shut up and hold on because I am going to take you all for a ride. And we here today, celebrate that ride.

MUSIC- Johny McDonald
EULOGY- (Aunt Linda to do eulogy)

Hi my name is Linda. I am Scott's sister- which means Jessica's, Justin's and Jedidiah's aunt. But to Jedidiah I am one of the cousins. He called all his aunts, uncles, and cousins: cousins. Because cousins were just fun friends to play with. So I am Linda, one of Jedidiah's Idaho cousins. And when I look out here I say, "WOW Jedidiah has done the same thing with his community". I look out and see young kids, Jedidiah's age, which I would expect to his friends, but also teenagers, and young adults, middle aged and older people as well. The wide range shows Jedidiah saw and befriended anyone, young or old, just like he did with his family, we are all cousins, and the community is all friends, just fun people to play with.

When Scott and Cynthia asked if I would speak and deliver the eulogy I told them I would be honored, scared beyond belief, but honored. I asked them what do you want me to say or read, and Scott and Cynthia said, well, would you thank some businesses and people because without their support we don't know what we would have done. So the three of us started compiling a list of thank yous. Scott and Cynthia genuinely appreciate all the prayers, hugs, handshakes, cards food that has been given to them. So on Scott and Cynthia's behalf I would like to say thank you, really thank you to:

1. Barbra: Town Hall Theatre (Family Pass)
2. Plumas Christian School: (School Play was awesome!)
3. Cheryl Arthur: Dinner at Pangaea Café for Jedidiah's Fund Raiser
4. Mike Taborski: Feather Publishing (J,J,J and Scott loved the plane ride)
5. Lisa Wallace: Hair –it-is, (Cynthia's and Jessica's haircuts)
6. Tim and Michelle Low: their generosity with Pet Country Feed and Tack
7. Subway Sandwich: Gift Cards for the Lusk Family
8. Barker Construction: Showed up to build a Ramp for Jedidiah to get his wheelchair into the house.
9. Richard Daun Designs: (Planned & Construction of the front deck)
10. Nurse Debbie Deselle: Setting up the Jedidiah Wellness Fund at Plumas Bank and all for her kindness in the E.R.
11. THANKS to all people who made contribution to Jedidiah's Wellness Fund

12. Dr. Kepple: Even with his busy workload, he offered to be Jedidiah's doctor when he came home from the hospital
13. Jim Boland: Central Plumas Park and Rec District
14. Curt Neiman: American Valley Speedway (Jedidiah loved fast cars and the family enjoyed their season pass)
15. Plumas National Forest Employees : (volunteered their time on two separate days for work parties)
16. Plumas National Forest Service SO : (for the gift cards)
17. Beckwourth Ranger District
18. Mt. Hough Ranger District
19. Michael Donald: (told Jedidiah he would take him to Disneyland, but Jedidiah said how about a weekend in his cabin, which Mike happily obliged).
20. Deputy Shawn Webb: MANY thanks for sharing your life with us! We miss you very much!!
21. Sergeants Todd Johns and Carson Wingfield, Chad Herman- Plumas County Sheriff Deputies SWAT Team (For coming down to visit Jedidiah when he was in U.C. Davis Medical Center. Jedidiah was very proud of being an Honorary Member) Thanks also to PCSO Sheriff Greg Hagwood.
22. President John Twiss, and John Helmer : National Smoke Jumper Association
23. Bill Cramer: Alaska Smoke Jumpers
24. Mike McMillian: Alaskan smoke jumper and photographer for Jedidiah's trip to Alaska. Also a wonderful writer who contributed to this book.
25. All the courageous Smoke jumpers who participated by giving money in "Jumping for Jedidiah" program, summer of 2010.
26. Johnsonville Jr. Ski team A great program that Jedidiah loved
27. Coach Kim Wilbanks: For giving ski lessons and the ski tickets. Also contributed a great story to this book.
28. Corky Lazzarino : Sierra Access Coalition. Shared a wonderful Jeep ride with Jedidiah
29. Dan and Andrea Seiler: fixing the International Scout
30. Ron Collins: Cal Trans (Jedidiah loved his motorized toys and they don't get much bigger than the one he got to operate) and the Bridge Dedication invitation in 2012.

31. CC Meyers Contracting: The Spanish Creek Bridge & the memories are Awesome!
32. Kory Felker: Plumas Physical Therapy
33. Andy Feinblum: Sierra Cycle
34. All the staff and students at Quincy Elementary School: (the support was tremendous) Mrs. Lemnah - Jedidiah's 3rd grade teacher and Mrs. Hochrein- and her entire 4the grade class that gave Jedidiah such an incredible reception on his return to school
35. Dan Torrance: Redmond Air Center (allowing Cynthia the Time Off)
36. Eric Graff: Redmond Air Tanker Base Manager- Extraordinaire. (and thank you for the friendship with your special family: Dale & Gracie, Moosie, Benjamin, Evan, and Zuzu
37. Dee Vagart: Use of your 4 wheeler
38. Pastor George Tarleton: (Sharing his wisdom and the wood splitter)
39. First Baptist Church of Quincy: All the very kind people
40. Quincy Ward of the Latter Day Saints: For the generosity
41. John Fehrman : Fehrman Mortuary (for his extended kindness)
42. High Sierra Grants: Cathy Rahmeyer- (It was really nice that Scott and Cynthia could just send their unopened bills and Cathy would sort them and pay them, in fact, one time they sent over Justin's report card.)
43. Sequoia Dreams: Hans and Michele Jemez-Holtz
44. Quincy Auto, along with Quincy High School "S" Club and Dr. Segura- for the van, that Jedidiah loved and made sure all his cousins got a turn opening and closing the ramp
45. FRC Rodeo Team: Jesse Segura and all the talented FRC Rodeo Team
46. Greenville Rotary: Centella Tucker and others
47. Make-a-Wish Foundation, Sacramento Chapter- Thank you!!
48. Northern Nevada Children's Cancer Foundation: Lizzy Dalton
49. Roberti Ranch Inc.: Rick Roberti
50. Quincy Les Schwab: Ron & Stephanie Horton
51. Delleker Les Schwab: Bill Coates
52. To all of Jedidiah's Cousins: Making the effort to come to Jedidiah's 9th Birthday Party. Also thanks to all his Cousins who met for the All You Can Eat/Swim Weekend in Reno

53. Uncle John and Aunt Stevie: Untiring & Dedicated support in Sacramento (while Jedidiah was in the hospital at U.C. Davis- with endless supply of Love, food, and time. Much appreciated!
54. All the community who participated in Jedidiah's Celebration Day in May: and especially Jenay, Jace, and Zac Cogle for spear heading it
55. String Beans: Beautiful music
56. Johny McDonald: for her love for music and teaching Jedidiah and composing the song, "Ode to Jedidiah".
57. To all the people who read Jedidiah's CaringBridge and sent prayers and positive thoughts, and the people who wrote in his journal so Scott and Cynthia could read to Jedidiah.

Thank You

This list is incredible! I am sure I have missed so many others, and for that I apologize. Scott and Cynthia appreciate all of you, from the bottom of their hearts. Every bit of kindness that has blessed them, they appreciated so very, very much!

Scott and Cynthia asked me to tell a few stories about Jedidiah. The three of us started telling stories Friday morning and continued all day long. With each new story Scott would say, "Yes, include that one," or "Oh that's a good one. Tell that one too!" I looked at him and said, "Scott, that one also? We won't have time for the rest of the ceremony! Scott's answer was, "Well, we do have the church until 11 pm tonight!"

Jedidiah was smart and clever, especially for such a young boy. He had creative smarts, and he knew what he wanted. Being the youngest of three children he learned to think for himself and did not go along with things just because Jessica and Justin did or told him to. Scott and Cynthia enrolled Jessica in dance when she was a young girl and she loved it! She would dance around at home after her practices. Scott and Cynthia also signed Justin up for dance when he was old enough. He learned to dance and enjoyed it too. (Plus, he got to dance with pretty girls!) Jedidiah had been brought along to dance class, too, right along with the two other children, since he was born. When dance class enrollment time came along when Jedidiah was 5 or 6, they signed him up, with Jessica and Justin. Jedidiah went to class, because he was told to. Soon after, he developed his own opinion of dance class- which was unique to him since he did not share the same excitement as his siblings. He would come home from class and say, while imitating the moves:

"I AM NOT GOING TO DANCE. I AM NOT GOING TO PUT MY HANDS ON MY HIPS LIKE THIS AND WIGGLE MY FEET LIKE THAT. I AM NOT GOING TO PUT MY HANDS ON MY HEAD AND TWIRL JUST BECAUSE JESSICA AND JUSTIN DID!"

Jedidiah always thought for himself, even from a very early age. One Christmas Justin asked Santa for a "Flying Blue Mouse". On Christmas morning Santa brought Justin a stuffed blue mouse, tied to a string that he swung over his head to make it fly. A couple years later, Jedidiah, being a clever little guy, asked Santa for blue puppy. He added that the puppy needed to be a "real live blue puppy", not a stuffed animal, like the mouse. Christmas morning came and Jedidiah saw what Santa had left. He was quite flabbergasted and said,

"WAIT A MINUTE! ALL I GOT WAS A BLUE ELK WAGON TO MOVE HAY, WHATS UP WITH THAT?"

Next Christmas, Jedidiah asked Santa for a real live red rocket that could go to the moon. Santa realized Jedidiah was a clever one and he needed to be a little sharper than last Christmas. When Jedidiah came downstairs Christmas morning he saw that Santa had left a huge red rocket! When the rocket was ignited, it travelled hundreds of feet up into the sky. (It also caused one of the horses to run thru the fence, the first time they ignited the rocket at home!)

Jedidiah was happy and enjoyed that rocket for years. But, he did notice that Rocket did NOT go all the way to the moon... which made Jedidiah kind of question the notion of Santa Claus. Even though Jedidiah became skeptical of Santa at an early age, he is still the only Alaskan Smokejumper- that after passing his Rookie Training- sat upon Santa's lap during a visit to the North Pole! Being young and kind-hearted, Jedidiah, put in a good word with Santa for his friends, JD and Nano, and JD's little brother, Quinn.

Besides being clever and smart, Jedidiah was a very active and energetic boy. For his Grandpa Bobby's 80th birthday party, all the cousins meet in Oregon to celebrate. The cousins were all in a circle playing Hacky Sack with a soccer ball, when the ball went rolling down towards Scott's pickup. I noticed the truck had a huge dent in it. I yelled, "JUSTIN! Did you have a fender bender in your Dad's truck?" Immediately Jedidiah spoke up and said, "Oh, that? No, that dents not Justin's, that's nothing… really." Well come to find out, Jedidiah was riding his snowmobile at his house and he was not going slowly. (I don't think he ever knew what gear slowly was!). The snow was kind of heavy and he was having trouble turning. So, as Jedidiah goes flying by on his snowmobile trying to turn, Scott starts yelling, "Jedidiah, TURN!.... TURN!.....". He couldn't turn it soon enough…..he gunned it, trying to get it to turn quicker….and WHACK! The snowmobile rammed smack into Scott's truck! Scott goes running over to Jedidiah, knowing for sure he is going to have to pick up a broken little boy. As Scott approaches, Jedidiah gets off his snowmobile, glances back and forth from his snowmobile to the truck and asks, "How's my snowmobile?" He then saw that it looked ok and said, "Whew, I thought my snowmobile would be all broken, but all I did was dent the truck…"

Jedidiah liked going fast! He loved his snowmobile, his go cart, his dirt bike, and his mountain bike. When Make-A-Wish Foundation came over to ask him what he REALLY wanted, he said, "I WANT A POLARIS 6X 6 RANGER".

The Make -A-Wish representative said, "I am sorry, we can't grant that wish because it has a motor and we can't allow motorized vehicles. So Jedidiah thinks again and says, "Okay, then I want a Polaris 6X6 Ranger without an engine, and my Dad and I can put it in later."

Again, the Make-A-Wish lady said, "Sorry we can't do that, it still is a motorized vehicle with wheels. But think of anything……. anything else, a cruise, a trip to Disney land, a ball game? Or whatever else it is that you REALLY want."

Jedidiah said, "Okay, how about a Dragon 1,000 Snowmobile!? It has no wheels! And I'd REALLY like one."

Again, Make-A-Wish was like, "Uumm, no, that won't work. Tell you what, let's try a new strategy…….What would you like to be when you grow up?"

Jedidiah answered, "When I grow up, I want to be an Alaska Smokejumper like my Dad!"

Jedidiah's wish was granted, and he became an Alaskan smoke jumper.

Scott and Cynthia wanted to grant any and all his wishes. Scott told him they would get him a Polaris 6x6 anyway even if Make-A-Wish would not. After looking at the price, Scott said to Jedidiah, "Ouch that is expensive!! But I am a promise keeper, so let's see what we can do."

But Jedidiah said, "Hey Dad, I know those six- byes cost too much. How 'bout you get me a Chihuahua, and we will call it even?".

Scott and Cynthia did not really want to get "a little rat dog", so they tried to persuade him to choose something else. Jedidiah knew what he wanted and he informed his dad, "Well, Jessica got that Cocker Spaniel, "Angel", Justin got his Blue Heeler, "Spot", and I NEVER got a blue puppy from Santa."

Later, he told his mom, "Mom, do you really want me to die unhappy? Then please get me a Chihuahua!"

Cynthia found a Chihuahua in the paper and family went to see them. Jedidiah had his checklist in-hand. Again, Jedidiah did not let anyone else influence his decision, though his family had their opinions. Scott and Cynthia said, "Jedidiah, check out this little grey one! Let's get him. He is really cute..." And Justin said, "Hey, I like this black one Jedidiah! Can we pick him?"

Jedidiah firmly said, "Nope! None of you gets to pick. This puppy has chosen me!" The tiny, tan female Chihuahua had jumped up and put her paws on Jedidiah's wheelchair.

Pep, like all of us, knew how special Jedidiah really was!

In closing, I just want to add that throughout all of Jedidiah's life with cancer, he never once complained. He never asked, "Why me?" Nor whined, "Oh pity me...." With each new challenge that he encountered, he embraced it with grace, embraced it head on, and with a positive mental attitude. Even when he no longer could do his self-transfers from bed to chair, he commanded Cynthia to, "Fly me over to my Brown Chair, Mom!" Instead of feeling sorry for himself, he wanted to make it fun! Cynthia said she never knew which bird he would be, as he would sing, "Tweet, tweet tweet..." as she carried him to his favorite chair. He was always positive and loved life.

Jedidiah has touched and changed so many of our lives. I know he has given me a greater appreciation for life, family and friends. For that, I will try to

Always be positive for Jedidiah!

PASTOR GEORGE:

Born March 30, 2001

In need of another angel, our Lord called Jedidiah Craig Lusk to his eternal home Monday evening, January 3rd, 2011. He died of a Glioblastoma multiformes brain tumor. His loving family was by his side at his home in Cromberg, California.

He was born in Quincy, California, to Scott and Cynthia (Nichols) Lusk. Jedidiah was currently a fourth grade student at Quincy Elementary School where he enjoyed the friendship of his fellow students but hated the homework assignments. In other words, he was very normal.

A talented skier, Jedidiah was a member of the Johnsville Junior Ski Team where he competed as Bib #21 on Fire and Ice. As second fastest on the team, he constantly strived to be first. A passionate lover of the outdoors, he was a member of the Bucks Lake Snowdrifters. Jedidiah found great enjoyment riding his snowmobile and dirt bike: really fast! He also enjoyed playing the fiddle. Jedidiah memorized O'Keeffe Slide on his fiddle in order to earn his first snowmobile.

Following in family footsteps, Jedidiah passed Rookie Smokejumper training as the Class of 2010 and earned a position as an Alaska Smokejumper with the BLM. He was an Honorary Deputy of the Plumas County Sheriff's Department and a S.W.A.T. Team member. Jedidiah was an accomplished Marksman and a safe firearm handler.

Jedidiah showed Naked Neck chickens at the Plumas-Sierra County Fair as a member of American Valley 4-H. He was an active member of the Quincy Boy Scout Troop 130, and earned the High Point Award by selling the most Popcorn in 2009.

In passing, Jedidiah leaves his parents; Scott and Cynthia (Nichols) Lusk, brother; Justin and sister Jessica Lusk, grandmother Donnal "Blue

Nanny" Nichols, all of Cromberg, grandparents; Bob and Betty Lusk of Coeur d' Alene, Idaho, three aunts, four uncles, and ten cousins. He will be remembered as a kind hearted, funny friend to all.

As I read Jedidiah's obituary for the first time and all the things this young boy accomplishes in so brief a time and the energy he had, I was reminded of a few lines from the science-fiction movie *Blade Runner,* that Rutger Hauer said,

"I've seen things you people wouldn't believe. Attack ships on fire off the shoulder of Orion. I watched C-beams glitter in the dark near the Tannhauser gate… **"The light that burns twice as bright, burns for half as long."**

Jedidiah lived more in his brief nine years than most people would live in two lifetimes. Though Jedidiah's light did not burn very long, it did indeed, burn very, very bright.

MESSAGE

I had the privilege of baptizing Jedidiah and his brother Justin a few months ago. And it is my practice to tell a joke before the sermon. Knowing that Jedidiah likes jokes, I had him tell the joke. This was his joke:

A cat died and went to heaven. St. Peter met the cat at the pearly gate and said, "Welcome. Is there anything you didn't have on Earth that I can get for you, here in heaven?" The cat thought a moment and said, "Why, yes. I always had to sleep on a hard floor back on Earth, could I possibly get a warm soft bed to sleep on?" And Poof! The cat had a nice soft bed to sleep on.

Next, four mice died in a tragic farming accident and went to heaven. St. Peter asked the same question, "What can I get for you here in heaven?" The mice thought a moment and answered, "Yes, on Earth we were always running away from people with brooms and other hazardous things. Could we please have roller skates here in heaven so we don't have to run anymore?"

"Say no more," said St. Peter. And Poof! It was done. All four mice were outfitted in perfectly fitting roller skates!

A few days later St. Peter saw the cat, and asked how he liked his soft bed.

"It's great." said the cat. "But even better are those 'Meals on Wheels' you've been sending by!"

When Cynthia first called me last year and told me about Jedidiah being diagnosed with terminal brain cancer, with only about 6 to 8 weeks to live and would I do his service? Like all of you, I was devastated. I was angry at God for dealing him and his family such a crummy hand. I thought to myself, what will I possibly be able to say at the memorial for a nine year old boy? I was at a loss with my anger at how to deal with this and it was not even happening to <u>me</u>. It was happening to the Lusk Family.

Well, as we know, Jedidiah made it through eleven months, not six to eight weeks. And during that time, watching Jedidiah and his family dealing with this tragedy they were going through, I learned a lot. I learned how to rejoice even though God had not healed Jedidiah. But God did give him and us, eleven incredible months with those that loved him. The doctors said, "No way." But God said, "My way."

Jedidiah was the sum of the characteristics of his whole family: his mom, his dad, his brother and his sister, and his "Blue Nanny". And those characteristics are in the passage that Cynthia asked me to use for my message today.

Phil 4: 4-9

4 <u>Rejoice</u> in the Lord always. I will say it again: <u>Rejoice!</u> 5 Let your <u>gentleness</u> be evident to all. The Lord is near. 6 <u>Do not be anxious</u> about anything, but in <u>everything</u>, by prayer and petition, <u>with thanksgiving,</u> present your requests to God. 7 And <u>the peace of God,</u> which transcends all understanding, will guard your hearts and minds in Christ Jesus. 8 Finally, brothers, whatever is <u>true</u>, whatever is <u>noble</u>, whatever is <u>right</u>, whatever is <u>pure</u>, whatever is <u>lovely</u>, whatever is <u>admirable</u>- if anything is <u>excellent</u> or <u>praiseworthy</u>- think about such things. 9 Whatever you have learned or received or heard from me- put it into practice. And the God of peace will be with you.

Phil 4: 12-13

12 I know what it is to be in need, and I know what it is to have plenty. I have learned the secret of being content in any situation, whether well fed or hungry, whether living in plenty or in want. 13 I can do everything through him who gives me strength.

- *Rejoice in the Lord always.* How does one do that when faced with tragedy? Through all of these difficult months, the Lusk Family rejoiced in the Lord each day that Jedidiah was with them. They rejoiced in the Lord each day he woke up, raised his hands, and said, "I'm alive!" They rejoiced in the Lord for the wonderful things they got to do with him. They rejoiced in the Lord for his lack of pain and his quality of life, despite the thing that was growing inside his brain. They rejoiced in the Lord for his continual sense of humor that he kept until the very end. They rejoiced in the Lord for all his friends and family that gathered around them in love and support. They rejoiced in the Lord for the incredible outpouring of love and support from the community. They rejoiced in the Lord for each encouraging word that was entered on his web page. And they rejoiced in the Lord for each other and their continued ability to lead a normal life with Jessica and Justin, instead of putting their life on hold.

Jedidiah was not anxious about dying. He had a peace with his fate that was incredible to be around. His family and friends continued with prayer and petitions to God instead of giving up. And they were thankful to God that every day they had something to rejoice about. And through all of that, God gave them peace, a peace that was certainly beyond my understanding. The Lusk's are not saints, and I am not trying to paint them as such. But compared to many of us, myself included, they were saints through all of this. They were indeed worthy of our praise.

So, what is the secret to being content, that is, strong enough to get through even terrible situations? It is knowing that Jesus will give us the strength to get through the bad times, to get through the times we think it would be impossible to go through. I grieve for those that face tragedy without Jesus in their lives to get them through it.

John 11: 21-27

21 "Lord," Martha said to Jesus, "If you had been here, my brother would not have died 22 But I know that even now God will give you whatever you ask." 23 Jesus said to her, "Your brother will rise again." 24 Martha answered, "I know he will rise again in the resurrection at the last day." 25 Jesus said to her, "I am the resurrection and the life. He who believes in me will live, even though he dies; 26 and whoever lives and believes in me will never die. Do you believe this? 27 "Yes, Lord," she told him, "I believe that you are the Christ, the Son of God, who was to come into the world."

Jesus could have healed Lazarus before he died, but he did not. But when Jesus got there, he did raise Lazarus from the dead and gave him some more time on this earth, but Lazarus did eventually die for good.

Jesus did not heal Jedidiah from his cancer but he did give him eleven more months. And the key to all this is what Jesus told Martha.

"I am the resurrection and the life. He who believes in me will live, even though he dies; and whoever lives and believes in me will never die. Do you believe this?"

Well, Jedidiah believed this. And so does his family. I know, I baptized him and his brother. Jedidiah and his family were able to deal with the hand they were dealt because they believed in Jesus and loved God with all their heart, and all their soul and all their strength. And they knew that even though Jedidiah would physically die, he would live forever, not just in our hearts, but in heaven with God forever. And it is that certain belief that allowed them to rejoice always for each extra day they got with Jedidiah and gave them the peace of God, the peace that is beyond all understanding.

And you can have that incredible peace of God too, if you too give your hearts to Jesus.

REMARKS AND MEMORIES

MUSIC- Ode to Jedidiah
CLOSING PRAYER

Heavenly Father, thank you so much for the time that we had Jedidiah in our lives, no matter how much we feel it was too short. Thank you for what he and his family showed all of us throughout their trial. Jedidiah reminded us that each breath we take, each loved one, and friend that we have is a gift from you, gifts that should never be taken for granted. Help us to live each day and treasure each loved one and friend that we have as if they were as important as they really are.

May we live each day in the awareness that each day is but a moment in time and some day we too shall follow Jedidiah into the next life. Until that day, may our hearts be open to your word, and your guidance. May we live our lives in loving you and loving each other as you have commanded us to do and as Jedidiah lived.

And we pray that you would bring peace to our hearts in this season of our loss. We ask this in the name of your son Jesus the Christ. And all here said, Amen.

Contribution from Mike McMillian- BLM Smokejumper

The Bravest Jumper
By Mike McMillan

When the National Make-A-Wish Foundation called to ask if there was something special he wanted, Jedidiah Lusk replied, "I'd like a 6x6 Polaris Ranger please."

The representative gently apologized and explained why motorized vehicles could not be granted as wishes. Jedidiah paused briefly. "Okay. I'll take a 6x6 Polaris Ranger without a motor. My dad and I can put one in it."

Jedidiah learned that motor-less motorized vehicles weren't allowed as wishes, either.

He refused more common Make-A-Wish gifts, replying, "I don't want to go to Disneyland or meet someone famous." Giving it some more thought Jedidiah declared, "I want to be a smokejumper like my mom and dad."

The Lusk children had heard their share of smokejumper stories growing up. Cynthia has fond memories of her seven years spent smokejumping at the Redmond base in Oregon, beginning in 1987. Scott happily recalls the eight years he spent jumping from the Fairbanks, Boise, and West Yellowstone bases.

During Jedidiah's first visit to the pediatric intensive care unit, news of his brain cancer diagnosis spread through the smokejumper community. Scott got a phone call from former smokejumper John Gould. Gould was manager of the Alaska Fire Service (AFS) at the time. They began their smokejumping careers together in 1981 as rookies on the Alaska crew.

They hadn't kept in touch since their days swatting tundra fires and mosquitoes. But John felt compelled to express his support for Jedidiah and the Lusks. He asked if there was anything he could do to help.

Several months later the Make-A-Wish Foundation phoned John to discuss Jedidiah's wish, and John realized he might be able to help after all.

He visited Bill Cramer, crew chief of the Alaska Smokejumpers. It was mid-June, and lightning-fueled fires had Alaska's 70 jumpers spread across the state's vast interior. It was the fastest start to wildfire season in a decade.

Cramer embraced the chance to fulfill Jedidiah's wish, believing it was an opportunity and a challenge. "It would have been easy for anyone along the chain to say 'no' to flying a very sick little boy on a government-contracted jumpship. It's not a standard mission," explained Cramer. "But giving the Lusks a tour of our building just wasn't going to be enough."

He worked with his deputy crew chief Gary Baumgartner to plan the week's activities and foster support from fire and aviation management.

Gould contacted the national aviation office in Boise, describing the plan to fly Jedidiah and his parents on a Casa jumpship to drop streamers, jumpers and paracargo. Directed by Kevin Hamilton, the national office approved the plan, believing Jeddah's mission was important.

"There was no downside for the Bureau of Land Management," said Gould. "We were ready to help a beautiful kid and his parents, both who've dedicated their lives to the fire service."

Cramer discussed Jedidiah's wish with his crew. Some of the jumpers voiced concerns about the demands of fire season preventing them from carrying out a week of promised, well-planned activities.

But the idea gained steam, many volunteers, and a detailed itinerary.

Jedidiah's physical stamina weighed on everyone's minds. We wondered how much motion and activity he could endure, or would want to endure. We pondered whether Jedidiah would be strong enough to make the trip at all.

What we didn't realize was that Jedidiah - though dependent upon a wheelchair - was stronger at that moment than he had been in months. He was ecstatic about his family's upcoming trip to Alaska.

It had been four months since Jedidiah "came back from the brink," said Cynthia, describing how Jedidiah's radiation and chemotherapy regimen rendered him physically and cognitively incapacitated. His family braced for the worst.

Jedidiah's ninth birthday arrived on March 30, 2010, with Jedidiah in bed, unable to speak. Mom, dad, brother and sister gathered around his bed with presents. Jedidiah opened his eyes briefly and fell to sleep again.

In the spring, the chemotherapy gradually improved his strength, and Jedidiah was alert. Steroids reduced the swelling in his brain - with a side effect of weight gain. He ballooned from 68 to 150 lbs. Jedidiah's bright smile shined again, now framed by rosy, chubby cheeks.

He eagerly returned to school, talking openly about his medical treatments and changed appearance with friends, teachers and classmates.

By May, Jedidiah was "all there" again, recalls Cynthia. To the delight of everyone, he was even making up his own jokes again. "What's brown and sticky?" he'd ask. After a well-timed pause and the usual blank stares and headshakes from his audience, Jedidiah would smartly say "a stick!"

With summer approaching, the Lusks decided to make it unforgettable. They resolved to enjoy every minute together, knowing Jedidiah's diagnosis gave no hope for a cure.

On July 4, a black limousine arrived at the Lusk home in Quincy, California. Their bags packed for Alaska, Jedidiah, Cynthia, Scott, brother Justin, sister Jessica, and grandmother Donnal laughed and talked together on the smooth ride to the airport - once the limo navigated the family's dirt driveway to the main road.

They enjoyed the four-hour plane ride, and spent their first day with friends at Harding Lake, just outside Fairbanks. Justin and Jessica - with Jedidiah nudged between them - steered a paddleboat across the calm green lake. It was a sunny and warm afternoon, a perfect start to their trip.

Pike's Waterfront Lodge in Fairbanks accommodated the Lusks for their weeklong stay at no charge. The kindness of this gesture touched the family, helping to put their minds at ease. Jedidiah especially liked the 'duck motel' attraction on the Chena River shoreline, in front of the hotel.

On Tuesday, July 6, the Lusks parked their van outside the smokejumper base on Fort Wainwright and helped Jedidiah into his wheelchair. The morning was quiet. Many jumpers were out on fire assignments. Others worked on projects throughout the sprawling building.

Two large bay doors leading to the aircraft ramp were open, inviting a warm breeze to sweep through the ready-room.

Jessica guided Jedidiah's wheelchair with the family quietly following. The group stopped in front of the operations desk.

I said "hi" to Jedidiah and introduced myself. He gestured to shake. Jedidiah looked at me closely. "Can I ask you a question?" "Sure," I replied. "Can I have your autograph?" he asked smiling, handing me a well-worn notebook and pen.

Cramer and Gould introduced themselves to Jedidiah and the Lusks. A few more smokejumpers waited their turn. Behind the group stood tall ready-racks with four rows of hanging jumpsuits, harnesses and helmets poised for quick suit-ups during fire calls.

Jedidiah's wide brown eyes scrutinized his surroundings as the conversations of grown-ups swirled around him.

Each person Jedidiah met signed his autograph book – filled with names of firefighters and admirers he'd met in California and Oregon.

We gathered at the end of the first row of racks, beneath a nametag still in place today, reading "LUSK". Under the tag hung a brand new smokejumper jumpsuit, made of coffee-colored Kevlar fabric. It included jump pants, suspenders and a high-collar jacket.

Made just for Jedidiah, it looked like the smallest working jumpsuit ever made. Alaska's loft specialists spent many hours sewing and fabricating their special gift to Jedidiah.

Cynthia handed Jedidiah his jump helmet and flight gloves. He looked a little surprised, not quite sure what to do with all of his new gear.

"Ready to try on your new jumpsuit?" Mom asked. Jedidiah nodded yes without hesitation. We gathered up his gear. The family scanned the photos of fire and parachutes lining the walls as we walked down the hallway to the parachute loft.

Jessica helped Jedidiah stand from his wheelchair. Mom and dad helped Jedidiah step into his jumpsuit pants. After a few minutes of fussing over him, Jedidiah's last zipper was zipped. He took a step away from the gentle support of Jessica's hand.

Jedidiah stood proudly in his jumpsuit. We told him how sharp, how cool, how tough he looked. Jessica and Justin were thrilled to see their little brother in full smokejumper gear. The family gathered around Jedidiah quickly for pictures before he sat down to rest.

The Lusks spent the rest of the morning touring the jump base and aircraft ramp. Scott steered Jedidiah's chair up the reclined tailgate of the Casa jumpship, near the plane's open side door. Jedidiah practiced throwing 'streamers' – long rolls of bright paper Mache' used to check wind speed and direction – from the door. We were all excited to see this was easy for him.

A colorful lineup of air tankers and logistical airplanes were also parked on the ramp. Several pilots approached the family to offer tours of their planes and helicopters. The Canadian water-scooping CL-215s peaked Jedidiah's interest. Once the pilot was finished describing the ship, Jedidiah asked him a few questions in a soft voice.

That night the family returned to their hotel rooms, filled with anticipation for the next day's events. The itinerary was set – Jedidiah's rookie training would begin in the morning.

On Wednesday, July 7, the Lusks arrived at the jump base just before 9 a.m. and gathered in the ready-room for roll call. Surrounded by his family, Jedidiah waited intently. After dozens of jumper's names were called, the operations coordinator bellowed "Lusk!"

"Available!" yelled back Jedidiah, rousing applause from the roomful of smokejumpers.

Smokejumper Ty Humphrey – a rookie trainer, introduced himself to Jedidiah. "Are you ready to report for training, young man?" Ty asked sternly. "Yes sir" Jedidiah replied, staring up at Ty's long, graying beard. "Then let's go. Follow me," instructed Ty.

The Ram-Air parachute inspection tower had been transformed into a classroom with a red, white and blue parachute suspended across the brightly lit room. Jedidiah and Scott sat at a long table facing Ty, accompanied by a dry erase board and video monitor.

Ty spoke of aircraft safety and parachutes, and what entails a standard smokejumper mission. Jedidiah leaned into his dad's shoulder, whispering questions and observations.

Jedidiah was happy learning about how things work - cars, motorcycles, especially ATVs. Talk of planes and parachutes naturally sparked his interest and imagination.

After class, Jedidiah returned to the ready-racks and climbed into his jumpsuit with help from his brother and sister. Once suited up, Jessica hugged her little brother tightly. Justin kissed him on the cheek.

Jedidiah took a step away from his family – standing by himself, beaming ear to ear, playfully swinging his arms side to side, humming with delight.

Jedidiah sat down again. Scott steered his chair outside and onto the aircraft ramp and wheeled up the tailgate of the Casa jumpship. Two pilots took their seats for a mockup practice session, in preparation for the day's mission.

Spotter Gary Baumgartner took his place at the jumpship doorway with two jumpers standing beside him. Scott sat next to Jedidiah in seats near the open door. Once we agreed we were all ready, we disembarked from the plane and re-entered the base.

After a brief discussion we decided not to wait until after lunch - Jedidiah was already suited up and feeling well. We boarded the jumpship once again, took our seats and the propellers spun up. As we lifted off Jedidiah was smiling and talking to his father. The ship turned away from the airfield. We took off our seatbelts and moved into place for the mission.

Gary removed the plane's side door from its hinge, stowing it in the plane's tailgate. Jedidiah and Scott endured a steady blast of cold air. Winding rivers, green pastures and spruce forests rushed past. Cynthia leaned over Scott's and Jedidiah's seats, keeping her video camera and wide grin steadily in place.

Circling above the Nordale Road jumpspot, Gary radioed the smokejumper ground crew. Everyone was ready. Kneeling at the open door, Gary communicated with Jedidiah using hand signals while Jedidiah spoke by headset to the ship's pilots, relaying Gary's commands.

Gary wrote "RIGHT" and "LEFT" in big black letters on his palms, prompting Jedidiah to direct the pilots about how to stay on the windline. After a brief spat of commands – including "LEFT", then "RIGHT", then "LEFT" again, Jedidiah couldn't help himself. "No, your *other* left!" he said, ribbing the pilot, and getting a good laugh from the spotter.

At Gary's signal, Jedidiah threw a streamer out the door. The ship made a second pass and Jedidiah threw another streamer. As the plane orbited, we watched the long yellow strands flutter toward the ground.

The plane climbed to 3,000 feet. "One jumper!" boomed Gary over the roar of the planes' engines. Jumper Togie Wiehl waddled into position by the open door.

The windblast made talking almost impossible. Gary leaned in between Togie and smokejumper Derek Patton to give them a briefing. At the end of his talk, Gary instructed Togie to sit in the door and wait for Jedidiah's command to exit.

As everyone focused on their next moves, Jedidiah looked up at me stooping in the ship's tailgate behind the open door. He was grinning wide as I poised my camera at him and clicked. I took my face from the viewfinder, smiling and giving him a thumb's up.

Jedidiah was tightly belted into his seat, so he couldn't quite slap the shoulder of a waiting jumper. On Gary's signal, Jedidiah improvised and gave Togie a quick kick on the leg. Togie slipped out the door and fell from sight. Jedidiah leaned forward and looked out, then up at Gary, and then quickly to Scott, eyes wide open. Mom and Dad gave Jedidiah a hug and hearty pat on the back as the plane slowly banked left.

"One jumper!" yelled Gary, as Derek moved into place by the open door. Through his facemask he kept his eyes on Jedidiah. With a nod of approval he let Jedidiah know he was ready as he sat in the door, legs dangling. On Gary's signal, Jedidiah gave Derek a quick kick. He fell from the door, into the wind stream, and out of sight.

We watched from the plane as the two jumpers floated toward the jumpspot. Gary reattached the plane's door. We could all hear each other again. Scott and Cynthia were talking excitedly with Jedidiah about the jumps. The jumpspot crew confirmed that Togie and Derek were safely on the ground. The ship descended to 300 feet to begin paracargo operations. The pilot lowered the ship's tailgate, giving us a sweeping look at the ground and sky. Our field of view rushed past in a blur of green, black and blue.

Gary moved a large cardboard box into position and waited for the pilot's command. Moments later he pushed the box down the ramp and out the open tailgate. Just for fun, Jedidiah threw another streamer at the same time. It joined the paracargo chute and twirled toward earth.

Jedidiah's spotter mission was a big success, and we were all in high spirits as the jumpship landed at Ladd Field, taxied in front of the jump base and parked. Jedidiah drew a lot of admirers during lunch at the AFS dining hall that afternoon.

Word of Jedidiah's successful mission spread through the small community of firefighters and support folks at AFS. Many people stopped by the family's table with kind words and congratulations for Jedidiah.

After lunch, the Lusks drove to the Nordale Road jumpspot to watch a practice jump. Jedidiah held up streamers to help the jumpers check ground winds on their way into the jumpspot. As they landed, they scrambled from their gear and greeted Jedidiah one by one.

The day was warming quickly and it was time to rest. The family returned to the hotel to get ready for the evening's celebration.

The Lusks returned to the jump base late that afternoon. They quietly made their way past the operations desk and down the long hallway to the loft. The brightly lit room was filled with firefighters, fire managers, kitchen staff - everyone from the Alaska Fire Service who wanted to attend. The room buzzed with loud conversations, mostly of a blessed fire season.

Bill Cramer addressed us, introducing the Lusks before inviting Jedidiah and Scott to the front and center. As they made their way across the room, Jedidiah kept his eyes on his father. When they settled into place, Bill expressed his admiration for Jedidiah and handed him a small plastic box containing a rookie jump-wings pin. Bill reminded the audience that Jedidiah was the only rookie the Alaska crew had that year, and a great rookie he turned out to be.

Scott looked up at the crowd and spoke. The emotion in his voice conveyed the cruel reality of Jedidiah's future. The room was silent. Scott thanked Bill and everyone for welcoming Jedidiah and his family. As Scott spoke he looked at Jedidiah, and with tears rolling down his cheeks, said how happy he was to see Jedidiah become an Alaska Smokejumper.

More importantly, he said, Jedidiah was the son any father would be proud of.

Scott handed Jedidiah his original smokejumper belt buckle, and Jedidiah reached for his father's arm to stand. He helped Jedidiah to his feet and the two embraced for several seconds. Jedidiah sat down once again. The loft erupted in prolonged applause.

After the ceremony, the family had many more people eager to meet them. They stayed awhile longer before returning to the hotel.

Late the next morning the Lusks drove to a boat launch on the Upper Chena River. They were ready for the last activity we had planned for Jedidiah - his "rookie campout".

When the family got out of their van, Bill was already in his own boat, talking with a gentleman in another boat he'd enlisted for the day's trip. The two jet boats shuttled the family - and a small party of jumpers and friends – to a remote beach five miles upriver. The shallow water and narrow bends in the winding river made for an exciting ride.

We stopped and set up a large paracargo canopy over the white, sunbaked sand. Jessica pushed Jedidiah in his wheelchair to a shady spot under the candy-striped parachute. We spent the afternoon fishing for small grayling, grilling meat over the fire pit and telling stories.

When it was time to go, the Lusks loaded into one boat. Cynthia huddled close to Jedidiah, her arms around him as the boat sped along on glassy water. In the chilly breeze, mom and son smiled, laughed and hugged for much of the ride back to the launch. It was a great day to be together.

The next day was the family's last full day of the trip before returning home. In the evening I met the Lusks at Hot Licks, a local ice cream shop. I gave them an album full of the photos I'd taken of their adventure. We flipped through the pages and slowly finished our ice cream cones.

It was time to say goodbye. The Lusks loaded into the van with Jedidiah by the open sliding door. I hugged him, telling him what a great guy he was. "Can I ask you a question?" Jedidiah said smiling.

"Of course", I replied. "Can I have another hug?" he asked.

Before I could answer and hug him again, Jedidiah smiled and said, "It might be a long time before I see you again."

Jedidiah and the Lusk Family with the Alaska Smokejumpers in Fairbanks, AK July 2010. Photo by Mike McMillian. Back Row: Togie Wiehl, Justin Lusk, Cynthia Lusk, Jessica Lusk, Scott Lusk. Middle Row: Jedidiah Lusk, Donnal Nichols, Derek Patton. Kneeling: Bill Cramer and Gary Baumgartner.

Contributions by Justin Lusk

April 2012

    What he wrote when applying to the Lighty Leadership Scholarship Award (which he did win and became a recipient at Washington State University)

    A leader is an individual who acts on what needs to be done. He is a man who steps up in times of need to put other's interests before his own for no benefit other than the self-gratification it brings to himself. A leader is one who shields adversity with courage and remains confident throughout the toughest of situations. A leader is someone who sees potential for positive change in areas where others have overlooked. He must be willing to step out of his comfort zone to try new things. And most of all, a leader is a role model who accepts the responsibility of allowing others to follow in his footsteps.

    In the eighth grade, I joined a new club called Quincy Junior History Club. The mission was to learn the history of places of interest and then visit them. I have an avid interest in traveling and decided to join the group. With the organization being new, I decided to run for president and ended up becoming elected. Within the months that followed, we researched and presented new information on places in New York, New York and Washington, D.C. After a year of research and fundraising, our hard work paid off and we were able to see the sights that we had talked about for so long; such as the Washington Monument, the Lincoln Memorial, Ground Zero, and Wall Street. The trip was such a success that we decided to go on another trip. Two years later we visited Paris, France; Rome, Italy; and London, England.

    Throughout high school I have looked for opportunities to be a leader. I was Captain of my basketball team in tenth and eleventh grades. I demonstrated good work ethics and always tried my best both on the court and in the classroom by never missing a game or a single day of school. Throughout playing the past four seasons of high school soccer, four seasons of basketball, two seasons of track, one season of baseball, and one season of tennis, I achieved the Scholar Athlete Award each season for maintaining a 3.75 GPA or higher.

My freshman year was the first time in seven years that my school had a Track Team. I chose to step outside of my comfort zone and give it a try, despite not having any previous experience. I decided that is what leaders do; they challenge their mind and body to see how far they can improve their character and learn new things. I ended up being very successful in the mile and 800-meter events and my team went undefeated the whole season, eventually winning the Northern California Section Title Championships. Later that summer, I used my experience in Track, to run an ultra-marathon. The next summer I convinced a friend and fellow track teammate to join me in another ultra-marathon. I finished three hours faster than my previous time. This is what I thought being a leader was all about- pushing myself and my teammates until we reached our goals. I viewed leadership in this way until the day my life was changed.

It was on Valentine's Day of 2010, during my sophomore year in high school. My younger brother, Jedidiah, then nine years old, was diagnosed with a Glioblastoma multiformes brain tumor; the worst and most aggressive form of brain cancer. I, my family, and the community were devastated. Living in such a rural community in Northern California, my family really felt the close-knit love and affection. To show the community we appreciated their support, my family set up a website through an organization called, "CaringBridge". My sister, Jessica, started off by journaling Jedidiah's plight. This way, whoever was interested, could monitor the progress of my brother on their computer. We also had bracelets distributed throughout the community that had the words, "Always Be Positive for Jedidiah" printed on them. For the months that followed, my family packed as much living as possible into every day. At school, it was difficult to focus on my schoolwork for I was constantly distracted by the smallest of things; yet I tried my hardest to stay focused on my schoolwork at hand.

This is when a feeling inside of me, that only now I can describe as leadership, showed me the way to stay ahead of school and to not keep to myself. This was a challenge, considering hardly anyone at school could relate to what I was going through. I kept up faithful relationships with my friends and spoke often with my school principal about the difficulties I was facing. A true leader knows when to seek advice and use the help of others. My principal made me self-aware and insightful about my impact on others. She said my teammates and peers were looking towards me for inspiration and strength. It was not until this time that I realized the public attention I was receiving and the opportunity to use my situation to inspire and be a leader.

Eleven days short of eleven months after being diagnosed with brain cancer, my little brother and best friend passed away on the evening of January 3, 2011. I felt shaken to the core. The next day at school took the most courage I have ever mustered in my life. When school started, I met in the principal's office with two of my friends. I sat there red-eyed as my principal announced the news about my brother's passing over the intercom to the entire school. Afterwards, we sat there and talked until I was dismissed to go back to class. My second period class was already in session as I walked into the classroom. I could feel everyone watching me....Watching to see what I would do, how I would act, and what would happen next.

The next couple of months were the most difficult months of my life. But I made the decision to accept the challenge of staying positive and keeping a high self-esteem. My next soccer season, my senior year, I was appointed as Captain of my team. Half of the team were freshman and I took it upon my shoulders to lead by example. For many of them, it was their first time playing soccer. I used the experiences I had gained over the years to help them be successful. We ended the season with 20 wins and 5 losses, winning league, and eventually winning the Northern California Section Championships- the furthest my team could go. I was awarded team MVP and All-League Offense MVP. Furthermore, every freshman on the team ended up scoring at least once during the season. It was a great season, full of memories I expect to one day tell my grandchildren about.

These days I continue enjoying life- not taking a single day for granted. I continue leading my basketball team on the court, and am in the position of receiving a 4.0 this semester. I am sad my high school days are coming to an end, but am really excited about starting another chapter in my life. For everyone, experiences turn into memories on which they learn from. For a true leader, someone who does not flinch from adversity, he will take his own experiences and apply them in helping others be successful as well. Hopefully, that is what I will leave my community with. – Justin Lusk

Cynthia Lusk

JUSTIN LUSK

Senior Speech-May 30, 2012

    High School has been an adventure. Like a box of chocolates. I have learned and experienced a lot about life during my time here. So much has changed for me from four years ago, back when I was an unknowledgeable freshman; back when used to ignore my sister at school because of the fact she was a mighty Senior, back when we actually locked our lockers, back when Sav- Mor had a deli, and Quincy had a Taco Bell. Honestly though, if I could repeat high school all over again, I don't think I would personally change anything. I have really enjoyed taking advantage of being a Senior. I have made so many fantastic memories here at Quincy High School, and so many are just from this past year; like leading a parade with Adam and Zach T-H, being honored as MVP of our Section Championship Soccer Team as we kept on winning until there was no one left to beat, having an 11 game winning streak in basketball and winning league, being awarded Hoopla King, being accepted to Washington State University along with two of my best friends, going on the 4.0 Trip, breaking up a fight with Adam, having the opportunity to be a Johnsville Junior Ski Team Coach for my Senior Project, saving Zack Pruitt's life...but not really. Our secretive sun watching adventure up on Mt. Hough, going to the Prom with an amazing young lady, rocking out for our economics video, the reverse passing with Viet on the drives home, challenging Josh to beat my hallway record, the Polka Dot hitch hiker adventure, learning about physics on a field trip to Donner Ski Ranch, almost being killed by David, watching movies in Viet's teepee, and trying out the Tennis Team...and also winning league.

    All these things have been really awesome, but most of my memories from the past couple of years are about my family. We have gone thru a really tough ordeal, and gratefully, it has brought us closer together. My family has really taught me how to appreciate life to the fullest. They have shown me that life is not guaranteed and to enjoy every day. It wasn't the easiest lesson to learn. My brother's battle with cancer has been really difficult for me. My friend's and I don't really talk about it that much. I think it's because they don't know what to say, and frankly, I don't know what to say about it either. It is how it is and I'm still learning to accept it.

But my parent's unconditional love has never failed. They have remained strong and courageous through it all. They have taught me the importance of being real to myself and to make the best out of what we have been given. Jessica, you are my favorite person. Thank you for allowing me to tell you everything that's on my mind. Your positive outlook on life is overwhelming inspirational. You have the unique gift to make the most ordinary things extraordinary. Never forget the two rules. I will definitely miss you next year.

My brother's death has really taught me a lot about myself. It has been almost a year and a half since he passed away, but he continues to influence me in everything I do. For my nine year old brother to face death while maintaining such a positive attitude is still something I cannot fathom. His courage in the hardest of times has taught me what I could not have learned any other way. He has shaped my personality and will continue to affect my life more than I can say. I'm not a real serious guy but I am so grateful to Dr. Segura for taking the time to talk, and be serious with me during the toughest part of my life. For her to take me out of class and talk with me has made me realize and understand the larger picture. We're not just here to learn about similes and metaphors, and cosign functions and sole proprietorships. High school is a time to enjoy life, learn about ourselves and find our personalities, as we continue to grow as individuals and become active members of society. Come June 15th, we will no longer be classmates. We will be something more than that. We will be a family connected by the memories we have shared within these past years; something that no one else can ever take away from us. And that will always connect us and will be unique to the Quincy High School Class of 2012.

Lately I've lived by the saying that if you are in a bad mood, do something nice for someone. I figure it makes me a more enjoyable person to be around. I feel like when I leave here and head up north for college, I will leave Quincy a better place. And despite how this community, our community, may look in the next couple of years, school-wise, and teacher-wise and everything else, I will always take pride in knowing that *this* is where my roots are. For that, I thank the teachers, the coaches, my friends, and my family who have instilled that pride within me and have made me the person I am today. Right now, I don't know what I want to

do for a career for the rest of my life, but I know that I now have the tools to do amazing things and that's exactly what I plan on doing. Thank You.
-Justin Lusk

JUSTIN LUSK

Relay-For-Life Speech- Saturday, June 23, 2012

    All right, please bear with me for this speech. I didn't know I'd be giving one until Thursday. I wrote this yesterday, on the return trip from Student Orientation at Washington State University. I was crammed in the back seat of a car for 11 hours with my friends Adam and Henry. My sister has planned on giving the speech. Unfortunately, she could not make it today because she was asked to be a Camp Counselor at a diabetes camp in Redding. She asked me to give one instead. I asked her what the speech was supposed to be about. She replied that it was to say something positive about people who have died from cancer. What? How do you do something like that? ...Cancer is.... Is NOT a positive thing...It's a heartfelt, gut wrenching, emotional, roller coaster.

    I started thinking about what cancer did to my family; to my brother. I started thinking how it physically transformed him. How during his initial biopsy, the neurosurgeon paralyzed his left side, and how he was confined to a wheelchair from then on out. How the medication he was on, while reducing the swelling inside his head, had made the rest of his body all puffy....But then I remembered all his jokes.... And his laughter....And his infectious smile. The more I thought about my brother's mentality during the toughest part of his life, the clearer it became: that under the ugliness of cancer...there *IS* hope.

    Indeed, of everyone in my life, it was my nine year old little brother who taught me *how* to live life to the fullest, *how* to be positive, *how* to rejoice in the worst of times, and many more fundamentals I live by today.

    I would like to start off my speech this evening by reading a passage by Nicholas Wolterstoff, an American philosopher and a Harvard graduate. He said, and I quote, "If love for those around us is not expanded, if gratitude for what is good does not flame up, if insight is not deepened, if commitment to what is important is not strengthened...if hope is weakened and faith diminished, if from the experience of death comes nothing good, than death has won."

I follow this with the words my mom put on my brother's CaringBridge Website two days after his death. She wrote, "The passing of his spirit, I consider a victory over cancer. Though the terrible disease, and a part of the treatment, ravaged his little body, he NEVER, ever let the presence of a brain tumor overwhelm his incredible life character, or his love of life, family and God."

How true this is. That's what I have learned is the key to defeating cancer; to somehow find the strength, the courage and ultimately the ability, to find the positives among all else.

For me, one of the hardest parts of dealing with my brother's death from cancer is that there is no one to blame it on. It would have made it so much easier to blame his death on someone or something preventable, such as a drunk driver or a war... Something where someone was at fault... An individual to take my anger out on. But that's the thing I have learned about cancer. It is not fair and it is not justified. I also feel grateful for that. That no one sole individual has to live the rest of their life feeling responsible for his death. Spiritually, blaming my brother's death on a sole individual would bring me no justice in the end.

One of my friends who also went through a family battle with cancer- for that's just what it is- a family ordeal that everyone fights in- she told me, "Justin, now I know your pain and you know mine. You have made me realize that their death isn't the end of all life." I would like to extend that by saying it was Jedidiah that made *me* realize that death is not just a "dead end," so to speak. For my brother to be able to show me that message is still something I still cannot fathom. He has taught what I could not have learned in any other way.

These are the reasons we continue on, and remember our loved ones who have been taken by cancer. There is so much we can learn from them and apply to our own lives. We can use that to make ourselves and the place we live in, more enjoyable.

I would like to recite a quote my sister provided for me: "Miracles are simply a shift in perspective."

My brother's death from a terminal brain tumor in January- was almost a miracle in itself- a miracle in the sense that we were fortunate enough to enjoy him for almost eleven more months after his diagnosis. It was a time in which we knew was limited, and we knew to focus on making the best of it. Yet that is how we should face each and every day- by learning to cherish the moments we do have with each other, while knowing the best is yet to come.

One last quote I share with you today, states: "If life is fragile, then do your best to love what you have in that moment, in that time...choose life. Celebrate Life." On my brother's Make-A-Wish trip to Alaska we were eating dinner in the smokejumper's cafeteria one evening. I noticed a sign hanging in the dining hall that read, "Life is short- eat dessert first!" It was a silly little saying that made me realize, yes, our days here on earth *are* limited, and that every day we live is a gift.

It is on days like this Relay-For-Life celebration, when our passed-on loved ones are not able to share with us, that we remember them. We reflect on the strong individuals they were, and who they would be, if they were still alive with us today.

My brother's battle with cancer was not pleasant. But gratefully, he did not have to go through it alone. My family was always by his side, and furthermore, the presence of the community was always there for us. I suppose that is the positive side about people dying from cancer- it pulls and brings us together. It turns communities into families. And, if nothing else, cancer makes us appreciate life- that much more. Thank You. –Justin Lusk

Justin's Story

Cancer. It is not something you ever want to deal with; especially on Valentine's Day. But that is exactly what was unfolding before me. My best friend, my little 8 year old brother, Jedidiah, was diagnosed with cancer. Eight year old little boys aren't supposed to get cancer. Cancer is what old people get after a lifetime of smoking. At least up to that point that was my only interaction with cancer. To make things worse, Jedidiah was diagnosed with a Glioblastoma Multiformes brain tumor. I later learned GBMs are the most aggressive form of the 161 different types of brain cancers.

The weekend before, I was accompanying my brother and filming him as he excitedly ran about at his Boy Scout Derby car races. I was watching him play an expedition basketball game during the halftime of a college basketball game. I was watching as he recited "The Cremation of Sam McGee", a 120 line poem, at his school's talent show. And now he was being airlifted from our small northern Californian hospital to the big city.

"As soon as Jesus heard the word that was spoken, he saith unto the ruler of the synagogue, 'Be not afraid, only believe'." Mark 5:36, KJV

My brother lived eleven days short of eleven months after that life-changing day. It is within those 11 months that my life changed, I came to appreciate life to the fullest, and I found comfort in my faith.

GBMs are 100 percent fatal. The doctors told us that. I had the choice to live out the rest of my brother's life in disbelief, or what I found the courage to do, was come to accept that our time here on Earth is limited and to enjoy the time that we do have. It was not the easiest lesson for me to learn. Jedidiah spent 33 days at UC Davis Children's Medical Center undergoing radiation and chemotherapy treatments and then two more months in a Ronald McDonald House. During his initial biopsy, the neurosurgeon paralyzed Jedidiah's left side. From then on, he could not walk and was confined to a wheel chair.

Like all close siblings, my brother and I shared a special relationship over the years growing up. Being seven years his elder, I was old enough to babysit him yet young enough to still have the same interests he did. On February 14, 2010, I was a junior in high school; captain of my basketball team, and in the process of maintaining a 4.0 GPA. That day, the doctors told my parents they needed to life light my brother to a larger hospital, I was hanging out with my girlfriend, with not a care in the world. When I received the news, I did not know how to react. I was confused and worried. I did know one thing – it was serious and in knew I would not be able to get through this alone.

"And the angel said unto them, Fear not: For, behold, I bring you good tidings of great joy, which shall be for all people.' Luke 2: 10, KJV

My parents were with my brother much of the time in the hospital. I wanted to physically be there for them. But I had school. And quite honestly, I was scared. I did not want to see my brother in the state he was in. On the weekends I went down to visit him. The doctors told us he would get worse before he would get progressively better. I will never forget the first time I saw him lying there in the hospital bed. It was one of the hardest things to see. When I saw him, he was at the worst part of his battle. He could not speak, he could not eat by himself, and he was not mentally there. IVs, tubes, and wires ran all over his fragile body.

Then on his birthday on March 30th, he laughed, for the first time since his diagnosis. All of our cousins and aunts and uncles and grandparents were at our house for his ninth birthday. My mom was loading him into the car at the end of the day and was smothering him with kisses. And he laughed out loud. It was the best feeling and it could not have come any sooner. After that day, through the grace of God, Jedidiah began to regain his state of being. He was still confined to his wheelchair and his face was puffy from the medication he was on, but he was fully able to enjoy the time with us, his family.

"The Lord is gracious and compassionate; slow to anger and rich in love. The Lord is good to all; he has compassion on all he has made." Psalm 145:8-9

My family was fortunate enough to partake in the Make-A-Wish Program - a program with the intention of granting children with cancer one last magical wish. Most children wish to spend a weekend in Disneyland or to meet a famous person. My brother's wish was to go to Alaska and become an Alaskan smokejumper- just like my father. When I found out about the Make-A-Wish trip, my initial thoughts were Disneyland or a cruise. But now that I look back, I wouldn't have changed that trip, or any part of it, for anything. This trip was more than just a wish for my brother. It was a magical experience that my whole family benefited from. Me, my family, and the smokejumpers that worked with us to make it possible, all benefitted from this trip. It was unreal how much energy the smokejumpers put into that trip to make it as successful as it was. One evening when we were eating in the cafeteria, I noted a sign painted above the dining hall that read, "Life is short. Eat dessert first". It was this silly little saying that made me understand the depth of it all. I do not claim to know the meaning of life. It simply made me realize the importance of cherishing the moments we do have and forgiving and forgetting the wrongs.

"And these three remain: faith hope and love, and the greatest is love" 1 Corinthians 13:13

From then on, it was the small things that I began to appreciate the most. Jedidiah being able to lift his left hand above his head, being able to transfer himself from his wheelchair to the car, the mini cheese grater he randomly found on an isle at the grocery store that he insisted on having. It was only a cheese grater. But placed into my brother's hands became a token. A token worthy of its own song that he would sing and plead us to sing, as we grated dyed cheese together in the kitchen. I relished these times. I lived for them. It was these small things that turned into the big things on which memories were born that will withstand a lifetime.

For a while, my brother had wanted to get baptized. It meant so much to him to do, yet he did not want to do it alone. He pleaded with me to also be baptized alongside him. So on October 19th, my brother and I each got baptized at out church. A baptism means something a little different for each individual. For me, it was a time to not just prove my loyalty to the lord, but to infinitely express my pure love for my brother. I will always be grateful for this opportunity.

"I can do all things through Christ which strengthened me." Philippians 4:13

My brother passed away on January 3, 2011. The next day at school took the most courage I have ever mustered in my life. When school started, I met in my principal's office with two of my friends. I sat there red-eyed as my principal made the news about my brother's passing over the intercom to the entire school. Afterwards, we sat there and talked until I was dismissed to go back to class. My second period class was already in session and as I walked into the classroom I could feel everyone watching me. Watching to see what I would do, how I would act, what would happen next. The next couple of months that followed were the most difficult months of my life. But I made the decision to accept the challenge of staying positive and keeping a high self-esteem.

Gratefully, this ordeal has brought my family closer together. My sister and I now share a bond that no one else can understand. The memories we share and the hardships we leaned on each other for support have made us closer than ever before. I now also have a better appreciation for my parents. I am currently about to graduate high school. And as I reflect on my last 18 years of life, 13 years of school, and the last four years of high school, it is within those last 11 months of my brother's life that have had the biggest impact on my life and has shaped me to make me the man I am today. I don't know what I want to do for the rest of my life, but I am not worried. I am excited to head off to college and begin a new chapter in my life.

It was horrific watching my younger brother go through this battle. With great courage however, he remained positive and upbeat until the day he died. For my nine year old brother to face death and to accept it is something I still cannot fathom. He has taught me what I could not have learned any other way. His courage and faith in the hardest of times has inspired me more than I can say. While the bracelet I wear is a physical reminder, it is the memories of those small things we did together that allow me to never forget the most important lesson I have learned – to always be positive. My brother's death has taught me the importance of life and to enjoy the ones around us. And for that, I will forever be obliged to my brother- my little hero. –Justin Lusk

"We also rejoice in our sufferings because we know that suffering produces perseverance; perseverance, character; and character, hope." Romans 5:2-4

Jedidiah on his dirt bike- photo by Justin Lusk.

STORIES FROM JEDIDIAH'S MOM

I was standing in the kitchen of the Ronald McDonald House in Sacramento, repeatedly flipping open cabinet doors and closing them again. I could feel my self-control eroding away, second-by-passing second. A tear leaked out of the corner of my eye, followed by a salty trail of dampness. I bit my lip and mumbled, "Now where is a stupid pan?" as I opened and slammed shut some more kitchen cabinet doors. Soon the world in front of me was awash in watery blurriness. I could not find a cooking pan if it were right in front of me. I grabbed the kitchen counter to balance myself as I began to sob, "I hate this stupid place! Why do I have to stay here? It's not MY house! It's Ronald McDonald's house and I DON'T WANT TO BE HERE!!" A rain of falling tears fell into the kitchen sink as waves of self-pity washed over me.

Confused by and feeling guilty for my emotions I continued to sob and cry. It felt good to let it out and I know I needed to cry; but why was I so ungrateful for a place to stay so Jedidiah could continue his radiation treatments? I should have been happy to get out of that hospital! I had held it together, emotionally, for 33 long days in that frightening place...Now here was release, into a semi-private, semi-home-like environment, in a location that is within walking distance of the Cancer Center.

"It really can't get any better than this right now," I tried to tell myself, but just the realization of that fact caused me cry even harder.

After pondering my plight, I figured that I missed the supporting presence of the doctors and nurses that had cared for us this past month, in the secure surroundings of the hospital. As bad as I wanted out, I knew then help was just a shout away, that I had assistance readily available when I needed it; anytime, 24 hours a day, seven days a week. Now I understood why I felt at loss and why I was so sad. The change was a frightening one. I felt utterly alone! It was all my responsibility to take care of Jedidiah now. No doctors, no nurses, and no working professionals to lean upon. Could I do this? Could I take care of ALL of Jedidiah's needs? "What if?...." I asked myself, the self-doubts creeping in. "What if Jedidiah needs something that I am not capable of handling?"

I straightened up and tried to stifle my sobs. I really wasn't alone. Scott was still here with me for today. He was in the back bedroom with Jedidiah, unpacking our things and watching Jedidiah so I could cook some lunch for us. Besides, Uncle John and Aunt Stevie were still close by. A phone call and a ten minute drive would bring them over to help. Thankfully, they were still more than willing to assist whenever I needed it.

Wiping the tears and snot away with my sleeve, I tried to convince myself that everything would eventually be alright... "Okay, Lord," I breathed a quiet prayer. "I know you are here, I am NOT really alone. It's you and me here together. Please help me stay strong." I tried to take a few long, deep breaths. "I know we can do this...help me...forgive my ungratefulness." I bowed my head, sorry for my childlike outburst.

Slowly the sobs subsided into sniffles. What a mess I was... And still, no lunch was made yet. I felt weak and shaken. There was a slight buzz at my hip. My cell phone! "Hello?" I answered, my voice still choked with emotion.

"Cynthia! It's Kim. How are you honey?"

"Coach Kim, it's good to hear from you! Uh, well, ummm...It's not going too well right now. I'm kind of... sad..."

"Ah, sweetheart, what's wrong?"

"Well, we just moved into the Ronald McDonald House in Sacramento," I tried to sound thankful. "We get to stay here for the next four weeks, for the rest of Jedidiah's radiation treatments."

"That's great, honey! Do you need some help? I could come down there and give you a hand."

"Really? You would do that for me?"

"Of course!" Kim cheery voice assured me. "When do you want me?"

"Well, ... I don't know...Scott is heading back tonight. He has to work tomorrow."

"Tell you what, Cynthia. I will be down there the day after tomorrow! And that is final!" Kim said firmly.

"Okay... that... would... be nice," I managed to say.

"See you then! Bye now."

I pushed the 'end' button and put my cell phone back in its case. "Wow!" I thought, "I've got a friend!!" The idea that she would come to help me was both comforting and empowering. "Now, where's that pan?" I located a steel cooking pot under the counter, found the package of macaroni and cheese, and proceeded to make lunch.

"Thank you Lord. Your timing is perfect!" I humbly said, thankful for gaining back some strength. "How did you know I needed a good friend right now?"

GOD IS CLOSE

I was driving home! Out of the U.C. Davis Hospital and out of Sacramento for the first time since Jedidiah and I had arrived there in the Life Flight helicopter. How long ago had that been?...two weeks ago?.... ten days ago? I did not know. All I knew was that it had been a whole LIFETIME ago since I had enjoyed the security of my loving family surrounding me in the comfort of my own home. I was then struck by the fact that life would NEVER be the SAME again. Our family could never be whole again, not without our Jedidiah! I swallowed back the familiar lump in my throat that threatened to choke out my very existence, and focused on driving north out of the city of Sacramento. I followed the multi-lane Interstate 5 North until I reached the Highway 99 turn-off. I followed the signs that said, "Marysville/Yuba City", heading northeast out of the Sacramento Valley. Then I took an exit, once again, where Highways 99 and 70 split. I followed Hwy 70 to the city of Oroville. Once in Oroville, I stopped at a gas station to refuel my car.

I felt like a blank, empty and hollow. I was unfeeling, uncomprehending, very different and outside of my normal self. It felt as though anybody looking at me would see the truth- that my youngest son had CANCER! Terminal Brain Cancer, of all things. How could that have happened? I still did not UNDERSTAND it! Would I ever understand it? HOW?? This was the first time I was alone with my thoughts, able to mull it over in my mind, without the constant worry over Jedidiah's care. I wasn't sure I was ready to face it. When is one ever able and ready to face that sort of news?

Resuming the trip from Oroville, north on Highway 70, I began to gain elevation. Up Yankee Hill, the climb began in earnest and gravity slowed my Subaru. I pressed on the gas pedal and the Subaru responded with a surge of power. The transmission shifted down with a determined growl and the tachometer showed higher RPM's. Soon the speedometer was showing a faster speed. "Hey, thanks guys!" I said to the mechanical horsepower under the hood. I was very grateful for the "new to me" 2005 Subaru Outback. I had purchased it less than one year ago, to drive back and forth to my new job at the Redmond Air Tanker Base in Central Oregon. The job was one where I worked for six months on, and then I had six months off. In Federal Government vernacular, it was called a "13/13" position. It signified that I worked "on duty" for thirteen pay periods, and then was "off duty" for thirteen pay periods (a "pay period" being two weeks long).

This was my first winter being "off" and I had been thoroughly enjoying it. Previously, I had been working at a permanent, full time job for the past six years. I was tired of the constant juggling act of prioritizing my time between three active children, their busy schedules, my busy full time job, my husband, and his full time job. Plus, we had completed the construction of a new home on our five acres, approximately four years ago...(that was a year-long project in itself!)

The action and activity seemed non-stop in our lives...24/7, there was ALWAYS something happening...I felt I was well suited for the Assistant Air Tanker Base Manager position, and the 13/13 schedule was a welcome change. I could work hard in the summer, to make money to help support the family. I would be happy to take time off in the winter to spend time at home, and help the kids at school, attend their sports activities, volunteer in the schools, etc.

My grip around the steering wheel finally loosened as I approached the top of Yankee Hill. So much to do...So much to think about...that was the story of my life...I took a deep breath and pushed the Kepple CD "Living Room Sessions" into the CD player. I began to relax as the sound of familiar voices and wonderful songs of the Kepple Family filled the inside of my Subaru.

Something about the angle of the evening light made me glance over my left shoulder. What I saw there, was the most awesome sunset I ever witnessed in my life! The pillowy soft clouds over the coast range to the west were a golden glow of the most beautiful light. The sun was a crimson ball, slowly sinking into the depths of the surrounding clouds. Flaming yellow, orange, cream, red, pink, and scarlet arrows of light were radiating from the setting sun. The colors, absorbed by the clouds and reflected up to the sky were vivid; a rainbow smorgasbord for they eyes. It was a picture that no artist's palate could ever re-create. I pulled into the highway overlook to watch, awestruck by the beautiful scene displayed before me. The Kepple's music, an instrumental song, played along perfectly orchestrated with the incredible sunset. I stared, mouth agape, barely wanting to breathe for fear I'd ruin the moment.

I realized that only God could orchestrate such a beautiful sunset. It was a free gift to me. Just like His love, and the gift of His son, Jesus Christ. All we had to do was open our eyes and accept the gifts God provided. It was as simple as that.

Reluctantly, as the colors were fading, I turned the car around and continued my trip into the Feather River Canyon. The straight, wide open highway transformed itself into a narrow, curvy, winding road. I knew I had to focus on driving now. This was NOT the place to make the mistake of not paying attention. The geographical difference between the elevation of the highway and that of the North Fork of the Feather River below was hundreds of feet, even thousands of feet at certain points. Yet I could not help but marvel at the beauty of it all.

Around every few corners I would be treated to a glimpse of a cascading waterfall. They began somewhere up high, thousands of feet above me, and tumbling, milky white, they briefly splashed the roadside, before retreating into a culvert under the highway. Then, emerging from the other side of the highway, they continued their free-fall quests to join the Feather River far below.

The deep, emerald green of the vegetation stood out in stark contrast behind the white, wispy clouds that floated in open space over the gaping mouth of the canyon. I turned to cross the Pulga Bridge and saw the last traces of evening light, being reflected in the clouds to the east. Shades of light blue, lavender, and purple shined in the clouds above me. This world of ever changing beauty, the magnificent mountains, the deep canyons, the raging rivers, the whole majesty of the outdoors- this was my favorite world. My whole life through, the natural beauty of Plumas County never ceased to amaze me. It was one I never tired of enjoying.

Nevertheless, the nagging pain would not quit. How could my youngest son be, at this very moment, stricken with cancer and lying helpless in a hospital bed in the city?

Cynthia Lusk

April 19, 2011

"I had a dream last night...."

I remember when Jedidiah would wake up on his pull-out bed in the living room, post-tumor, and say that to me. Then he would ask me write down his dreams for him, detail by detail, until I had several pages filled with writing, and read it back to him. He would correct me, add stuff, and say, "No, change that!"

Now, it was my turn to dream about Jedidiah last night. He has been dead for over three months now. It was a very sad dream for me, but I felt compelled to write it down.

I don't quite remember the setting, but I was looking at some clear-ish garbage bags with things in them. I knew one of them held Jedidiah's dead body. I heard someone yell, "Cynthia, don't look in there!" But, I wanted to, I knew I had to anyway. Yes, I confirmed it was Jedidiah's dead body. He was all wet, and curled up in a fetal position. I grabbed him, and tore the bag away. It was Jedidiah's body before he had the tumor. He was lithe and slender, all long arms and long legs, with his cute little boy face. But, unfortunately, he was obviously dead. I sat down next to him, and pulled him into my lap. I embraced that body and hugged and cried with it. I cried and cried, with agonized sobs for long minutes. I cried with all the grief, sadness, sorrow, and longing for her son, that a mother can possibly cry. Broken hearted, I held that boy, in his little boy body, for as long as I could. I held him tight, hugging him with all the love and the strength I could muster. My tears felt as if they would drown me. My throat was so tight and constricted that I could not speak.

But I held on to Jedidiah, loving him, even in his death. His face was exactly as I remembered it, before he had his tumor. It was the same

Jedidiah as he was on that morning of February 14, 2009, before we took him to the hospital. It was not the Jedidiah that died in his Decadron swollen body on January 3, 2011. It was MY Jedidiah, my little boy that I loved and raised for over nine years. He was my special baby, as all children are special to the mother who raised them. I held him close, cradling that body, grieving that he was gone from me. "Oh, how I miss my Jedidiah!" my broken heart sobbed.

Then, in the midst of my pain and suffering, I heard a faint whispering of hushed voices. As it got louder, I realized it was a beautiful melody of angels singing praises to God. My eyes continued to rain tears, but my heart sang along with that incredible, soothing assurance that the presence of God was near. The sweet melody continued, strongly, asserting the praises of our Lord. As sad as I was, I now realized that they loved Jedidiah too. I was assured the ever encompassing, great love of God would surround me and comfort me. I continued to hold Jedidiah, and yet I knew who was holding me close- The Holy Spirit.

Then slowly, the brilliance of my dream faded away to gray.

I awoke, and continued crying, drenching my pillow with tears for Jedidiah. Sobbing and crying, for another hour or two, until I was exhausted, and no more tears would come. I looked at my wristwatch. It was 4:10 AM. Too early to get up and too late to get much more sleep, so I lay still and I reflected on my dream.

I prayed with gratitude, still singing the praise songs in my head. I was very sad, there is no denying that, but knowing that something deeper than my emotions, something very real in my life, would triumph. I knew that 'something' has the power, and the victory over death. I knew that 'something' was Jesus Christ, who was God's only son. Though his earthly body was cruelly killed on a cross, he rose again three days later, leaving an empty tomb behind, to join his Father in Heaven. Wow. I lay there contemplating for another hour.

Also, it occurred to me I had not mourned enough for Jedidiah's lost body. His REAL body, as a healthy, growing boy, NOT the grotesquely swollen, Decadron riddled, tumor-invaded body that developed during the last eleven months of his life. The body he died in, we all knew it wasn't really his. I missed his little boy body. I hated seeing how the drugs changed his little body into something monstrous.

His appearance changed so much under the influence of the steroid dexamethasone, or trade name, "Decadron".

Jedidiah's body became so bloated and swollen, his face almost beyond recognition, even to some of the children on the school playground. The students would come up to me, tug on my shirt sleeve and innocently ask, "Who is that kids over there in the wheelchair?"

"Why, that's Jedidiah." I would tell them.

They would look at me quizzically, waiting to see if I was just teasing them. When I did not say anything else they'd state slowly, "W E L L, it doesn't LOOK like Jedidiah…"

"No, you are right." I'd reassure them. "It doesn't really look like him anymore. He had to take lots of medicine after his biopsy operation. But, it really IS Jedidiah! Why don't you go talk to him? He would love to see you."

I spoke with Jedidiah about writing a book about him, while he was still in the hospital. I asked him what he thought it should be about. I asked him what we should call the book.

Jedidiah told us, "Always Remember Me!"

But of course, at that time, I really had no idea what the future would hold for all of us. I just knew I wanted to capture ALL of Jedidiah's courageous spirit, and how he dealt with his cancer.

Now I know all of the facts: Jedidiah was born on March 30, 2001, in Quincy, CA. He was diagnosed with a Glioblastoma multiformes brain tumor on February 14, 2010. Jedidiah died on January 3, 2011. It was 11 days short of 11 months, from his diagnoses, until his death.

He came home to celebrate his 9th, and last ever, birthday, at home in Cromberg, California. We hosted a party on March 20, which was on a Saturday, so all his cousins could come. They all rallied around him as he sat in the wheelchair, partially paralyzed on his left side from the biopsy of his brain tumor. He had just been discharged from the hospital on March 18th, after 33 days of being at UC Davis Medical Center. He had received 12 Radiation treatments thus far, before returning home for the first time since his diagnosis. At that point, I am not sure if Jedidiah recognized his cousins or not. He was just beginning to be able to speak again, and was using single words. He was still using "hospital pants" in lieu of being able to use the bathroom on his own. He hated the word, "Diapers" as it took away his dignity of being a grown- up, potty trained, kid.

That evening, after his birthday party, I was tucking him into the Subaru for his return trip back to Sacramento, and I heard one of the sweetest sounds I have ever heard. It started as a low rumble in Jedidiah's throat, and ended with a high hiccup noise. "What was that, Jedidiah?" I looked him in the eye. He looked back at me, with a crooked smile on his lips and did it again. He giggled!

"Scott!" I called excitedly. "Listen to this!" I poked my finger at Jedidiah's tummy like I did when I was attaching his seatbelt. A bubble of happy sound emerged from Jedidiah's lips.

"Hey," I called to some of Jedidiah's cousins. "He is saying good-bye by laughing! Come over and listen!"

That was the beginning of the long road to Jedidiah's recovery. And recover he did, to go on to spend a happy, wonderful, fun-filled summer with his family!

Having cancer might not be a character-building circumstance, but it certainly does reveal character. After his tumor was diagnosed, Jedidiah's true character was uncovered. He was a courageous, happy, and high-spirited child with an incredible sense of humor. Jedidiah had the courage to face an uncertain future, yet he was NOT afraid. He always saw the funny side of life. His sense of humor never failed him. He relished in telling jokes. He made me laugh when I wanted to cry. Throughout Jedidiah's treatment for brain cancer he never once whined. He did not get angry because of his brain tumor. He did not even ask, "Why me?" He always told and showed his love to his friends and family.

One of Jedidiah's quotes, at the time of his transfers between chair and bed, or between wheelchair and car, was this: "When Jedidiah stands, People get hugs!" and no matter what we were doing, anyone who was around at the time HAD to come over to where Jedidiah was and get a free hug. Often we would be in a hurry to get somewhere on time, but Jedidiah would not skip this important step! I would get exasperated, in a light-hearted way, and ask Jedidiah, "Haven't we had ENOUGH hugs, yet?" Jedidiah would look at me in his knowing way and say, "People cannot get too many hugs!" And he would continue on with his famous quote, and more importantly, giving out his special hugs on a daily basis.

Jedidiah had a unique way of turning a potentially sad situation around to something more positive. And to the surprise of many people, he would stay focused on the positive.

"What? You say I may be stuck in a wheelchair the rest of my life? Hey, it's cool! I get to be pushed all around town. It's kind of like riding in a chariot!"

"So, I can't run anymore? No problem- throw me in the pool- I CAN SWIM!"

"Too much Decadron? Hey, let's go to the All You Can Eat Buffet!! I can have seconds and thirds, maybe even fourths!! That way I can get our money's worth!"

"So, the Doctors told me my brain cancer is terminal, and they said I am going to DIE! Well, you know, we are ALL going to die, sooner or later. But let's just see how much we can LIVE first!"

When Jedidiah was home that late summer and fall, he would awake in the mornings and give a "Big Daddy Man yawn" and stretch, and then yell, "I AM ALIVE!"

From the day of his diagnosis, forward, we did not take any day for granted. Every single day was realized as special.

I am not sure where I first heard this quote, but I read it somewhere long ago. I still really like it:

"Yesterday is gone. Tomorrow may not come. But today is here, it is a gift from God. That is why we call it 'the present'."

Jedidiah with his special Dirt Bike Riding' Buddies: JD Holzer on the left, and Nano Jarmillo on the right.

"IT'S ALL ABOUT ME"

I read a book shortly after Jedidiah died. It was written by a mother whose daughter died of cancer at age 6. I wanted to read all about the life of that precious little girl.

And I did read about the life of that little girl- for the first half of the book. Then the little girl died, and the book transitioned into a story about the life of the mother. I was disappointed. I still wanted to read about that girl! How could the mother just write about herself? Why is it suddenly all about her?

Then I slowly realized that the life of that little girl was brief, as was the story directly about her life. She died, and was gone from this earth. But the stories of how this little girl's life affected other people continued on. Much the same way Jedidiah's short life affected others. I am still hearing about events in Jedidiah's life that happened, that I wasn't aware of, and how they changed another life in a positive way. It brightens my day to hear these stories from people all around me.

Jedidiah's death has forever changed me, as a person, as a wife, as a mother and as an employee. In some ways, I feel softer, more gentle and forgiving. I am definitely more aware of other people's grief and suffering. I feel empathy when others are hurting. I want to help them find a way to live with their pain and grief. I know you can't say, "Oh, just get over it!" Because as a parent, I know I will NEVER get over the grief, sadness and suffering of losing my youngest child. I just have to learn to deal with it, and live on, despite it.

In other ways I feel harder, more resolute. I don't want to waste time with petty issues. The phrase, "Don't sweat the small stuff" comes to mind. I know most of the things we deal with, and worry about on a daily basis, really are just the small stuff.

I have also developed more confidence in facing the future of my life to come. Watching Jedidiah face his own death, with courage and humor, has certainly changed how I face the present. From him I learned how to live the "No Fear" motto. We do not have to live our lives in fear of death. We should not fear in life, nor should we fear in death. It's that simple, "No Fear", EVER!

The Bible says perfect love casts out fear. Jedidiah accepted that love into his heart and life. He absorbed that perfect love from God, reflected it, and shared it with many people all along the way.

Only now am I beginning to realize just how many lives Jedidiah touched, in many positive ways.

I wanted to share their stories. I invited people to write down their story, so I could pass them along to you.

So, I have included other people's stories about their lives with Jedidiah. I wanted to give them an opportunity to tell their own story in their own words. None of us are "professional authors". I chose not to edit their content, correct the grammar too severely, or re-arrange their writing. I wanted it to be real, written from the depths of their heart. I am ever so grateful that friends and family wanted to contribute. Thank you to all who helped me by writing down your stories. Thank you for keeping Jedidiah's special spirit alive, by telling your story about him. I will always be grateful for the many people who inspired me to write down my story.

The Little Racer Who Could
By Kim Wilbanks

I first met Jedidiah in 2003, when he was just two years old. I was crewing for a friend on the Tevis Cup Endurance Horse Race. I was brand new to the endurance game, and I was nervous. I was assured that our crew boss was kind and experienced, and would keep me lined out. (That would be Sweet Cynthia) When I discovered that she was bringing her baby with her while we crewed the race I was worried anew. But all this worrying was before the race, and before I met Jedidiah. Those who know "Jedi" also know I needn't have been worried ... Jedidiah Lusk was no ordinary baby.

As Cynthia and I rushed from task to task and checkpoint to checkpoint during that Tevis race, I came to appreciate just what a special little guy Baby Jedidiah was. Not once during the long, hot day did he complain or require attention and entertainment. In fact, **he** provided **us** with entertainment – giggling as he rode along in the tack wagon, playing contentedly in the oats, climbing into the water buckets, snacking on the horse's carrots, and snoozing under bushes. Needless to say, by the day's end I was smitten with Baby Jedi.

Two years later, in 2005, I found myself involved in a different kind of "endurance situation": I became "Coach Kim" of the Snow Leopard's Developmental Ski Team, the entry level group for the Johnsville Junior Ski Racing Teams. According to the club's policies, my "developmental racers" have to be at least 6 years old and must be able to follow directions and work in a group setting. Our club goal is for the children to promote out of this developmental team onto a regular racing team within the first few races.

That year Jedidiah was 4 years old. He was well below the cut off age for our program, but as I said Jedi was a pretty special little guy. In light of my first impressions of him from the Tevis, I agreed to try to help Cynthia and Scott when they came to me with this "Jedidiah problem": Jessica and Justin were both on a Johnsville racing team, and Jedidiah didn't like being left out AT ALL. He wanted to be a racer, too … there wasn't much Jedi wanted more than to be a part of the Johnsville program. (Well, maybe he wanted to be on a snowmobile even more than he wanted to be on a racing team, but that's a different story).

We decided to try Jedidiah out on the Snow Leopards, with Scott shadowing the team in case of a meltdown. The "four year old meltdown" we feared never happened, as from day one that little guy was on his skis and "on his game" as a racer. Scott was soon off "shadowing duty", as Jedi became a Snow Leopard fixture. He truly was a "fixture", as he **had** to be on the "Leopards" for two years, until he was 6 years old. Age requirements aside, he was just too small to be promoted to a regular racing team - he couldn't even get on the chairlift because he was so short!

But good things come in small packages, and Jed was such a good thing for our developmental team. Before the end of his first year with us he became my "Assistant Coach". He was soon the best (and the most fearless) skier on our team and many times I'd have him lead the team down the hill while I worked with a child who was struggling with stops and turns.

Jedi volunteered to race the regular team's courses that first year, just for fun. Through his example and encouragement he lead many of his older, more timid team mates to try the race courses, too. By the time he was five he was turning in times that beat some of the regular racers! He soon became a sort of "Johnsville Ski Team Mascot". He became a real favorite of Program Director Elliott Smart, who dubbed him "Mr. Biscuits and Gravy". (Don't ask me - you'll have to ask Elliott about that one!)

Even though he was stuck with the Leopards "farm team" until he was six, Jedi had a blast. With the enthusiasm and love of life for which he is so well known, he smiled his way through each Saturday, and what an impish little smile he had J. I am so fortunate - those two years with Jedidiah as my assistant coach were some of my best years of coaching. Jedidiah truly was the "little racer who could" ... he could keep up with his big sister and big brother; he could inspire his team mates to be their best; he could find joy everywhere and share it, through his smile, with others; he could always enjoy a good joke; and in the end he could even bravely face death.

Thank you for the good times, and the important lessons, Little Buddy. Don't worry - we *will* ALWAYS REMEMBER, and we will always love you.

XO from Coach Kim <3

WHAT ABOUT THE GRIEF?
By Cynthia Lusk

Oh yes, the grief. The PAIN... The LOSS... The anxiety and the hurt. I have felt ALL of it, every day since his diagnosis on February 14, 2010. And ESPECIALLY since his death on January 3, 2011. I have asked myself a lot of questions in the past two years. What about the lifelong after-effects of losing a beloved family member? Why was my son taken before he could grow up? I felt like the first and only mother, ever, to lose a child. How long would the sadness last? How could I possibly go on living a longer life than my youngest child? How do I help my torn heart to heal? How do I overcome this overwhelming loneliness? Will it ever heal?

Yes, I read a few of the books. I know what "the experts" said. I learned some of the psychology of grieving, the proposed "steps" I was supposed to "go through".

It's true, there are so many aspects of that kind of pain, the emotional torment. Worst of all, to me, was the haunting knowledge that I would never, ever hold my child in my arms again. As a mother of a child only 9 years old, I knew my job was not finished yet. I was supposed to raise him up to adulthood. I needed to be there for him, to help him through school, to pick him up when he fell, to coach him in Little League, soccer, basketball and 4-H. He was just getting to the "Fun Stage" where he could participate in all kinds of really fun things! That was my job- to help him grow up. I was expecting to have him around another 9 or 10 years. How could I do that now, he is dead? What about my unfinished business? Was I supposed to forget all about being a mother, just like that?

During the almost 11 months that Jedidiah lived with his cancer, I remember feeling so very vulnerable. It was a thin veneer I wore as the outside shell that covered me. I felt like a chocolate covered cherry. If any crack occurred in that coating, then the soft gooey interior would come oozing out. If my outer coating received a larger gouge, then I felt as if my insides would come gushing out. Like my lifeblood would drain right out of me in an instant. I had a desperate need to protect myself. But how? I felt like Jedidiah's cancer had stripped all of my defenses away from me. Helpless- that is how I felt. And I was. Helpless to stop the growth of my son's brain tumor. Helpless to stop the cancer. Helpless to stop those rapidly, ever multiplying cells. No matter what I did, I knew the insidious growth of that tumor would eventually kill my baby. How can a Mom face that?

May 24, 2011

I had another dream about Jedidiah last night. He was alive this time!
Jedidiah was skipping and running through the woods, a happy, healthy eight year old boy. I was watching him through a large, clear cabin window. I was inside a cabin in the woods. As Jedidiah approached closer, I could see a perplexed expression on his face as he looked around, scanning the cabin and looking for a door to get in. I knew he wanted to come to see his mama. I tried to motion through the window, to show him where the back door was. It appeared that he did not even see me at all. After he ran back and forth a few times, he finally found the back door to the cabin. He burst through the door and into my open arms! I hugged and hugged Jedidiah and held him tight! I did not want to let my little Jedidiah go....... ever again!! I deeply inhaled of his little boy smell, felt his soft, sandy brown hair against my cheek, and squeeze his healthy body. Oh, it was so good to see and hold him again!

Then he started wriggling and squirming within my arms, as little boys often do, when they are confined too long and want to be free. As much as I wanted to hang on to him, I knew I had to let go eventually. So, he gradually slipped free, and I awoke, crying.

My tears flowed down my face, and into my ears. I checked my watch. It was 0330.

"Just sad, nothing worse," I told myself.

I just wanted someone to hold me tight, and tell me it is all right. But I was in Central Oregon, sleeping alone in my little travel trailer, and my husband was at home in Cromberg, California, sleeping alone in our large, king-sized bed- 440 miles away.

June 15, 2011

I had another dream about Jedidiah early this morning. It was a happy dream. Jedidiah was happy and full of life. I did not wake up crying, or with a sense of dread.

Jedidiah was doing his normal little boy stuff, and I was doing my usual Mom things. He ran up, looked me in the eye, and kissed me on my cheek, and ran away again, laughing and playing like little boys do. I was gathering up a pile of kid's things, after dance class. Ms. Eileen Cox was there, being nice like she always is, supporting, encouraging, and being her usual dance teacher self.

It was a reassuring dream. A reminder that things are going to get back "to normal", and things are going to be okay.

SIXTH GRADE GRADUATION SPEECH

June 13, 2013

Good Evening! My name is Cynthia Lusk and I am Jedidiah's mom. That empty chair over there was put aside in honor of my son, Jedidiah, who died two years ago of a brain tumor at nine years old.

When I was first invited to this Sixth Grade Graduation to make a Speech, I did NOT want to come. I thought it would be too emotionally difficult for me to follow thru with it. But then I thought, "What would that be teaching Jedidiah's classmates? They would think it's ok to run away from uncomfortable situations, and not face your fears."

So, I decided that I WOULD and COULD do it, and I would rather teach the class that you DON'T need to duck, dive & dodge your fears, but it is possible to face your troubles HEAD ON! And succeed!

They told me I had 5 minutes to speak, so I would like to present to you: five important points, that I think Jedidiah would like you to know.

When Jedidiah got diagnosed with the Glioblastoma multiformes cancer in the brain, he qualified for a Make-A-Wish. We were told his brain tumor was Terminal and that he would die soon. After much negotiations with the Make-A-Wish Representatives over Jedidiah's' wish for a 4 wheeler, six by six or snowmobile, he then chose to take a trip to Alaska, where he said he wanted to be an Alaska Smokejumper- like his Dad. It was a Trip of a Lifetime for the whole family! When we walked into the Cafeteria at the Alaska Fire Service Base-there was a sign on the wall for all to see- It read, **"LIFE IS SHORT- EAT DESSERT FIRST"**. And Jedidiah adopted that motto for the rest of his life. So that is my first Point- ***Life IS Short, Eat Dessert First***. Referring not just to your meals, but also to the fact that you need to enjoy life at the present time, and it okay to put your troubles on the back burner to have fun!

My second point is: **BE KIND TO EACH OTHER**. Continue to show the same kindness throughout your life, that you showed to Jedidiah, here at this school, when he returned after his cancer treatments. His hair fell out, his body doubled in weight, & he came back to school in a wheelchair. He was pretty much unrecognizable from the little boy they all knew in Mrs. Lemnah's Third Grade Class. But NOT once did I ever hear any child in this school make fun of him. You all showed upmost kindness and respect to him. I was very much impressed with you all, and sure did appreciate the way you conducted yourselves.

Point Number Three is: ***When you are Climbing the Ladder of Life- Pull Others up with you.!***. Everyone climbs at their own rate. If your buddies need help below you, don't hesitate to help. Pull them on up! Don't worry if others climb higher or faster than you, encourage them anyways. Maybe you think someone got a better deal than you, and they somehow got ahead of you. But remember… those are the ones who will be pulling you up when you need it!

Point Number Four is: **_LIFE is NOT Fair!!_** It's TRUE! Life is NOT fair….Don't expect it to be. Get used to that fact, the sooner the better. Don't waste time whining & complaining that life is NOT fair. Get over it and move on. Jedidiah & I spoke about that a lot. Personally, we agreed that God is in control, and He knows the overall Big Picture. But we don't always get to see ALL the pieces to the puzzles at one time… so we don't always understand what is happening at the present time.

Point Number Five is: **_HELP OUT WITHOUT BEING ASKED._** Take the initiative to help your parents around the house. Help make dinner, wash the dishes, take the trash out or clean your room…Taking Responsibility is IMPORTANT!! If everything works out well for you- In six short years you will be graduating High School SENIORS!!! & well on your way to becoming full-fledged adults! We welcome you! Congratulations on your Sixth Grade Graduation!!

July 20, 2013

I had a dream about Jedidiah very early this morning.

I was in a motel room in Carson City, Nevada, getting ready to run the 50 K Tahoe Rim Race. I was having a hard time sleeping…knowing I had to get up soon, make race preparations, and head up the hill to Spooner Summit, for the start of the run. I looked over at the night stand and the clock read 0230. Also on the night stand was one of Jedidiah's favorite old stuffed animals- it was the zebra! For some reason I had started to bring that silly little zebra with me. It had ridden in my backpack on several hikes and a couple of overnight camping trips. And it had wormed it way into my packed bag full of running clothes on this trip.

So, that zebra was sitting there staring at me, and I stared back, thinking of Jedidiah. Then I finally drifted off to sleep…

Then, there was Jedidiah! Clear as can be, looking just like the little boy I sweetly remembered. I was so happy to see him in my dream.

He was standing right next to me. I leaned over to talk with him. He kissed me on my face, near my temple, and said, "I miss you, Mommy!"

And I said back to him, "I miss you too, Jedidiah!" Then he faded away.

DEFENSE MECHANISMS

I heard that armadillos curl up in a tight ball to protect themselves. They keep their soft underbelly to the inside, while turning their tougher, armored exterior towards the danger. And hedgehogs, too, and porcupines, all have the ability to curl up like that, while displaying a prickly, proactive coating on the outside of their bodies, so no one bothers them. I know some people that act like that, any time someone annoys them. They bristle up, and emit a kind of psychological, exterior sharpness. It is not a nice feeling to get too close to those prickly kind of people!

At times I sure wish we humans had a little more protection, instead of just this thin layer of soft skin, physically, mentally, and emotionally. I had never experienced the tougher side of life, to feel like I needed more protection than just putting on a nice, thick coat, like protection against an icy blow of winter wind. But when dealing with cancer, and children's deaths, boy, I sure wish I had more protection! Something to keep the pain away. Why do we have to feel it? Why does it keep coming back?

Now, do ostriches really put their heads in the sand? Or is that just an expression someone made up? I have never seen one of the big birds do that, so I don't know. But it sounds like a good plan. Stick your head under the ground, and it makes the world go away!

THE LAST CHAPTER

I realize that everything in life is temporary. In fact, this life we are now living is only temporary. Our bodies are temporary and so is everything on this earth. Of course, you have the option of looking at that in a negative way, or turning it around into something positive. I chose to keep my thoughts positive, to maintain a positive attitude in all ways I can. An "attitude of gratitude" is something worth cultivating. Especially, gratitude towards our Maker, and all that God has given us. He has given us SO MUCH, and it is up to decide how we want to utilize what He has blessed us with. I believe He wants us to use our gifts, helping others in this life He gave us.

In this life we are offered tiny slices of incredible beauty. But we have to realize that we are only offered these for a brief moment, and likewise, we can learn to appreciate and embrace these short moments. Just like our Jedidiah, who was taken from us after such a limited time. One can argue that, after all, we DID get to enjoy Jedidiah for over nine years. But we wanted to keep him longer!!

So, I began to write down some of those wonderful moments in my life that I was privileged to experience. These are so special, yet they only last a few seconds, or maybe a minute or two. These are the images that burn into your brain. They burn so deep, that they can sustain you through the grayer times throughout your life. The sights, sounds, and smells, of these events can still stir awesome feelings in my soul.

The predawn hush after the night time snowfall.

The golden evening alpenglow on a snowy, craggy peak.

The suckling sound of a newborn foal when it finds it's mother's warm udder of milk.

The sights, sounds and smells of a summer thunderstorm in the mountains.

The majestic stare of a golden eagle looking down from atop a pine tree, feathers ruffling in the wind.

The downy soft of a day old chick cradled between your hands, as your child sticks out a tentative finger to touch, and squeals in delight.

Watching the night stars dancing like purest diamonds on a cover of black velvet.

The sweet scent of wood smoke on a brisk autumn day.

The wiggly pink of an earthworm your child is dangling from his fingers, "Look, Mom! IT'S A WORM!"

The taste of a hot, home-cooked meal after a hard day's work outdoors.

The beauty of your dancing daughter at her ballet recital.

That colorful rainbow in the sky after days of dreary drizzle.

The perfect pattern of orange and black on the unfurling wings of a newly hatched monarch butterfly, as your child watches in wide-eyed wonder.

The cotton candy pink of sunset clouds after a fun day at the fair.

The exhilarating feeling on standing on a tall mountain peak, looking down at the landscape far below.

Always Remember Me

The "Good morning, Sunshine!" you hear waking up next to your loved one.
Seeing the cheerful orange of dancing flames in your warm wood stove, as you watch the snowflakes pile up outside your window.
The warmth of a loved one's clasping hand on yours while saying grace before eating dinner.
The bubble of laughter from young girls at a slumber party.
The oh so deep azure blue of a cloudless summer sky in the mountains.
The fresh clean smell of a child just out of the bathtub.
The feel of a newly laid egg, still warm from the hen's body.
The sigh of utter contentment you hear from yourself as you watch your child safe in bed, deeply sleeping.
The ability to breath....And the feeling of deep inhalation of clean mountain air- when you can feel your lungs expanding in appreciation.
The feel of clean sheets on your bed.
The finish line - at the end of your first marathon!
So many, wonderful, incredibly precious things of beauty in our lives!! Dwell on the beautiful and positive!! It is all a matter of choice of your perspective.
ALWAYS be positive!
always BE positive!
Always be POSITIVE!
ALWAYS BE POSITIVE!

Yes, Jedidiah, we will always remember you!